The Whaling Indians

WEST COAST LEGENDS AND STORIES

Tales of Extraordinary Experience

told by Tom Sa:ya:ch'apis, William, Dick La:maho:s, Captain Bill, and Tyee Bob

PART 10:
SAPIR-THOMAS
NOOTKA TEXTS

Prepared by
Edward Sapir,
Morris Swadesh,
Alexander Thomas,
John Thomas, and
Frank Williams

Edited by Eugene Arima, Terry Klokeid and Katherine Robinson

Mercury Series
Canadian Ethnology Service
Paper 134

Published by
The Canadian Museum of Civilization

CANADIAN CATALOGUING IN PUBLICATION DATA

Sapir, Edward, 1884–1939

The Whaling Indians: West Coast legends and stories: tales of extraordinary experience

(Mercury series, ISSN 0316-1854)

(Paper/Canadian Ethnology Service, ISSN 0316-1862; no. 134)

Text in English and Nootka.

"Part 10 of the Sapir-Thomas Nootka texts told by Tom Sa:ya:ch'apis, William, Dick La:maho:s, Captain Hill, and Tyee Bob"

ISBN 0-660-17836-2

1 Nootka Indians – Folklore.
2. Nootka language – Texts.
3. Indians of North America – British Columbia – Vancouver Island – Folklore.
4 Tales – British Columbia – Vancouver Island.

I. Arima, Eugene, 1938–
II. Klokeid, Terry
III. Robinson, Katherine
IV. Canadian Museum of Civilization.
V. Canadian Ethnology Service.
VI. Series.
VII. Series: Paper (Canadian Ethnology Service) ; no. 134.

E99.N85S26 2000 398.2'089'97097112 C00-980062-X

Published by
Canadian Museum of Civilization
100 Laurier Street
P.O. Box 3100, Station B
Hull, Quebec
J8X 4H2

PRINTED IN CANADA

Senior production officer: Deborah Brownrigg

Cover design: Purich Design Studio

Front cover: *Whaling Canoe* ʔOʔO:taqsats
Photograph by A. Curtis
Supplied by Washinton State Historical Society #19238

Back cover : *Return from the hunt*
Photograph by A. Curtis
Supplied by Washinton State Historical Society #20182

Canada

OBJECT OF THE MERCURY SERIES

The Mercury Series is designed to permit rapid dissemination of information pertaining to the disciplines in which the Canadian Museum of Civilization is active. Considered an important reference by the scientific community, the Mercury Series comprises over three hundred specialized publications on Canada's history and prehistory.

Because of its specialized audience, the series consists largely of monographs published in the language of the author.

In the interest of making information available quickly, normal production procedures have been abbreviated. As a result, grammatical and typographical errors may occur. Your indulgence is requested.

Titles in the Mercury Series can be obtained

by calling 1-800-555-5621;

by e-mail to <publications@civilization.ca>;

by internet to <cyberboutique.civilization.ca>; or

by writing to
Mail Order Services
Canadian Museum of Civilization
100 Laurier Street
P.O. Box 3100, Station B
Hull, Quebec
J8X 4H2

BUT DE LA COLLECTION

La collection Mercure vise à diffuser rapidement le résultat de travaux dans les disciplines qui relèvent des sphères d'activités du Musée canadien des civilisations. Considérée comme un apport important dans la communauté scientifique, la collection Mercure présente plus de trois cents publications spécialisées portant sur l'héritage canadien préhistorique et historique.

Comme la collection s'adresse à un public spécialisé, celle-ci est constituée essentiellement de monographies publiées dans la langue des auteurs.

Pour assurer la prompte distribution des exemplaires imprimés, les étapes de l'édition ont été abrégées. En conséquence, certaines coquilles ou fautes de grammaire peuvent subsister : c'est pourquoi nous réclamons votre indulgence.

Vous pouvez vous procurer les titres parus dans la collection Mercure

par téléphone, en appelant au 1 800 555-5621,

par courriel, en adressant votre demande à <publications@civilisations.ca>

par internet à <cyberboutique.civilisations.ca>

ou **par la poste**, en écrivant au :
Service des commandes postales
Musée canadien des civilisations
100, rue Laurier
C.P. 3100, succursale B
Hull (Québec)
J8X 4H2

Alex Thomas singing in Ottawa in 1968
(Photo: Clarke Davis, MCM/CMC J-21201)

Abstract

"TALES OF EXTRAORDINARY EXPERIENCE" IS THE second of four parts in *West Coast Legends and Stories*, or *Nootka Legends and Stories*. These Native texts were collected between 1910 and 1923 by Edward Sapir and Alexander Thomas from the Nuu-Chah-Nulth — once known as the Nootka — of Vancouver Island's west coast. This volume is part 10 of the extensive "Sapir-Thomas Nootka Texts", and contains thirteen tales of supernatural encounters and spirit power. In addition to documenting thought and behaviour in Native ethnography, as Sapir intended, these tales are equally engrossing as simple stories from a world other than our own.

Résumé

« TALES OF EXTRAORDINARY EXPERIENCE » EST LA deuxième de quatre parties consacrées aux légendes et récits de la côte ouest (ou des Nootkas). Ces textes ont été recueillis auprès des Nuu-Chah-Nulths – jadis connus sous le nom de Nootkas – de la côte ouest de l'île de Vancouver, par Edward Sapir et Alexander Thomas, entre 1910 et 1923. Ce volume est la partie 10 d'une série plus grande de textes de Sapir et Alexander concernant les Nootkas et contient treize légendes qui ont trait à des rencontres surnaturelles et au pouvoir de l'esprit. En plus de documenter la pensée et le comportement des Amérindiens – l'intention réelle d'Edward Sapir –, ces légendes sont captivantes comme tout récit d'inspiration populaire provenant d'un monde différent du nôtre.

The Whaling Indians: West Coast Legends and Stories

TALES OF EXTRAORDINARY EXPERIENCE

Prepared by
Edward Sapir, Morris Swadesh, Alex Thomas, John Thomas, and Frank Williams

CONTENTS

Frontispiece: Alex Thomas singing in Ottawa in 1968 (Photo: Clarke Davis, MCM/CMC J-21201) iii
Abstract v
Preface viii
Introduction x
References xxiii
Place name maps xxvii

Narratives		translation	text
113.	Shaman and Ghosts	1	79
114.	Bone Game at Nitinat	12	96
115.	How a Man Mishandled Beaver Power	18	105
116.	Sa:ya:ch'apis Meets a Storm	21	109
117.	Kanop the Shaman	27	118
118.	Ch'it'oqwin'ak Becomes a Shaman	32	125
119.	The Youth Who Followed a Shag	37	132
120.	A Runaway Slave Comes to the Chief of Wanin	39	135
121.	Wealth From a Shag	42	139
122.	Tla:tla:qokw'ap Sees the Thunderbird and Gets Power from a Sea Egg	53	155
123.	How the Nitinats Got the Thunderbird and Lightning Snake	57	161
124.	A <u>H</u>iko:lˀat<u>h</u> Sees the Thunderbird and the Northern Lights Women	59	163
125.	A M'o:<u>h</u>o:olˀat<u>h</u> Youth Visits the Thunderbird	62	167
Endnotes		69	

PREFACE

The Ts'isha:ʔath̲ or "Tseshaht" of Barkley Sound and Alberni Inlet, Vancouver Island, are the people who are the primary source for the extensive collection of Nuu-Chah-Nulth or "Nootka" texts gathered in the 1910-23 period by the outstanding linguist Edward Sapir and his second chief interpreter Alexander Thomas. Sapir was the first head of the Division of Anthropology, Geological Survey, Canada Department of Mines, the institutional ancestor of the Canadian Museum of Civilization.

The collection of these texts was begun before World War I by Sapir who made two field trips to Port Alberni in 1910 and 1913-14. During fieldwork Frank Williams was the main interpreter and native collaborator, as is duly recognized in the authorship of this volume. Alex Thomas became the principal collaborator only toward the end of Sapir's visits. He was the grandson of the leading informant, Chief Tom Sa:ya:ch'apis. Most of *Tales of Extraordinary Experience* are Ts'isha:ʔath̲ accounts by Sa:ya:ch'apis and others, though just texts nos. 116, 122 and 124 centre on them as subject. A lesser, though still important, tribal source for the collection are the Yo:loʔilʔath̲ or "Ucluelet", thanks particularly to Chief Kwishanishim who furnished much of the already published vivid accounts of the fierce wars around Barkley Sound (Sapir and Swadesh 1955:356-443). In the present part which is not concerned with war, text 118 is about a Yo:loʔilʔath̲. Another group near the latter, the Tlaʔo:kwiʔath̲ or "Clayoquot" feature in text 117 about a shaman doctor. Groups to the east featured in this part include the Ho:ʔ̲i:ʔath̲ or "Ohiaht" of east Barkley Sound in texts 113 and 114, and the Di:ti:dʔa:ʔtx̲ or "Ditidaht" or "Nitinat" of text 123. Still others around Alberni Inlet who figure in the volume are and the H̲o:choqtlisʔath̲ or "Uchuklesaht" around the inlet entrance of texts 115, 119 and 120, and the Ho:pach'asʔath̲ or "Opetchesaht" who provide text 125. These exotic sounding First Nations are but part of the many to be acknowledged as the ultimate sources of the texts.

The patient support of National Historic Sites over many years in the preparation of the last third of the Sapir-Thomas corpus is to be most gratefully acknowledged. The two other institutions to be cited especially are the Canadian Museum of Civilization and the American Philosophical Society Library so ready to help with copies of the original documents in their safekeeping. On the native side to be thanked in particular is John Thomas who translated most of what has long been known as the "Third Volume" of the "Nootka Texts" (nos. 85-147) in academic circles. Knowing all three West Coast languages, he was a godsend. Not long after completing his vital task he suddenly passed away, underlining the last minute nature of this undertaking. Alex Thomas must also be singled out, he who wrote down the majority of the texts with interlinear glosses. His lively encouragement sustained the work through times of difficulty and doubt. Then there are the renowned linguists, Edward Sapir and Morris Swadesh, who brought out the first two volumes so masterfully, and for the third can alphabetically be nicely listed at the start of the authorship to aid library referencing. Lastly, let us remember with warmth the storytellers themselves for passing on these now rare accounts before they disappeared in the mists of time.

INTRODUCTION

Tales of Extraordinary Experience is part 10 of the West Coast native texts gathered by Edward Sapir and Alex Thomas in 1910-23. It is the second of the four parts comprizing the last "Third Volume," as it has been referred to over the years, of the corpus of these fascinating narratives. The three volumes of "Nootka Texts" were named by Sapir and Morris Swadesh, his accomplished student, as follows: **Nootka Texts** (Sapir and Swadesh 1939), **Native Accounts of Nootka Ethnography** (Sapir and Swadesh 1955), and **Nootka Legends and Stories**, the present effort. However, as noted already in the Preface, the last title has been altered to **West Coast Legends and Stories**. Authorship of the Third Volume would no doubt have remained Sapir and Swadesh had the latter not died before bringing it out. Now it seems fitting to add the two leading interpreters in the field, Alex Thomas and Frank Williams, and also the main translator, John Thomas, who worked on the texts over half a century later.

Since the one who passed on the torch in person was Alex Thomas, we may introduce the material starting from his vantage point. Alex, or Alec in conversation, was absent from the Ts'isha:ʔath reserve at Alberni during Sapir's first fieldwork there in 1910. As mentioned, following governmental educational practice of the time he was sequestered in the Indian Residential School just a few hundred yards away from home but may as well have been gone to the moon. His grandfather, Chief Tom Sa:ya:ch'apis, became Sapir's principal informant (Cf. Sapir 1921). When Sapir returned in 1913 for his second fieldwork session, Alex was home on holidays. Watching over Sapir's shoulder as he recorded narrative texts and other linguistic and ethnographic information in his notebooks, Alex picked up the notation system and started imitating it. Seeing Alex doing so, Sapir taught him all the details, then said he would not have to come to the West Coast anymore since thenceforth Alex could do the recording. Alex, born 1895, was about nineteen as he began his now invaluable documentation of his own culture, society, and language. He truly was a professional native ethnographer and linguist for this work was his principal employment over the next decade as he sent in thousands of pages of text, at 50 cents a page, and other materials to Sapir in Ottawa at the then newly built Victoria Albert Memorial Museum. Sapir had begun the Division of Anthropology within the Geological Survey of Canada, Department of Mines, which became successively the Human History Branch of the National Museum of Canada, the National Museum of Man, and currently the Canadian Museum of Civilization. No doubt this last name will change again for some political convenience or another.

The "Boasian" notation system used then by Sapir and taught to Alex was not yet fully the modern unit symbol per phoneme representation, and couple of digraphs were used, notably **ts** and **tc** (for "ch"). Sapir was trained by Franz Boas, the undoubted father of modern American anthropology. Another notable representation is **o**, used by Sapir in his fieldwork and in the first volume, but later changed for the second volume by Swadesh to **u** which is less accurate though seemingly more in accord with recent linguistic convention. The **o** of *Nootka Texts* is continued in the present volume after due consultation with Don DeBlois, the museum's latest linguist, now retired, who has special interest and experience in native literacy development. In practical terms **o** has the real advantage of ready recognition as an "o" sound by the ordinary English literate reader, native or non-native, whereas **u** is generally taken to be an "a" sound as in "cup", particularly when met in new settings.

In the 1960's the old system used by Sapir and Alex was slightly modified for the standard English typewriter keyboard to give a practical orthography (Thomas and Arima 1970). Alex was using it in native literacy classes at Alberni until his sudden death in 1971, quite happy with its workability. But the orthography was designed for the typewriter as far as mechanical execution was concerned. With the arrival of the computer age in earnest in the last quarter of the 20th century, a practical orthography, used here in English contexts like this Introduction and the translated narratives, is preferably to be geared to word processing in a manner usable by the comparatively unsophisticated in computer terms. The present representation is thus kept within the confines of the common keyboard with a minimum of extra operations. If available, macro buttons may be created for underlined symbols. Vowel lengthening is by the colon. While doubling vowel letters is easier still, Alex noted that in Nootka doubling is liable to be confusing and indeed expressly said not to double vowels. When handwriting the single dot is fastest. By hand one may also link the digraph letters if wished, enlarge glottal stops for capital forms perhaps, and reduce the labialization "w" (dispensable in more abstract representation, says Klokeid, since governed by phonological rules).

The glottal stop hook traditional in linguistics could be obtained on the old typewriters by filing the dot off the question mark; however, with just simple word processing the commoner procedure of whiting out the dot may be followed, at least in mechanical representation. In handwriting the traditional hook is no problem, of course. The apostrophe is used to indicate the glottalization of consonants. Digraphs are used departing from the unit symbol per phoneme linguistic ideal. Where the digraph unit might be unclear a dot is inserted, in the first few pages more often than is strictly necessary to assist first time readers. The writing system employed may be listed as follows:

English-adapted Orthography

p t ts ch s sh k m n w y h *l* - English-like sounds

l - lateral made with tongue tip on the palate edge at the root of the top front teeth and the breath escaping off the tongue sides, somewhat like in "athlete"

tl - l preceded by stopping breath as in t and releasing

q - like k made farther back, voiceless back velar stop

x x̲ - like in German "ich" and "ach" respectively

h̲ - like h made far back in the throat, laryngealized

kw qw xw x̲w - made with lips rounded forward, labialized

p' t' ts' ch' tl' k' kw' q' qw' m' n' w' y' - glottalized

ʔ - glottal stop or catch like in "uhʔuh"

ʔ̲ - laryngealized glottal stop made with back of tongue retracted toward back wall of throat like in Arabic

i e a o̲ o - vowels like in "kit, kept, cat, cot, coat"

i: e: a: o̲: o: - long vowels

i::: o̲::: etc. - extra long as in cries

Variable length vowels need not be indicated separately since they vary by phonologic and grammatical environment. Although designed for Nootka, the orthography can represent Nitinat and Makah with the addition of **b, d,** and ***l̲***. Underlining, used for **x̲, h̲, ʔ̲** and **o̲**, the latter rare, goes with backing of the articulation point of the sound. When writing by hand the subscript dot may be substituted. The kind of pen, whether ballpoint or more flowing, will determine which of the two marks is easier to make. Glottalization of the nasals and semivowels is rendered as for glottalized consonants with the apostrophe mark coming after the letter as **m' n' w' y'** since Sapir, working with Alex, has established "... the phonologic reality of a glottalized class of consonants which included both type p' (with prior release of oral closure) and type 'm (with prior release of glottal closure)" (1949:56). The normal Nootkan lateral is with the tongue tip contact farther back than with us in English and has thus been represented by an ordinary l while the infrequent English-like lateral has been italicized. The latter on its rare appearances occurs mostly in loan words, e.g., ***l*om** for rum, **Mito*l*i** for

Victoria, and, if desired, the whole loan word can be italicized with native pronunciation to suit. The inclusion of some capitalization and punctuation provides visual and symbolic advantages. When a word to be capitalized begins with either of the glottal stops, the following letter is made the capital since those stops lack the form. These capitals and punctuation marks have been found to facilitate reading as a visual process. Further discussion on orthography details will be found in part 9, *Legendary Hunters*.

Many native places are mentioned in these accounts, and some of them have been located physically as indicated in the endnotes. Since the region of chief concern is Barkley Sound, Denis St. Claire's detailed study of place names and groups, *Barkley Sound Tribal Territories (1991)*, has been most helpful for locating them. Their establishment on the ground, so to speak, brings out a very real dimension of the narratives which might otherwise be missed, at least by the non-native audience.

Synopses, with remarks

When oral traditions were at the height of scholarly interest in the second half of the 19th century and into the first decades of the 20th, it was common to provide summaries of the often prolix accounts presented in order to facilitate the comparative study of mythology and folklore. Following this past academic custom and also for more general help to those such as Parks personnel who want just a quick overview, synopses of the *Tales of Extraordinary Experience* have been prepared along with a few explanatory remarks. Those readers who do not wish to have the stories spoiled by prior revelation in bare outline should pass on directly to the real narratives in all their rich fullness.

In *Tales*... there are thirteen texts numbered from 113 to 125. All feature encounters with assorted supernatural beings, spirits of the native cosmology who generally confer valuable powers for success in undertakings to the human individuals involved. If possible the person seizes the supernatural which often then turns into mere foam or a fungus. Perhaps hallucinogens were known. But the one encountering a supernatural can also be paralysed, overwhelmed by the powerful spirit forces in close proximity. Whatever substance is obtained is carefully wrapped in moss or a piece torn from one's robe, commonly of woven cedar bark, and then usually put up in the forks of a young cedar or yew to become "medicine." The supernatural itself may also come in a small enough form convenient for pack aging as is into medicine, for example, a miniature whale. Or what is obtained might be something given by the spirit such as food which changes form upon reaching the human world, for example, salmon that turns into wood.

Immaterial things like songs and names were no less valuable, being good for prestigious public display along with the associated power obtained. In some cases, like an encounter with the Thunderbird, the spirit's appearance would be consciously retained for graphic representation later in painting, sculpture such as mask, and dance.

Following a supernatural encounter, the individual must remain in some sort of isolation from everyday existence in normal society for a period of time, often four days, or suffer ill effects from the power turning against him. The existential distance between the sacred and the profane is great and not to be recrossed suddenly. Since spirit encounters usually occur at a distance from home, the person often stays off in the woods. But sometimes he, or she, stays isolated in the house, as when the spirit is met at sea and return ashore is to the home location. Or both kinds of distancing might be implemented for extra insurance against adverse effects. Whatever the case, the power obtained is dangerous at first while the person is as if charged with it electrically, and usually he has to observe rites such as the basic ?o:simch purificatory bathing and tabus like fasting. He might rehearse for relevant activities such as doctoring. Behind the variety of observances lies a common rationale.

Also these stories show the individual's desire for supernatural experience and heighten it by dwelling on the extraordinary, all the while claiming prestigious family association with the supernatural and its fantastic powers. Again the underlying concern is with status, with standing in rank-conscious West Coast society. This basic theme surfaces in a variety of ways. For example, no. 121, "Wealth From a Shag," begins with the hero disowned by his chiefly father as unmanly because his wife did not bear children. Without offspring to continue the family line, he is discarded as useless by his father, but the hero attains lead stature by becoming very wealthy with supernatural assistance, wealth and chiefship being synonymous. Since the narratives can vindicate family claims to illustrious forebearers and high rank when publically validated with wealth display and distribution, they are themselves very much part of the status game. With these preliminary general remarks, those less familiar with West Coast native culture may more readily understand the accounts presented and appreciate the outlook they embody. Some stories are not about the origins of the acquired spirit powers but rather the applications of them.

No. 113 leads off with three comparatively recent occurrences involving about ghosts and shaman doctors as recollected by Dick La:maho:s. The first episode presumably took place among the narrator's people, the Ho:choqtlis?ath who used to live around the mouth of Alberni Inlet or "Canal" on the east side. A foretelling dance called the N'a:chn'a:cha after the presiding shaman is started by children who are then spirited away by the ghosts. One

boy does not want to participate but is imprisoned along with the rest inside a big rock, a ghost's house. A woman shaman doctor retrieves the children and restores them to their parents except for the boy. Eventually he is rescued without ill consequence from his longer captivity. Evident in the account is the strong West Coast socialization pressure with all the children having to participate. That the children are said to start the dance is the usual ceremonial fiction whereby the adult organizers put their young in the public forefront to further their status. This capture by ghosts is an instance of social initiation involving separation from the secular community and return with enhancement by supernatural contact. The spirits are employed to renew group identity and cohesion with each new generation.

Next, La:maho:s is on a gift visit to ʔOse:l or Ozette south of Cape Flattery. There in the course of formal socializing, a woman doctor made pieces of wood walk about by themselves. Then a shaman of the visiting party performed, going outside to communicate with ghosts and returning to say they were to the south side in a highly excited state and that the next day there would be news of what was exciting them. It turned out that a drift whale had stranded, a prize find.

The third ghost story is about Chief ʔOwimy'is at Sarita. At death his property was destroyed except for some valuable oil stored in stomach bladders. When the people try to stage the greatest West Coast ceremonial of the Tlo:kwa:na or Wolf Ritual, the proceedings are disrupted by an awful whistling whenever the spirit power singing and dancing are started. Frightened, the people retreat to their homes. When ʔOwimy'is in his coffin had been taken out into the forest behind, there had been a shrieking sound like by a ceremonial whistle. A shaman doctor, again a woman, sees in a vision that it is the dead Chief's spirit that is angry because his oil was not poured on the fire to brighten the proceedings. The oil is poured on, the fire blazes spectacularly, and all is well. It was a flamboyant way to display one's greatness.

Text no. 114, "Bone Game at Nitinat," still by La:maho:s, tells of playing lahal (Selish), the popular gambling contest involving guessing which hand conceals a marked bone. A number of tally sticks, often ten, are taken or lost according to right and wrong guesses, the game being won when you get all the sticks, hence "stick game" also. Ha:naʔa is the Nootka name. Going on a gift visit to the Ni:ti:naʔath, his party travels from Barkley Sound on the steamboat *Tees* which disembarks them past their destination at P'a:chi:naʔa or Port Renfrew. Since it is a personal account, in both text and translation the names of places and peoples are given in the Nootka speech of La:maho:s rather than the Nitinat of the area visited. Stormy weather delays the travelers at Port Renfrew for five nights, during four of which our narrator does ʔo:simch ritual training for the anticipated ha:naʔa game. He trains in

bitterly cold, snowing weather, kneeling on the beach where the waves would wash over him, singing his gambling songs and praying to win. A motor launch comes and takes the party to Nitinat where they arrive with their gift of eight boxes of Pilot biscuits. Feasting occurs, repeatedly, and Ni:ti:naˀath social ceremonialism is vividly pictured. In his speech La:maho:s stresses peaceful relations with intermarriage between the Ni:ti:naˀath and the former great enemies of east Barkley Sound, the Ho:ʔi:ʔath, both sides actually alliances of several tribes. After the ceremonies are finally over, the bone game begins and lasts through the night with the visitors winning all three games thanks to the efficacy of the arduous ritual bathing and praying undergone earlier by La:maho:s. Telling his team mates not to play any more since they might lose, he leaves for home, walking to Tsaxts'a:ˀa or Bamfield. However, they play again, losing three times. The necessity of doing ˀo:simch ritual to be a winner at the bone game is underscored. La:maho:s's narrative is more verbose than the others and of interest as a first hand description of the period.

No. 115, "How a Man Mishandled Beaver Power," by Tom Sa:ya:ch'apis the old blind chief storyteller (Sapir 1921), is comparatively short. An older man goes Sockeye fishing and arrives at a place called ʔO:qtl'as where two young men with ritual branches on their heads invite him to a big house to visit their Chief. Inside are a lot of people, all wearing branches and busily adzing out things. A feast of blubber is held with four songs sung before beginning. After, a bunch of leftovers is given to the man to take home. Returning to his own house where he lives with just his wife and a small daughter, he goes in and tells the girl to go and fetch the take home food in the canoe. But the girl returns empty-handed having found no blubber there, only a bundle of wood. The wife is sent and comes back in with the wood whereupon alder sticks poke out from inside the man all over his body. He should have known that those he met were not human since the place had no house normally and he should not have returned home immediately. After meeting supernaturals one was supposed to stay several days off by oneself ritualizing and fixing the power substance received. Before he dies the man sings the four songs of the beavers to his wife. The woman then goes with her child to Ho:choqtlisˀath. This account is a typical historical explanation of a hereditary family right justifying public display. It can also serve to instruct the young as to proper procedure when power is received in an encounter with spirit beings.

In no. 116, "Sa:ya:ch'apis Meets a Storm," Alex's grandfather tells him about a great storm during the commercial fur sealing days when West Coast canoes were carried to and from the Bering Sea aboard schooners out of San Francisco. Caught in the storm coming home in the fall of 1886, the Ts'isha:ˀath on their schooner are resigned to death. Sa:ya:ch'apis, however, sallies forth to utter the magic spell of his great ancestor Na:we:ˀi:k to make the storm abate. It clears and a few of the Outer Islands of Barkley Sound

become visible, but the waves remain huge as they seek safe harbour. Two other schooners are seen, one a large three masted ship, going in at Homo:w'a or Village Island. The schooner of the Ts'isha:ʔath̲ anchors at the other, north end of the island, and they disembark in their canoes only to upset in the big breakers at the beach. Sa:ya:ch'apis though calms the sea with Na:we:'i:k's spell and, with his son, lands safely. Canoe and all they are picked up and carried to their house by ʔ̲A:h̲o:sʔath̲ from the big boat. To them it is clear that Sa:ya:ch'apis had used special power to calm the sea and he is asked to tell about it. He only remarks that it is very rough out and that he would be surprised if a schooner didn't perish. Later it turns out that the boat with the Qiltsmaʔ̲ath̲ went down. Sa:ya:ch'apis gives a feast of rice to the ʔ̲A:h̲o:sʔath̲ for pulling up his canoe, gaining their esteem. None of the others who had upset in the breakers had thus paid back their rescuers. The account is a lesson on how to succeed in life with its instances of the application of inherited spirit powers and of practicing public generosity to good effect. As in virtually all these texts, there are numerous illuminating details on the West Coast native world.

No. 117, "Kanop the Shaman," is again by Sa:ya:ch'apis. One moonlit night Kanop is sitting on the beach near a little creek in the Tlaʔo:kwiʔath̲ or "Clayoquot" village of Hopitsʔath̲ or "Opitsat" when a war party in a great canoe comes charging around the point and stops opposite him. Out jump two young men with buckets to get water. Then, all being supernatural, the various spirit beings in the canoe very loudly voice their characteristic utterances and songs, Otter and Wolf talking deafeningly, the angry Warrior yelling terribly, T'ama song singers singing away, the Shaman singing a doctoring song, the Whaler singing his ghost song, and the Chief performing his Ya:tya:t ceremony. Kanop is supposed to grab whichever one whose power he wants, but his legs go shaky and he just watches helplessly. When the young men return with the fresh water to the canoe and it departs, Kanop regains his legs, dives in where the raiding party had halted, and gets some of the foam created by the paddling. He goes home but is sick the next morning and in a vision sees the raiders still there where he saw them before. They tell him that to get better he has to be speared right through the body. Kanop is starting to die when several warrior friends are fetched. Two of them in turn spear Kanop, but he takes the weapon out. Now he spears himself in the belly and cuts off the intestines which fall out, then rubs the wound, magically making himself well. He runs out into the woods for four days, returns singing a song, and demonstrates his newfound power by pouring gunpowder into the fire and recapturing it falling back from the smokehole onto a mat, miraculously unburned. Next he burns all his blankets following the orders of his helping spirits. Then the Tla'o:kwiʔath̲ perform the Tlo:kwa:na ceremony but during the proceedings the people, beginning with the three Chiefs, start dropping dead. Kanop revives all the dead with his doctoring power the proceedings the people, beginning with the three Chiefs, start dropping dead. Kanop revives all the dead with his doctoring power and is paid well, amassing more blankets than he ever had before. He becomes wealthy and highly respected, the standard success story based on spirit power acquired through a dramatic supernatural encounter.

No. 118, "Ch'it'oqwin'ak Becomes a Shaman," by Sa:ya:ch'apis, is about a Yo:loˀilˀath̲ who excels at catching "shags" or cormorants sleeping on the cliffs at night. In this perilous undertaking as in others, proper ritual training is necessary to succeed. Ch'it'oqwin'ak, "War Club Dancer," decides to go after the Chief of the shags, one with dentalium shells inside, and trains diligently from the spring for the next winter shag catching season. In the fall when the people move up the Alberni Inlet to Nam'int for the Spring salmon run, he ascends the Nam'int River toward a mountain called M'itlow'a and at a certain spot finds small magical looking fish one of which he grabs. He climbs up M'itlow'a, and when night comes hears the fish in his hands singing doctoring songs whenever he falls asleep. Also he sees shamans. After four days he is descending when he sees a fireball tossed back and forth by the trees which event encourages him to become a shaman. He makes medicine of the magic fish, wrapping it in moss and pieces of his blanket. He forgets about doing ˀo:simch ritual for the special shag and imitates doctoring sounds. Back at the village someone sickens and dies. Ch'it'oqwin'ak has the coffin opened and puts his hands on the deceased who revives. He becomes a widely sought doctor and wealthy. At a Ts'a:yiq doctoring ceremonial he shows his power by breaking apart a bundled up mountain goat blanket then reassembling it whole again, symbolizing his revivification of the dead.

No. 119, "The Youth Who Followed a Shag," begins with a youth shooting an arrow into a shag. Together with his younger brother in a canoe, he follows the wounded shag up the river at H̲o:choqtlis, through a lake and up a headstream to a clump of ferns on the bank into which it disappears. Parting the ferns he sees a beautiful land abounding in Spring salmon. He goes home, then returns to the land with his sister with whom he has two boys. After four years he sends the boys back to the village seeking their grandfather. The grandparents receive them happily and feast the village with the many dried winter Spring salmon brought by the boys. When all the people go to sleep the boys slip away back home. After two more years of absence the young man with his sister as wife goes to the village taking bear meat and bearskins. The sister, when mocked by a woman for her incestuous relationship, replies by a song boasting of wealth, but later she becomes ashamed when her old father again feasts the village. After everyone falls asleep, the brother and sister depart undetected, never to return. In West Coast tradition incest can be the start of a new, or renewed, group in isolation, a widespread motif.

In account no. 120, "A Runaway Slave Comes to the Chief of Wanin," Sa:ya:ch'apis gives the origin of the Wanin?at<u>h</u>. Three brothers in a canoe see a hair seal on a rocky point which is suddenly clawed on the head by a creature which is taken for a cougar by two of them but is seen by the third to be the supernatural Head-On-Both-Ends. They take the seal home and while it is cooking talk about what attacked it. A slave listening in figures out that it is the Head-On-Both-Ends which alone does such a thing. In the evening he goes fishing with his boy and returns at night to find everyone dead from eating the seal. Taking the late Chief's valuables, the slave paddles away with his boy, hiding in bushes during the day lest he be killed as a runaway. The second day he hides near ?O:qwa:tis when at another spot in the vicinity called Wanin, a Ma:ktl<u>?</u>i:?at<u>h</u> named Ho:<u>h</u>inkwop comes at dawn to sit on the beach. The latter's boy is going about shooting little birds and reaches the hiding place of the runaway slave who tells him to tell his father. Ho:<u>h</u>inkwop gets his younger brothers and goes to fetch the runaway slave and his boy to the house. He gives a feast to the Chief of ?O:qwa:tis, giving coppers. The latter reciprocates with a feast and gives the Coho stream called Wanin to Ho:<u>h</u>inkwop who settles there with his group to become the Wanin?at<u>h</u>. Encounter with the supernatural began the chain of events leading to the origin of a tribe and its Chief to whom the narrator traces ancestry.

No. 121, "Wealth From a Shag," is a long account by Sa:ya:ch'apis about a young Chief called K'o:k'ots'itl'i:k or "Getter-of-Small Mussels" of the Ots'o:s?at<u>h</u>, the people around Flores Island who were killed off in the early 19th century by the <u>?</u>A:<u>h</u>o:s'at<u>h</u> of Vargas Island (Drucker 1951:344-53). Since his wife bore no children, K'o:k'ots'itl'i:k is cast off by his father as unmanly, but his uncle becomes his advisor. For days at a time he and his wife go off by canoe to get small mussels, also doing bathing ritual for success. Once when returning home he sees a great shag on the beach, seizes it and obtains two live <u>H</u>i:xwa: or dentalium out of it, a mated pair. The <u>H</u>i:xwa: multiply tremendously and being the native currency make the hero wealthy as canoe parties come from far and wide to trade goods for them. He and his wife continue to go off to get mussels for food. On one excursion a mother and infant of the Ya<u>?</u>i: spirits are met and the wife captures the baby. For its return the Ya<u>?</u>i: mother gives baby items which become medicine powers. Next the hero finds a cave full of seals and, together with his uncle, begins taking seals back to the village, cutting them to simulate harpoon wounds. He says he found them as dead drift seals, and the village hunters claim them as their own lost catches, giving feasts with them. Then the hero starts carrying a sealing harpoon in his canoe sticking out of the bow. The people surmise that he is harpooning the seals whereupon the false claimants are shamed. He increases the number brought in at a time to twenty-five and holds a feast at which his father gives him a new name. He declines the name. Next he buys a full whaling outfit and when the season begins, goes out with his uncle as steersman and four slaves as the rest of the crew. As a whaler he has great success, holds dorsal fin feasts shaming the people who used to laugh at him, and gets ten whales that year. Through supernatural powers he has attained complete success in West Coast terms.

No. 122, "Tla:tla:qokw'ap Sees the Thunderbird and Gets Power From a Sea Egg," told by William, is about a whaler who is successful through gaining supernatural powers. At the beginning he is trying in vain to get to a fleeing harpooned whale when a cloud comes up with rain and thunder, so he ties up with the canoe of his younger brothers. His whale now stays surfaced. It hails as the Thunderbird picks up the whale and drops it on the sea repeatedly. The giant supernatural bird then flies off, leaving the whale to be easily killed. As the whale is being towed home to Ts'isha:, it is noted to be unusual with a large fin and a small. What was seen is remembered well for making into a topa:ti or family property right. On the next outing, a younger brother harpoons a whale with a one-sided tail. Then a broken-tailed whale is taken. A feast is given with the three dorsal fins at which Tla:tla:qokw'ap displays the Thunderbird as a topa:ti privilege in a painting on a wide board. They go out again and get two whales. The next time the youngest brother harpoons, but the whale cannot be killed in two days of trying. At night it speaks to the youngest brother in his sleep telling him to sing to it. He does so, and the whale swims in to Ts'otsit or Sail Rock, towing along the whalers. Inside it had two fat liver-like organs. Again they go out and this time attack the giant halibut which accompanies whales, but the harpoon draws from its soft flesh. Four whales are killed and towed in together. But the next time nothing is caught. Depressed, Tla:tla:qokw'ap swims from Ts'isha: to Ts'otsit about a mile away, picking up a supernatural sea urchin on the way. He makes medicine of it on top of Ts'otsit, returns home and observes the required period of ritual tabu. Whaling success returns to the brothers, the eldest getting two at a time. This account might have been put in part 9 which features whaling, often with supernatural elements; however, here the latter seem more primary since the whaling brothers do not have to work particularly hard for their successes.

No. 123, "How the Nitinats Get the Thunderbird and Lightning Snake," by Captain Bill, starts with the great flood when the tide kept rising to cover all the land except the top of Ka:ka:piya: or Mt. Edinburgh. Xitlxitl'iˀi lands there in a canoe with his daughter. The flood recedes, but they stay on the mountain and the daughter gets pregnant by a Yaˀi: wood spirit. A boy is born and grows rapidly, being supernatural. Descending from the mountain, the boy, now a young man, starts whaling with the whales coming right on to the beach while he just watches from the house. He has two children, a boy and a girl. The boy grows up, is told that he owns the mountain Ka:ka:piya:, and climbs it. On top he sees the Thunderbird. When he is back down, his sister has her first menses and is isolated behind a board screen at the end of the house. The youth paints the Thunderbird on the screen. The girl has a vision, seeing the Lightning Snake giving birth. Her father makes medicine of it, getting a name and designing a headmask. The youth designs a Thunderbird and also builds a house with the Lightning Snake on the side. The father holds a Wolf Ritual Dance in honour of his children, having the son dance as the Lightning Snake, telling of what the girl saw, and giving her the name Gliding-Out-of-the-Corner-of-the-House. All of these ceremonial features are family privileges, of course, of Captain Bill who was part Nitinat.

No. 124, "A H̲iko:lʔath̲ Sees the Thunderbird and the Northern Lights Women," is another by William. The H̲iko:lʔath̲ were a leading division of the greater Ts'isha:ʔath̲ sociopolitical union. A man sets off on foot alone, does ritual bathing and rubbing for four days, falls asleep, and is awakened by some being who is immediately gone without being seen. He bathes again, walks on, and sees a large feather fall from the sky. He grabs it and falls unconscious but is told by it that he would see something. Reviving, he hears thundering approaching from afar, sees a Lightning Snake fall and then the Thunderbird which lands. Paralysed, he cannot get near it but observes its appearance. After the supernatural creature flies off, he does not go home for a period. He has another supernatural experience, coming across ten women of the Northern Lights by a great fire. Now he returns home, tells his younger brother of the things seen which would be made their topa:ti right. The Thunderbird had bestowed many names. He painted it, the Lightning Snake, and the feather on a wide board and used it in his daughter's puberty rite ceremony, a major social event at which prestigious, supernaturally acquired family prerogatives were publicly displayed with feasting and wealth distribution, and thus recognized. The account is typical and again helps in understanding the rationale of West Coast ceremonial representations.

No. 125, "A M'o:h̲o:lʔath̲ Youth Visits the Thunderbird," told by Tyee Bob, is a well detailed treatment of a visit to the mighty mythical creature in his mountain top home. The M'o:h̲o:lʔath̲ are one the three originally Salishan peoples around the head of Alberni Inlet who became the present Ho:pach'asʔath̲. An uninstructed inept youth goes off to bathe and rub arduously and repeatedly. Told by dream to go to the Thunderbird's home, he tries to climb Thunder Mountain but is blocked by a sheer cliff around it. His mother advises him, and he bathes and rubs still harder, praying for a pathway up the mountain. On the second ritual attempt he finds a pretty little supernatural bird. After that he finds a trail up past the cliff and reaches a house. Entering he is told to sit and finds many Lightning Snakes inside which are repelled by the cedarbark he has brought along. A chamberpot calls out four times that he had entered the house, and the Thunderbird comes home from afar. He tells the youth who is hiding to emerge, boils up blubber, feasts him, and gives him a

Lightning Snake. He is pleased by the cedarbark the youth has brought. Part of a whale is given to the youth for taking home. Then the Thunderbird flies the him back to his place. The youth becomes a great bear hunter, repeatedly feasting the people. A seal hunter competes with seal feasts. The youth makes his father overeat bearfat and die in revenge for not teaching him how to hunt. He distributes bearskins as he validates rights to a masked Thunderbird dance and many names for himself and his sister. That it is bear hunting prowess which the youth gains from his supernatural experience reflects the land orientation of the Ho:pach'as?at<u>h</u>.

The foregoing synopses are only outlines, of course, lacking the richness of the actual narratives. Storytelling was a well developed West Coast art, and is often enthralling even in translation. Evocative atmospheres, dramatic moments, bold speech, and sometimes song enliven the account. When characters speak their individualities are sharply rendered, including idiosyncrasies. For the West Coasters these narratives tell of true events and are history. Their plots and details reflect the native worldview, the cosmology structuring reality in terms of the supernatural and marvellous which through encounter bring prestigious power to individual and family. These *Tales of Extraordinary Experience*, like those of *Legendary Hunters*, are of the psyche - West Coast wonder tales. They may seem to be from another planet though, so different is our world view today, even from the time when they were gathered by Sapir and Alex Thomas not a century ago. In native outlook there is enough continuity still to keep the accounts current.(EA)

References

Arima, E.Y., Denis St. Claire, Louis Clamhouse, Joshua Edgar, Charles Jones, and John Thomas
1991 Between Ports Alberni and Renfrew: notes on West Coast peoples. *Canadian Museum of Civilization, Canadian Ethnology Service Mercury Series Paper 121.* Ottawa.

Cook, James
1967 The voyage of the *Resolution* and *Discovery*, 1776-1780. *The journals of Captain James Cook on his voyages of discovery, ed. J.C. Beaglehole, vol. 3, pts. 1 & 2.* Cambridge: University Press for Hakluyt Society.

Drucker, Philip
1951 The Northern and Central Nootkan tribes. *Smithsonian Institution, U.S. Bureau of American Ethnology Bull. 144.* Washington.

Ha-Shilth-Sa
1978 Nuu-Chah-Nulth-Aht not Nootka. *Ha-Shilth-Sa* 10 Nov 1978, p. 4. Port Alberni.

Sapir, Edward
1921 The life of a Nootka Indian. *Queen's Quarterly* 28:232-43, 351-67. Kingston.
1949 *Selected writings of Edward Sapir in language, culture and personality.* Ed. D.G. Mandelbaum. Berkeley and Los Angeles: University of California Press.

Sapir, Edward, and Morris Swadesh
1939 *Nootka texts. Tales and ethnological narratives with grammatical notes and lexical materials.* Philadelphia: Linguistic Society of America.
1955 Native accounts of Nootka ethnography. *Indiana University Research Center in Anthropology, Folklore, and Linguistics 1; International Journal of American Linguistics 21(4), pt. 2.* Bloomington.

St. Claire, Denis
1991 Barkley Sound tribal territories. In E.Y. Arima et al., Between Ports Alberni and Renfrew, *Canadian Museum of Civilization, Canadian Ethnology Service Mercury Series* 121:13-202. Ottawa

Thomas, Alexander, and E.Y. Arima
1970 t'a:t'a:qsapa - a practical orthography for Nootka. *National Museums of Canada, National Museum of Man Publications in Ethnology 1.* Ottawa.

MAPS

1. Location and languages of the West Coast Indians xxvi
2. Barkley Sound First Nations, later 18th century xxvii
3. United Ts'isha:ʔath area, Barkley Sound xxviii
4. Ho:m'o:w'a (Village Is.)........................... xxix
5. Ma:ktlʔi: (Wouwer Is.) xxx
6. Ts'isha: (Hawkins Is.) xxxi
7. T'oqwa:s (Turret Is.) xxxii
8. ʔAlachmaqis (Dodd Is.) xxxiii
9. Timqimliml (Wiebe Is.) xxxiv
10. Momo:ssqomiktli (Jaques Is.) xxxv
11. Tl'iho:wa (Nettle Is.) xxxvi
12. ʔA:siml (Hand Is.) xxxvii
13. Hi:kwis (Equis) xxxviii
14. Chihamil (Canoe Is.) xxxix
15. Hach'a: (Alma Russell Islands) xl

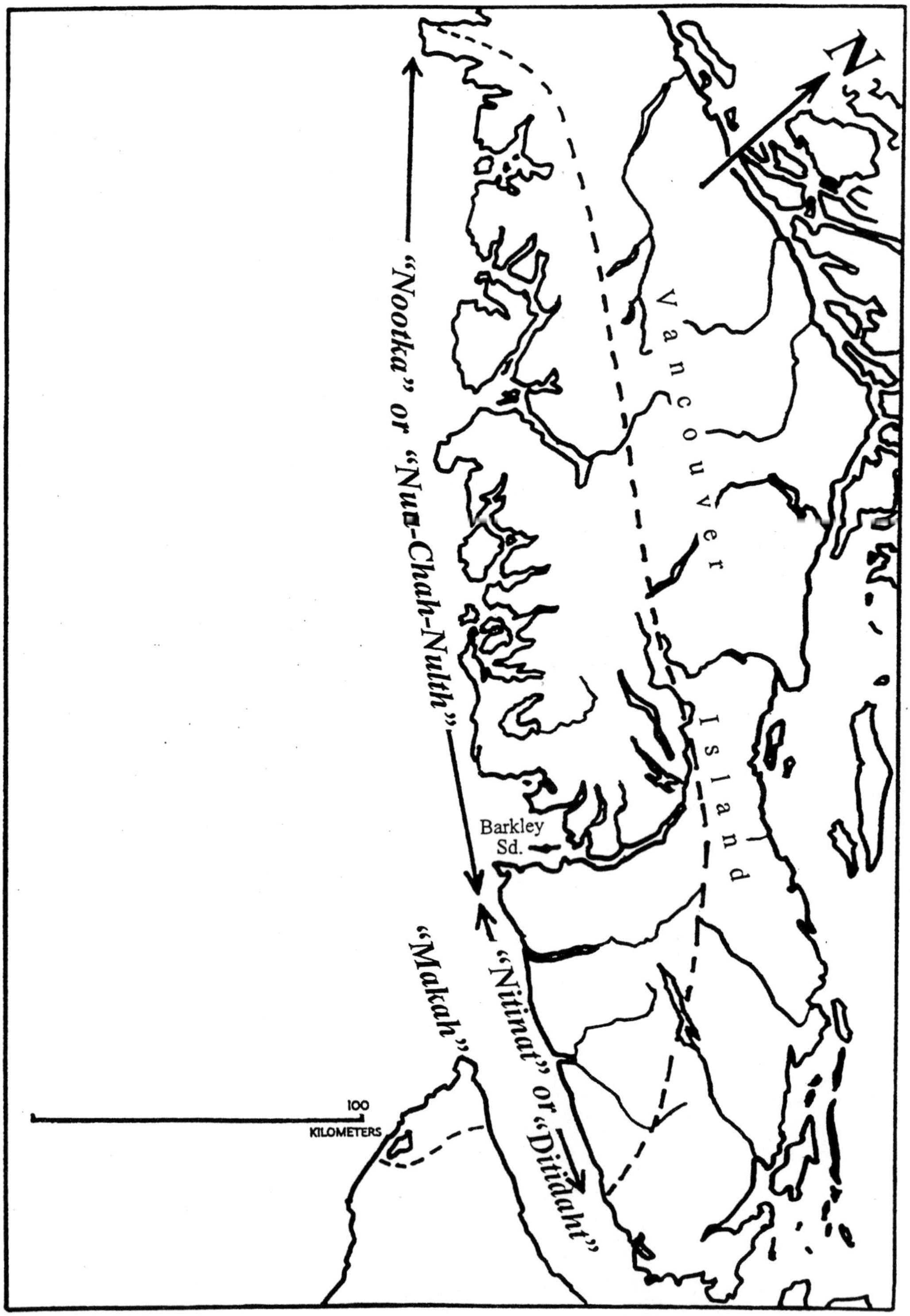

Map 1. Wakashan languages of the West Coast Whaling Indians of Vancouver Island and Cape Flattery

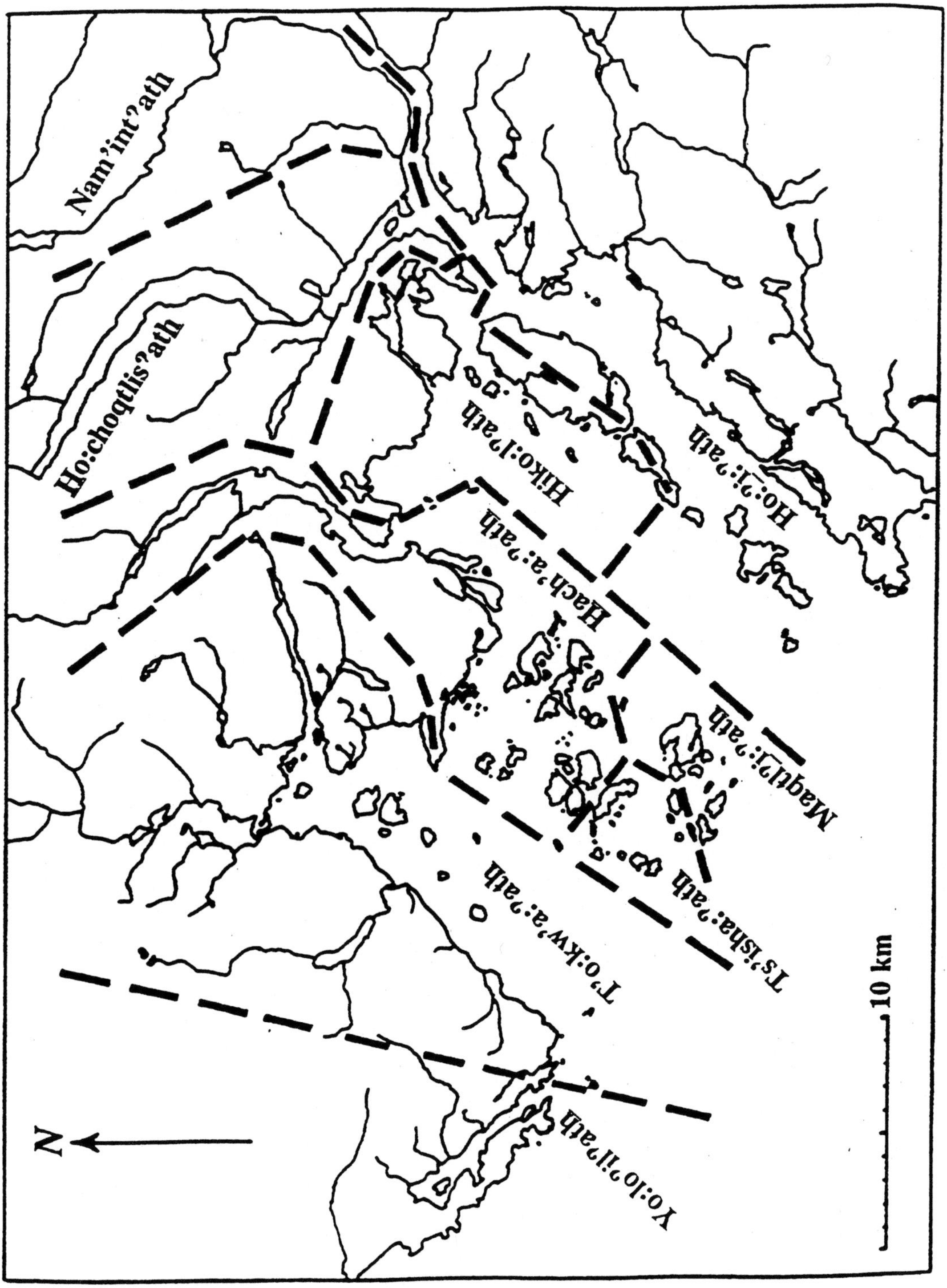

Map 2. Barkley Sound First Nations, later 18th century
(After St. Claire 1991:29, 34, 35, 39, 46 maps 1-5)

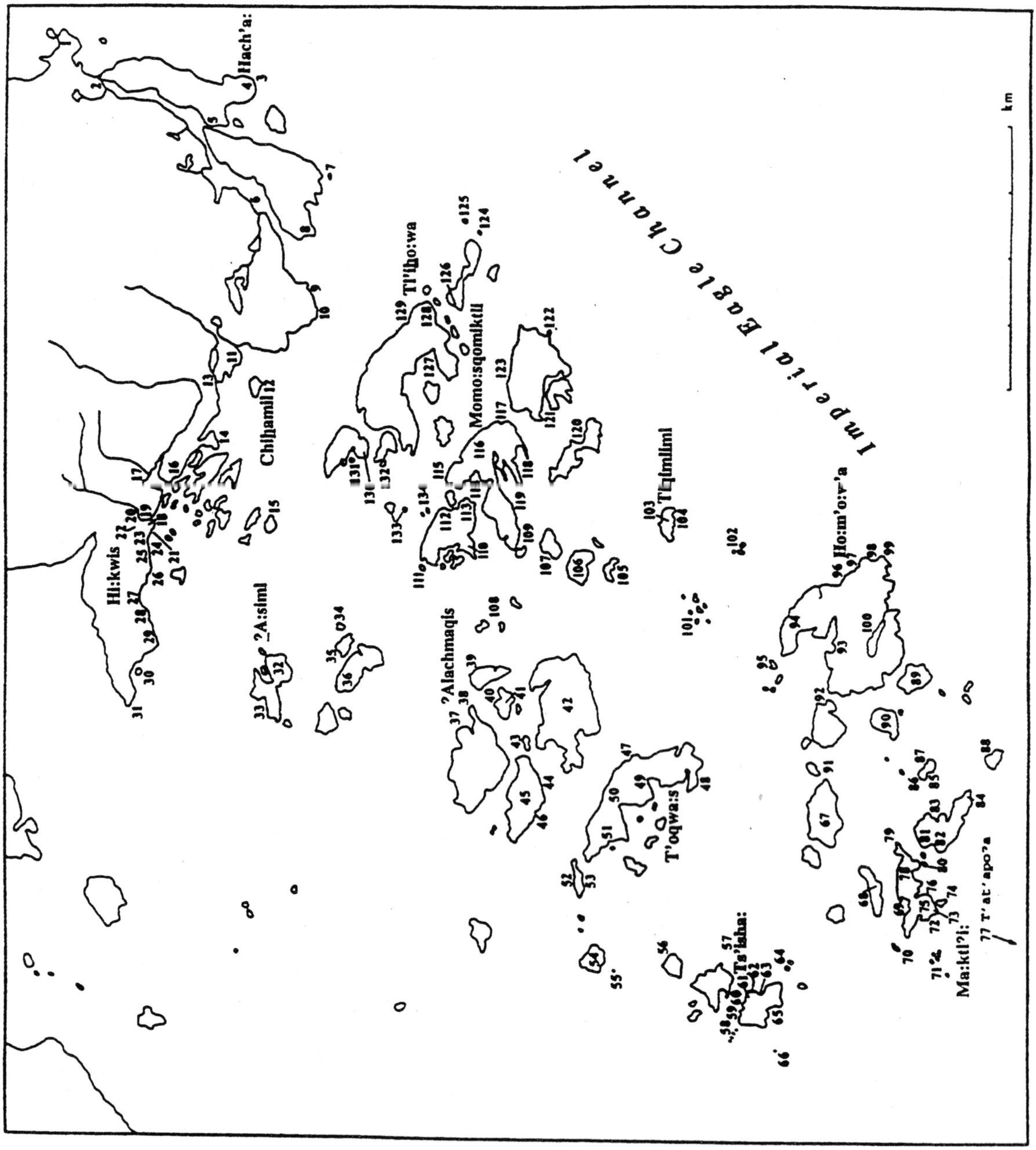

Map 3. United Ts'isha:ʔath̲ Area, Barkley Sound
(After St. Claire 1991:129 map 12, for endnotes place identification and to key larger scale maps to follow)

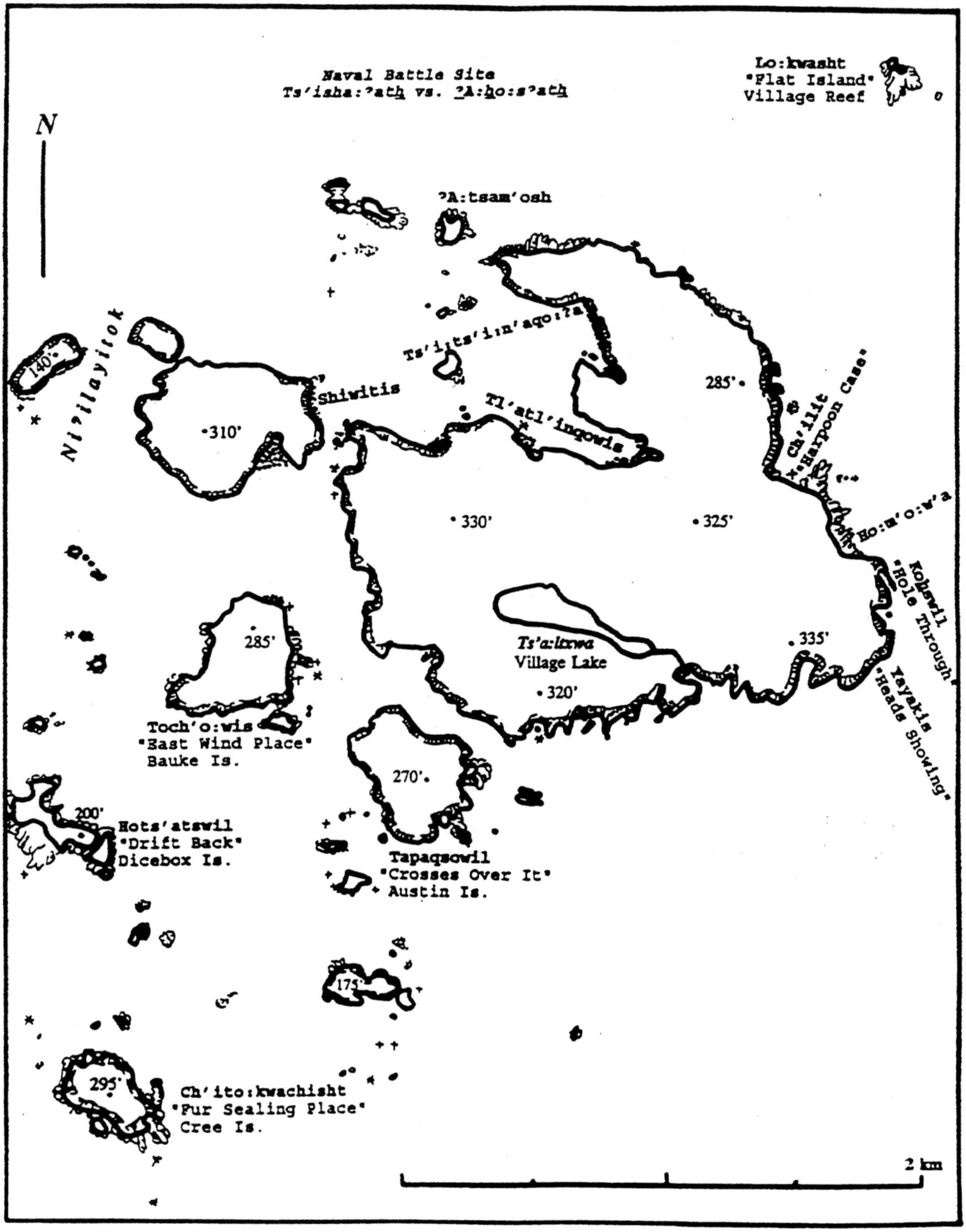

Map 4. Ho:m'o:w'a (Village Island, recently renamed Effingham)
(After St. Claire 1991:129 map 12)

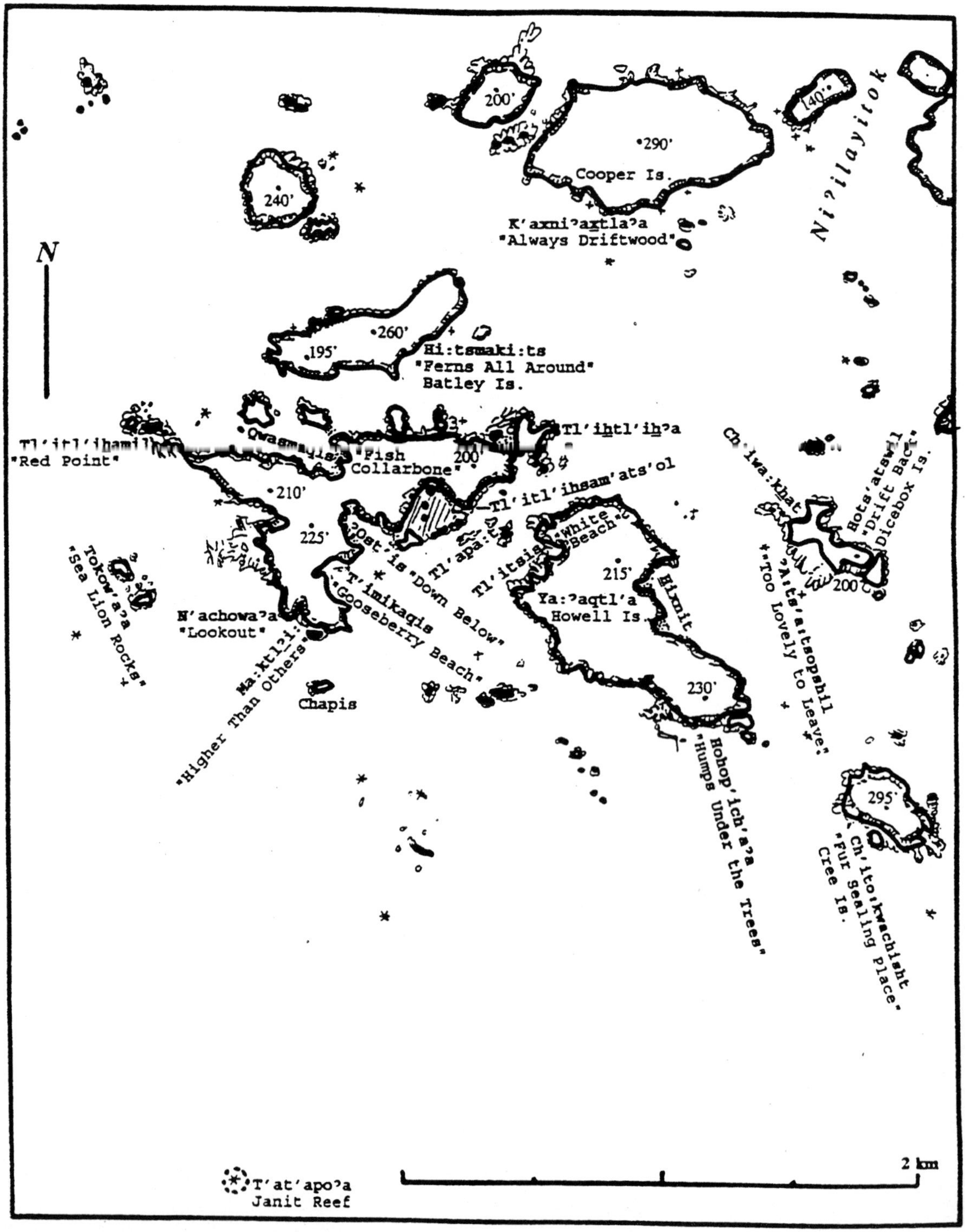

Map 5. **Ma:ktlˀi:** (Wouwer Is.) (After St. Claire 1991:129 map 12)

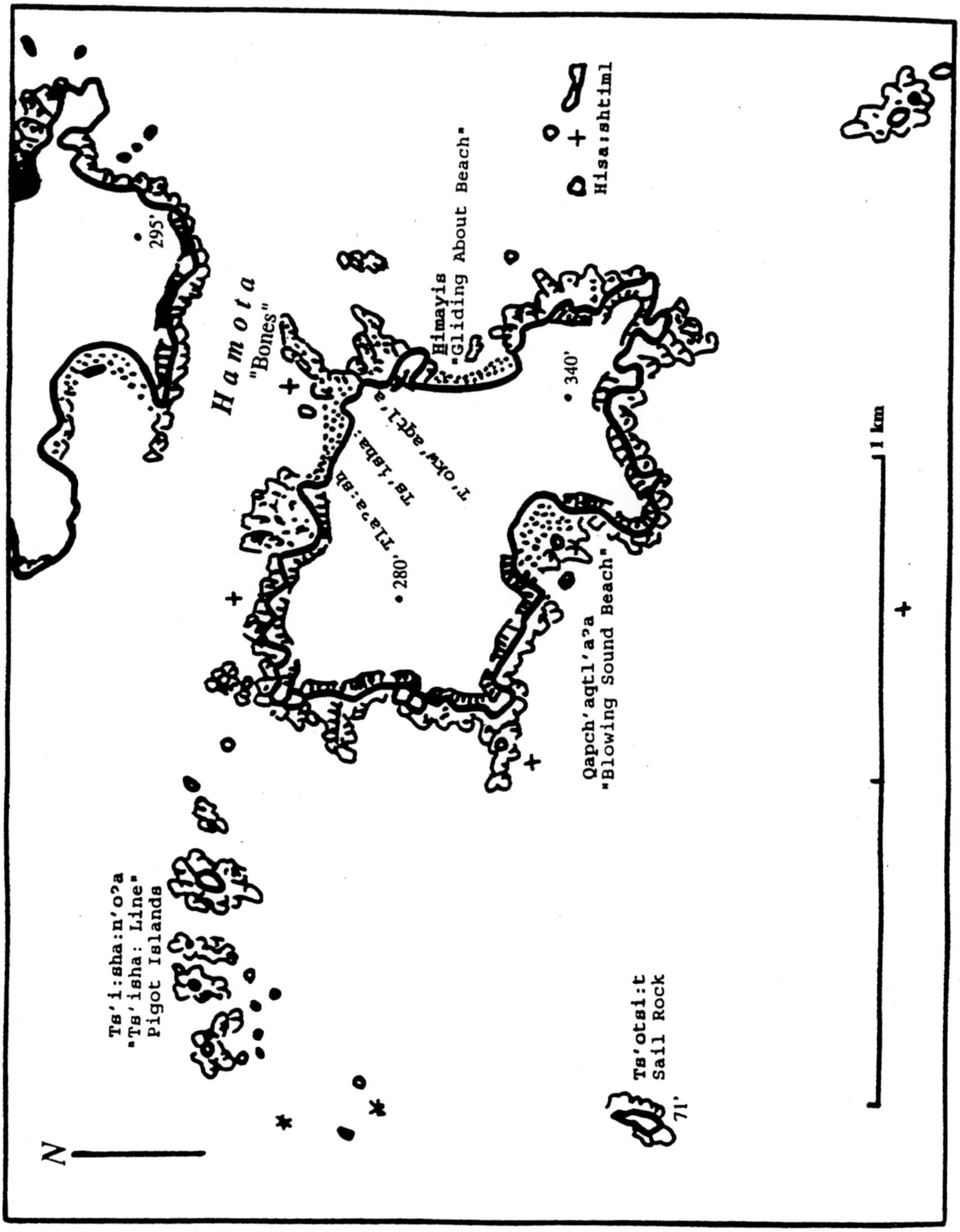

Map 6. Ts'isha: (Hawkins Is., recently renamed Benson)
(After St. Claire 1991:47 map 6, 129 map 12)

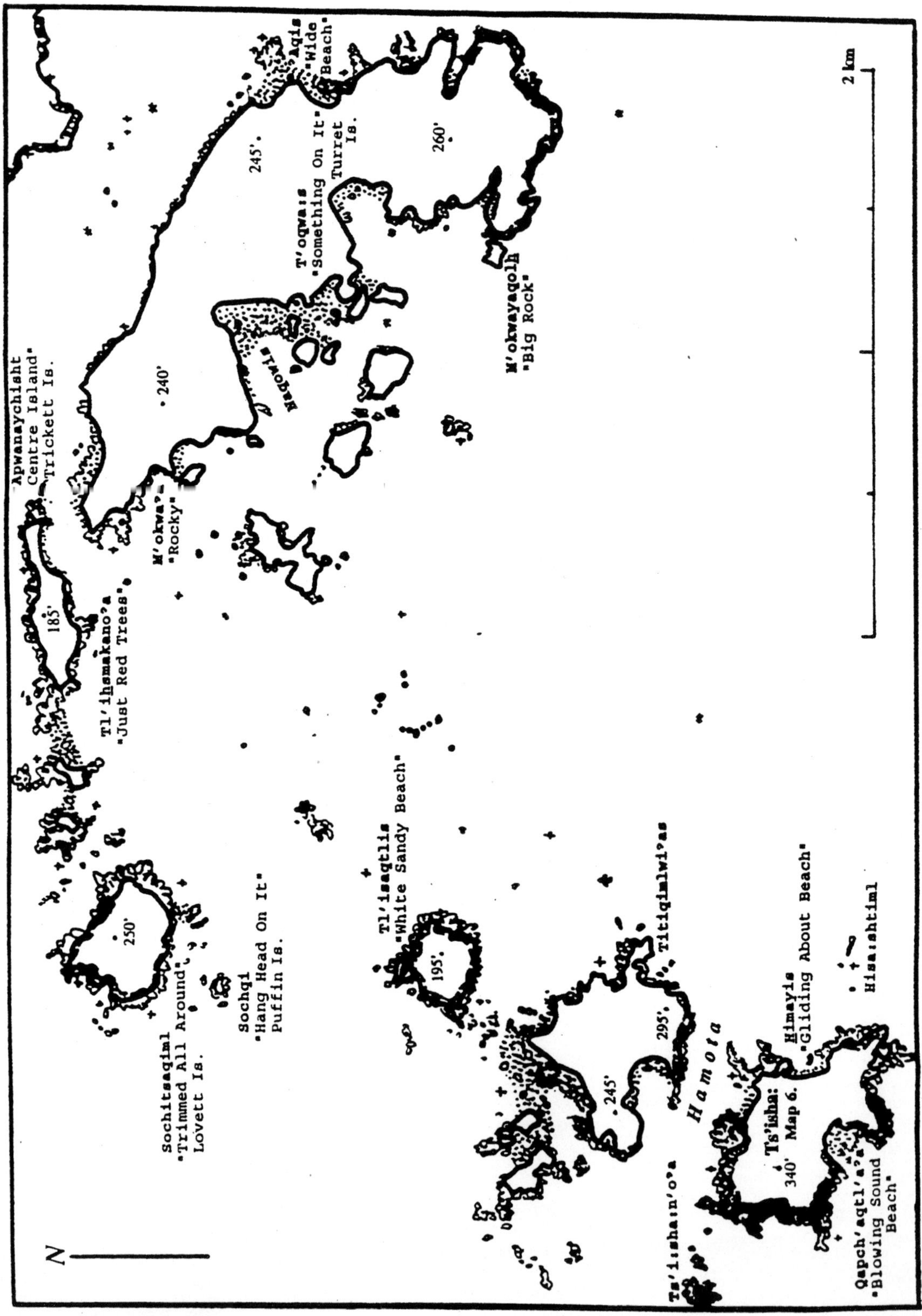

Map 7. T'oqwa:s (Turret Is.) (Ibid.)

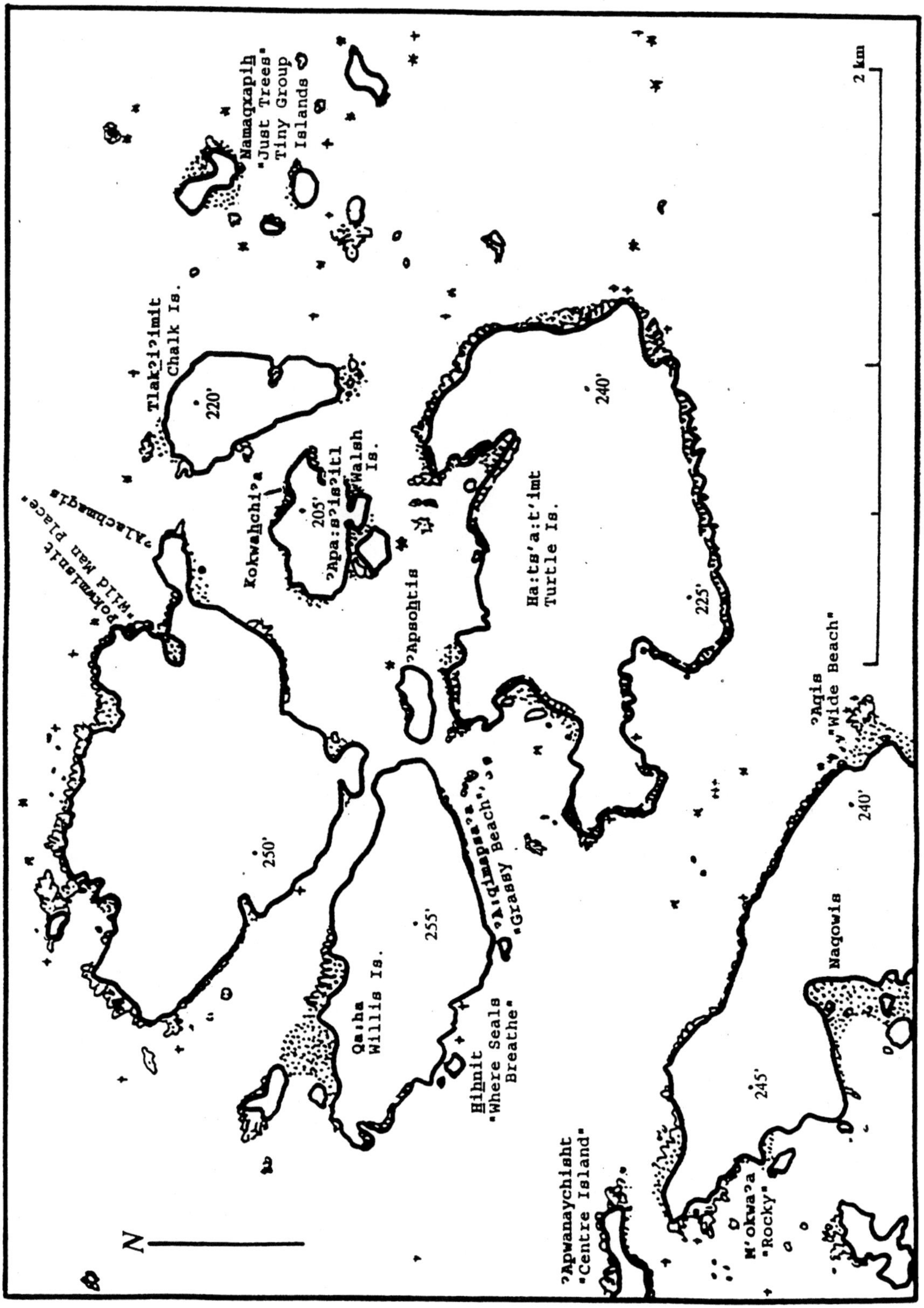

Map 8. ʔAlachmaqis (Dodd Is.) (Ibid.)

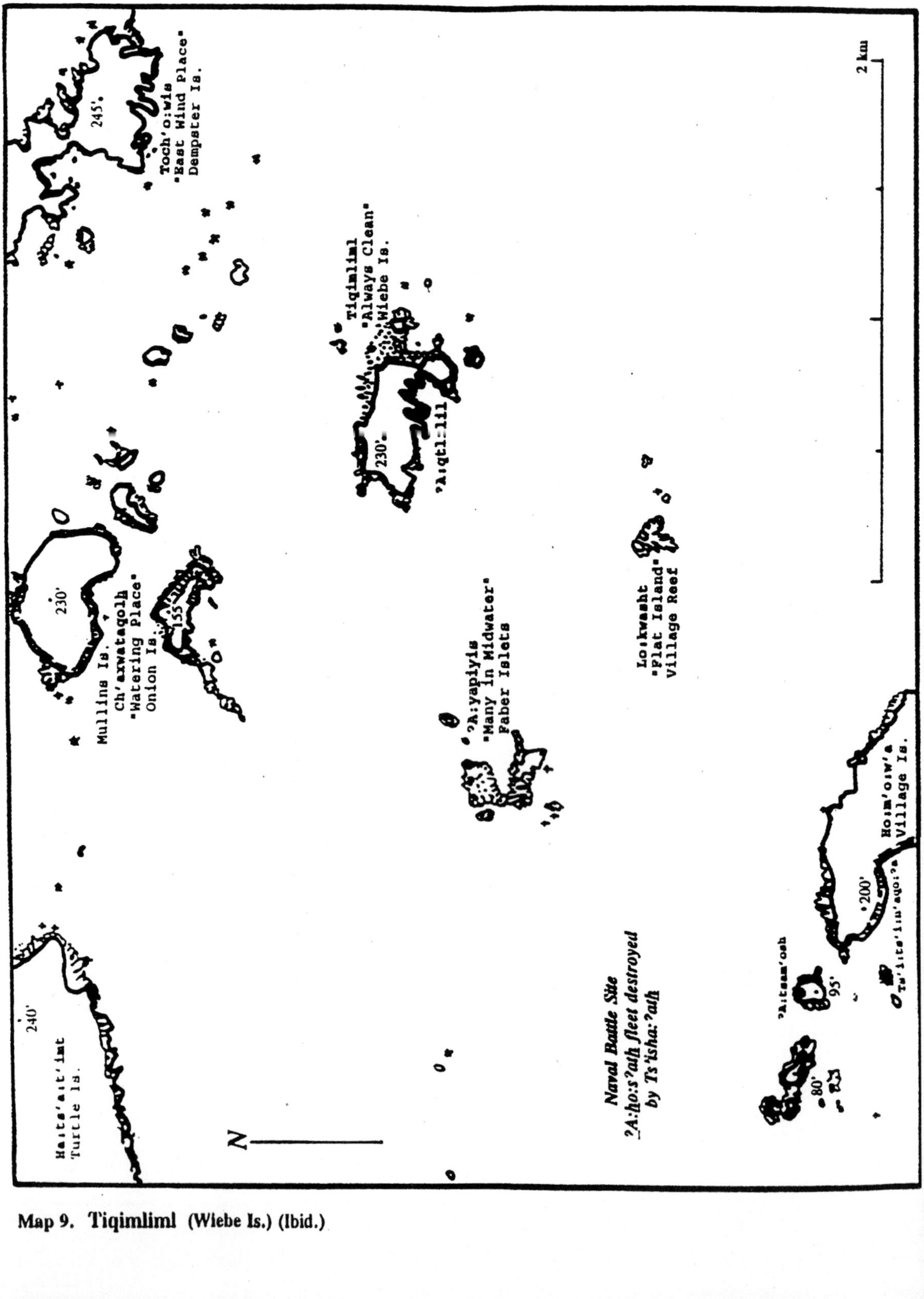

Map 9. Tiqimliml (Wiebe Is.) (Ibid.)

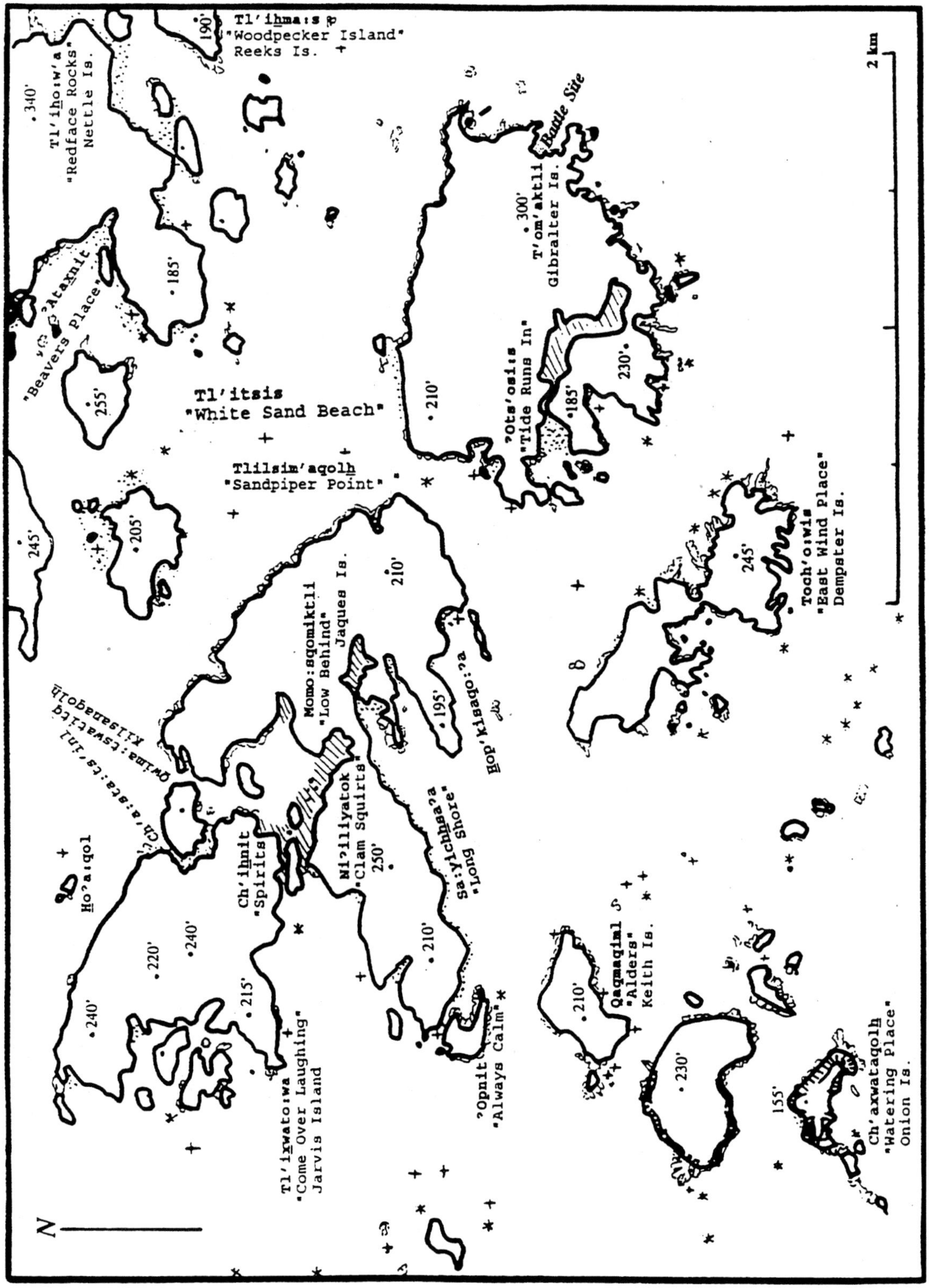

Map 10. Momo:sqomiktli (Jaques Is.) (Ibid.)

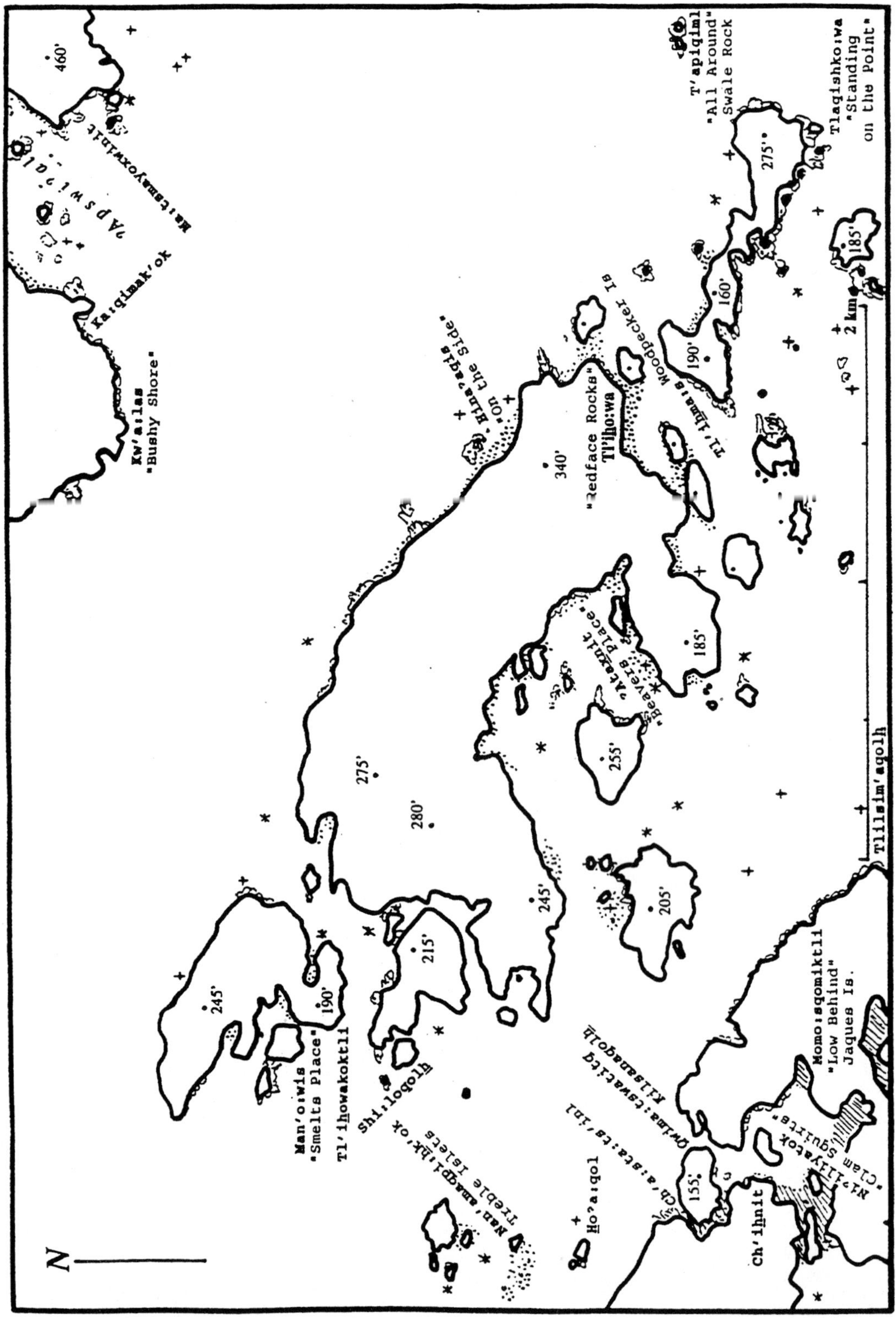

Map 11. Tl'iho:wa (Nettle Is.) (Ibid.)

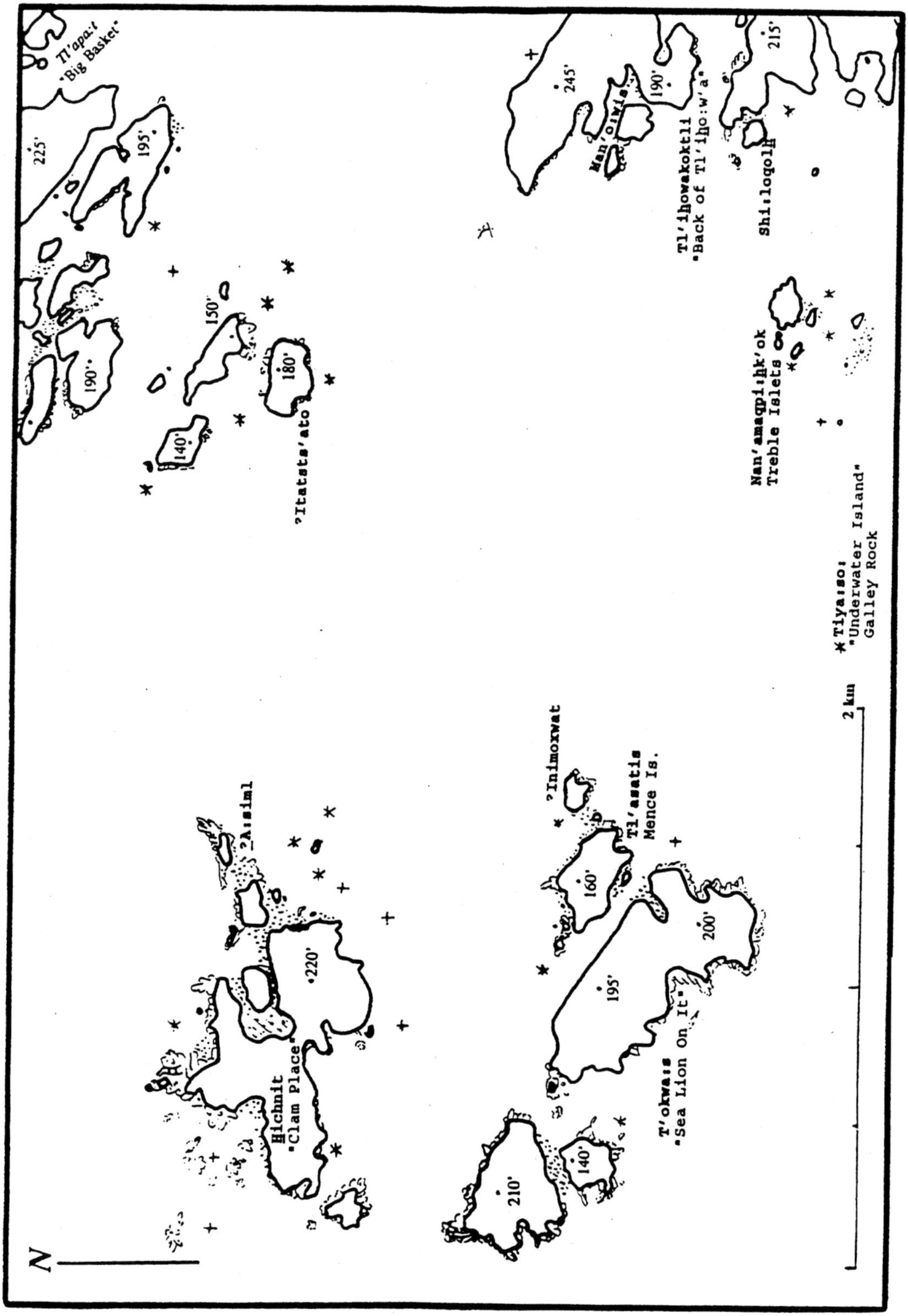

Map 12. ?A:siml (Hand Is.) (Ibid.)

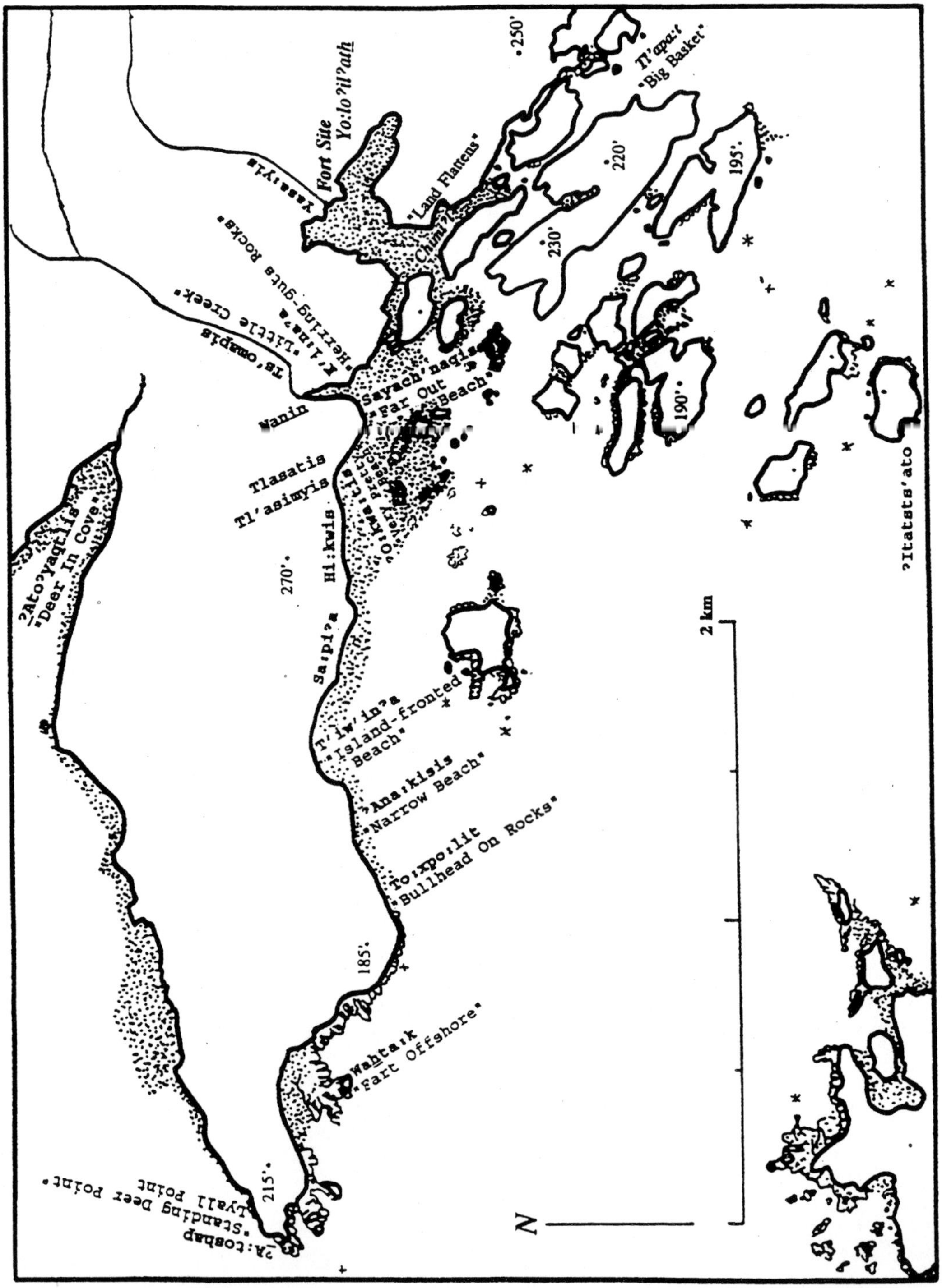

Map 13. Hi:kwis (Equis) (Ibid.)

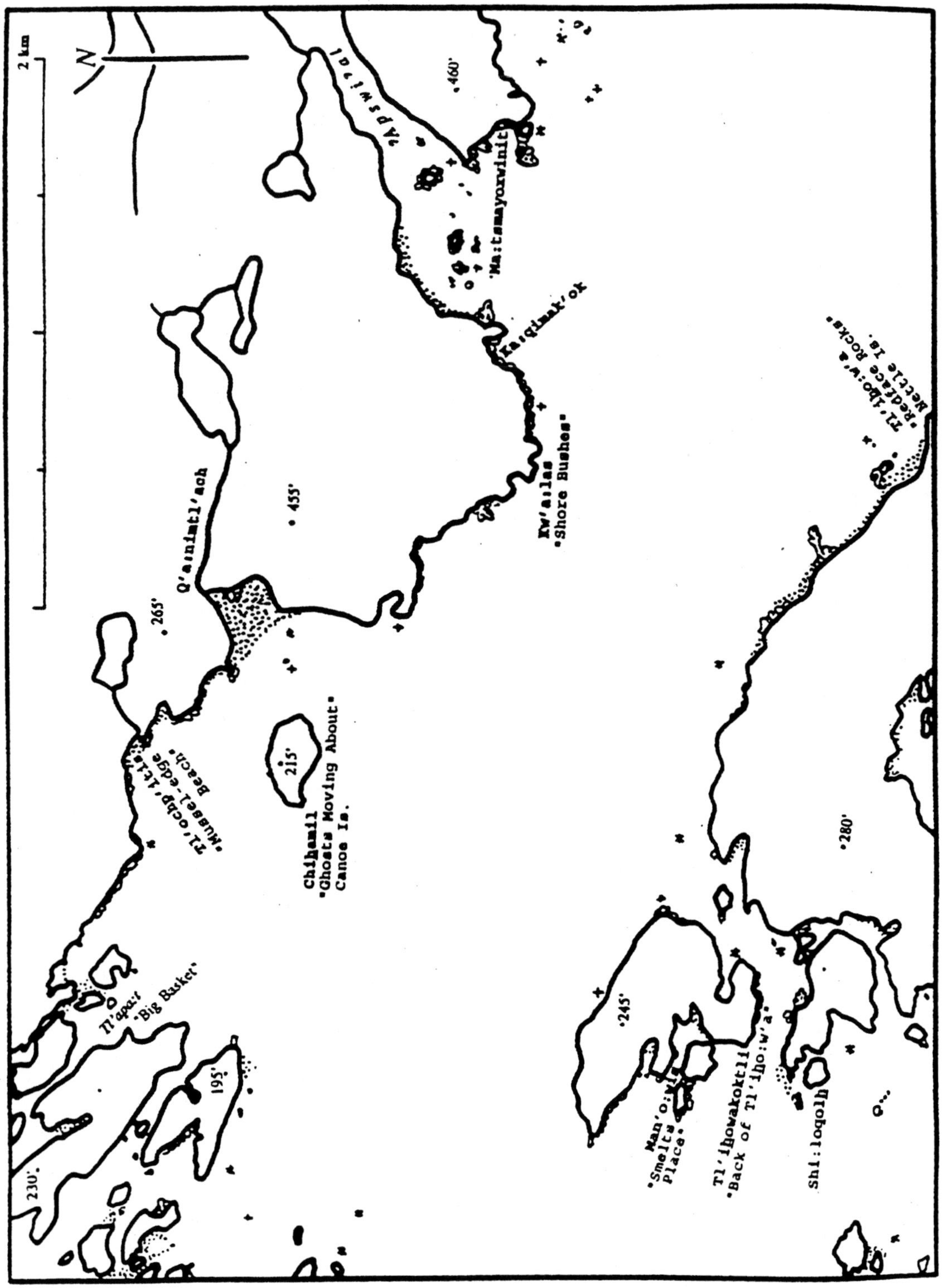

Map 14. **Chihamil** (Canoe Is.) (Ibid.)

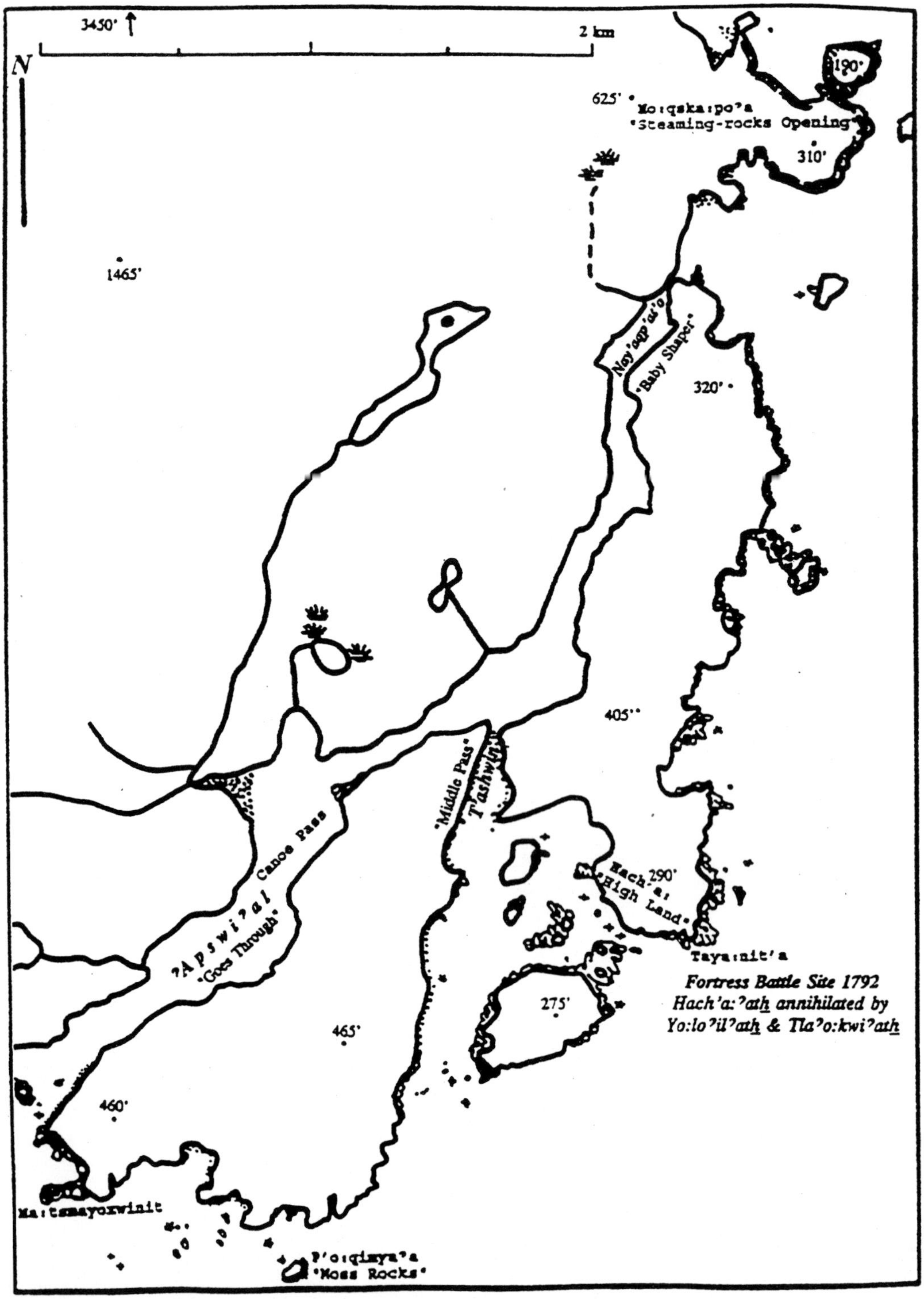

Map 15. Hach'a: (Alma Russell Islands) (Ibid.)

NARRATIVES

113. Shamans and Ghosts (La:maho:s)[1]

All right. They were starting a N'a:chn'a:cha or foretelling ceremony.[2] The children were starting a N'a:chn'a:cha dance, those many children were starting the N'a:chn'a:cha. The shaman doctor was performing the N'a:chn'a:cha because, they said, the children were taken away by those people who were long dead, those who were already ghosts. The N'a:chn'a:cha said that all the children should be taken, all those that started the dance. They took those who had small children and brought them to where the N'a:chn'a:cha was. The N'a:chn'a:cha was very excited![3] She was very fierce looking now. Her name was Wawatso:poˀotl, the N'a:chn'a:cha woman. The N'a:chn'a:cha said it was fearsome now: the ghosts were all excited about the children who had been taken. One of the boys did not want to participate. The one who did not want to was named Chapiqtlil. The little boy was taken, the one who protested, by his mother and she told him,

"You are now the only one not there where the other children are who are going to dance this."

The boy still said no, he didn't want to.

The N'a:chn'a:cha used to go outside, going into the woods back of the house. Lots of people followed her, men and some women. They used to come back and go inside. The woman was very fierce looking now, dirty faced. She had dirt on her face because she was digging up the ground. Then the N'a:chn'a:cha said,

"It is hard now but you should go and get the absent boy. The ghost has him inside the big rock at the ghost's house."

Again the doctor said, "You should go and get him. Try really hard. They have his soul, the ghosts do."

So then two women went to get the boy, the mother and an aunt; the two of them went to get Chapiqtlil. They arrived where the boy was.

"You are the only one absent. Come along now, you are becoming a nuisance," they said to him.

The boy then spoke: "I guess they will have to leave me in this rock."

The two women got ugly.[4] One on each side of him they took the boy along, trying to make him stand up, making him stand up. Still the boy said he would not do it.

He said the same thing again: "I guess they will have to have me remain in this rock."

Now the two women got very angry and started to scold the boy, just the two of them, saying he was a real stupid boy.

"You are a very stupid boy!" they kept saying to him.

The two women set out walking back to where they came from and said the boy wouldn't come.

"He really won't. Doesn't want to. We tried and gave up. He won't do it, the ugly stupid boy!"

All right then, the doctor set out walking, the N'a:chn'a:cha. She started jabbering away. None of us could understand what she was talking about because she was talking differently to the Ghost. The children went along, all of them, with those who owned them to the big rock which, they say, was the Ghost's house where he had the children's souls taken by the ghosts. They arrived there and gathered together, all those who came along. The doctor woman started to dig at the lower side of the beach. She made the dug out spot the size of her head, just right so that it entered underneath when she bent down her head. And while she was like that she would tilt her head and call out.

"Come!" she'd say, mentioning the names of those children in there.

Then she would grab at them under there while saying the names of the ones she took, the name of each child.

"This is so-and-so," she'd say and give it to the owner of the child.

The owner[5] would then take the child.

"Come, I have taken you," the owner of the little child would say.

She did that until all of the children were called out.

"All right, the only one still in there is Chapiqtlil," said the woman doctor. "We could not do anything because he did not come out."

Then the doctor woman went to where she lived. The mother of Chapiqtlil was nearly crying, and his aunt as well, because he was the only one left in there with the doctor woman unable to do anything for him. The mother and aunt were saying that they were very sad in their minds, that their child was the only one left in there. The others whose children had been called out were very happy because theirs had come out, taken out by the doctor woman, because they had gotten their children back. They began thanking the doctor; she was being thanked by all those who owned the children. The doctor now spoke:

"I can't do anything about Chapiqtlil who did not want to come out, she said. "He's being really held by the ghosts; they have hime inside the house."

All right then, the doctor started to counsel the parents of the little children.

"You make them bathe," she said. "Put something on their heads, and rub medicine on their bodies."

All the women began talking among themselves, those who were there. They were sad on account of Chapiqtlil being left behind inside the rock. All right, that's as far as it went. The group of women were saying that something would happen to him pretty quick because the ghosts still had a hold of him. The people spoke among themselves saying that perhaps something should happen; they really expected something to happen to him. They were very sad, the father, mother and aunt who were nearly crying for Chapiqtlil. And yet he is alive. He was never sick as he grew up and has lots of children today. ʔ̲I:la:wopshi:l is his name now. He has never been sick all his life.

* * * *

We went to Tl'a:ˀasˀath̲[6] a long time ago. I went with the one who was called Ho:kw'a:xin, a Ho:ʔ̲i:ˀath̲.[7] Ho:kw'a:xin was on a gift visit trip to ˀOsi:l.[8] That is the name of the place to the other side of Ni:ya:. Our canoe was at Ni:ya:. From there we started walking over toward ˀOsi:l. We went with the doctor called Nopots'iqx̲aˀa, a doctor from Ni:ya:. He was related to Ho:kw'a:xin and was lame, the doctor, a great doctor who now lived on the other side of Ni:ya:. We set out in a whaling canoe, paddling towards ˀOsi:l at last.

We arrived at ˀOsi:l. People came down to meet us. The father of the young man who came with us was ˀAshk'iˀi:. We told them that we brought four boxes of Pilot bread. The son of ˀAshk'iˀi: said to bring two boxes to his sister. Then they brought us up the beach, inviting us. It became night, and we went to sleep.

Then it became daylight. We were invited again by someone else. Evening fell again.

All right, the next day came once more. We were told that

there were not many people living there, only about seven men.[9] That evening we were invited again. We went as guests inside the house. We heard them getting ready, the villagers. Ha! They came, arrived at the door and began to sing in the doorway. The song they sang was a Ts'a:yiq power dance song. They came in. Tied around their heads they had headbands of beaten raw cedarbark. All of them wore these, as many as there were, both men and women wearing the raw beaten cedarbark. They all came in, probably seven women. We were watching with interest. The doctor Nopots'iqxa?a was also watching. They stopped dancing, stopped their Ts'a:yiq song. The woman doctor spoke now, an old Kwinyo:t'ath[10] woman.

"I am going to see how strong my doctor powers are," she said.

She took off her shawl, didn't have it on now. Then she began singing her song, her own doctoring song, the shaman doctor woman. She took pieces of box wood, two pieces, each narrow. She was really dancing, starting the Tlo:kwa:na or Wolf Ritual dance. She put the box wood "spearing fashion" on the floor and was talking, praying that they would come alive. Her hands were shaking, the right hand held up in the air and the left one pounding the floor with the box wood endwise. For along time she did that but could not get them alive. All right, the woman then stopped singing.

All right, the other doctor took her turn, a woman again. She, too, began to sing; she also sang her song for doctoring. The woman began to do the Tlo:kwa:na. She was stronger powered than the other first doctor and caused the box wood to stand on end on the floor, her hand shaking. She was making noises, really gone into the Tlo:kwa:na. The beaters were really beating time as they were singing. All right, hers started moving around, the woman doctor's pieces of box wood started to move! The box wood really moved now, nearly going over on the floor; they began to "walk" by themselves, "spearing" themselves on the floor. They would go far one way and come back again, moving by themselves, nobody holding or touching them. They were made to come alive by the doctor! She was just shaking her hand while sitting down. Then she stopped singing. The doctor woman spoke:

"Don't you folks sit too close to the wall," she said to us. "The ghosts are moving about. There are lots of them behind the house there where you folks are sitting. The ghosts are extremely agitated now."

We moved out a little from the wall, got away from being close to the wall. We did what we were told to do. There was a graveyard on the upper side of the house close to the beach. It was truly close to the side of the house at which we sat, that's why we believed what was said to us by the doctor. She started to sing again. She did the same one again, sang the Tlo:kwa:na song. She did not use the box wood this time; she was just singing. All right, she stopped singing.

All right, it was at this time that Ho:kw'a:xin was talking to me:

"Our doctor should try, too, so we can find out for sure what kind of ghosts are going about here because now we are afraid. I am very much afraid," Ho:kw'a:xin said to me.

"All right," I said to Nopots'iqxa?a. "You are to try now!"

"All right, for sure!"

Right away Nopots'iqxa?a got ready. He took his little sack, reached inside and got his headband of cedarbark and his small scallop shells. He had some scallop shells held in each of his hands. He took off his shirt. He rubbed red ochre on his chest, also along his legs and on his face.

All right, he now began to sing, and his song went like this: that his hands are at the other side of the "veil", that his hands went through "because I am a doctor", so his song said, the rascal Nopots'iqxa?a. He began performing the Wolf Ritual dance, began the Tlo:kwa:na, and moved to the centre of the floor. He became fierce looking. All of our crew were singing, helping him, those of us on the gift visit. The ?Osi:l?ath[11] now watched while they sat there. Then our doctor went outside.

"Follow him, you folks, follow him," said the ?Osi:l?ath bunch.

They were amazed that he went outside because, it was said, there were lots of ghosts out there. He went behind the house straight up to where the many dead bodies were. Then it seemed that he went to the other end of the village, our doctor, singing while moving. He was gone a long time, then it sounded like he had returned. He was heard to sing from there at the doorway. He came dancing in singing an ordinary song, not his doctoring song. He came inside dancing. We started to sing again while the ?Osi:l?ath just sat quietly. All right, he finished, stopped singing at night. It was a dark night, raining. Now the doctor spoke, Nopots'iqx?a.

"They are not ghosts," he said. "They are not ghosts; they are live real people, those ones making noise. They are on that side over here," he said, pointing to where the Kwinyo:t'ath side was. "We will hear about it tomorrow or the day after whatever they are, what all the excitement is about," said Nopots'iqxa?a.

All right, that is as far as he went. All right, we then got ready to leave the next day. We went out and travelled homeward, went to Ni:ya: again and told about what they did to us at

ʔOsi:l.

Then the next morning someone came from ?Osi:l, one man, bringing the news that there was a drift whale on the other side of ʔOsi:l. For two days they were there, butchering the whale. There were lots of people at ʔOsi:l now, Kwinyo:t'ath, lots of people butchering. Nopots'iqxaʔa became very proud that he was the only one who predicted right when he told them that maybe the next day they would hear of what the "ghosts" were making all that noise about, that he had said that they were not ghosts that were making all that noise but humans when he was performing the N'a:chn'a:cha. They were amazed that what he had predicted was true. All right, that is what I saw, something I saw myself.

* * * *

All right, a man died at wintertime, the father of Qwintin'ox. The man who died was called ʔOwimyis.[12] He died suddenly, he was not sick very long. In a little while he was put away in a box. He was pulled up[13] from where he died; they did not even have to pack him out. Just as this happened a ceremonial whistle blew, when they lifted him up through the roof. The whistle blew again as they took him down at the back of the house onto the ground and into the woods, shrieking as they went along going towards a far off place. All right, now they threw away his possessions; everything he had they threw away. Whatever the person who died had, they threw away. But they didn't throw away his oil which was kept in stomach bladders: this was given to his widow. So that's what happened.

Then winter came, and they began the Tlo:kwa:na or Wolf Ritual which was started by the uncle, Gordon's late father. They started the Wolf Ritual dance; they took the children.[14] They took the one who was now the orphan, Qwintin'ox, whose father had died that winter. Many were initiated, other children, too. All right now, they then began trying to capture the Wolves who had taken the children. It was La:maho:s and Otto Taylor's father who were capturing the Wolves. There were three persons in canoes. They had boards across two canoes. There were many people watching those who were dancing the Wolf Ritual capturing dance. Their song said they are stepping on the saltwater because, they say, they are crazy Qi:shim spirits.[15] Then they did what their song said: they stepped onto the saltwater while they were far offshore. The three persons were dancing. The people were amazed that they were dancing on the water.

All right, just then those trying to capture the novices got them back from the ones trying to "bite". Now then they came into the house bringing with them the novices who were wearing ritual branches on the head. They called all the men only. The one who does the Ts'i:qa: power dance was asking for help. Then he started singing the spirit song. He started to Ts'i:qa: just then, saying,

"There is no trouble whatsoever."

Then the Ts'i:qa: dancer stopped and took Qwintin'ox, the new orphan, into the middle of the house.

"This one saw here father, the one who was here, the Chief of this house," said Ha:ya:lim. "This girl was told by her late father the house was bright with the fire going when they poured on the oil. All right, that is all he told her."

All right, he started to Ts'i:qa: again and while singing, he stopped.

"You people keep quiet," he said while still performing Ts'i:qa:.

Then we all heard this whistle whistling. It was as if we could not find out from which direction the sound came from. It seemed as if it was up in the air, very loud! Then the whistle came from back of the house. We all ran outside; all of the people ran outside. We all ran to our homes, all of us people of the Ho:ʔi:ʔath. Those who stayed home said that it was real fierce out there, that they nearly broke down the doors, for the spirits were really running wild! The whistling stopped, the sound of many. Then came two men.

"You all go and walk to where they are dancing the Tl'o:kwa:na. Hurry!" they told us.

We went there.

"We saw something awful," he said.

The people went into the house. It was he who had died that got angry, the one who died last winter. He it was who had gotten agry on account of the fact that they did not pour his oil on the fire. The one who was sleeping was Ch'ihin'ak, she was the one asleep. They say that the famous shaman doctor was the one who saw, while she was sleeping, that the one who died got angry because they did not pour his oil, which was contained in stomach bladders, on the fire.

"Ch'ihin'ak said this," said the one who told of this.

All right, then the people found out about it, that it was a spirit, not a Wolf, that opposed them. All right, the people, all of them, got ready. They put ritual branches on their heads to perform the Wolf dance. The men got ready. The men took off their clothes, their shirts, keeping only their pants on. On their bodies they rubbed blood, and also rubbed the blood on their faces. All finished getting ready to perform. They started making torches made from split up boards, big ones. There were to be two men to carry those torches because they were huge ones, long, thick and heavy. There were four torches all together. All right, they planned that there would be two going into the house repeatedly and two remaining outside holding the torches. On the outside they started performing as a Ts'i:qa: song was sung by two women, not young women but old women. Both of them had fierce P'ishxi:nak ritual gear: axes and spears. Some had guns with them. There were two of them who had bearskin robes on and were wearing wolf masks on their heads. All right then, they set out.

"Let's go," they said, "Let's go to the other house."

We came to the front door. We started to sing Ts'i:qa: first. All right, then the Wolf dancers began, two of them; they went in and started performing. The P'ishxi:nak also went in, performed by the naked men. They danced right around the house and out again. There was no trouble; we did not hear anything bad. We went into the house called Hilst'oʔas, a big house. Then we set out again heading for the house called Saya:ch'a. We came to the front door. We repeated our performance again: the Wolves went inside, two of them. They were always the first to enter. The P'ishxi:nak also circled the house and went out again without any problems. We set out again on foot towards a house called T'akaqtl'as. We entered the same way. Again those doing the ceremony repeated their performance.

And then while there, just then we heard a whistle again from the back of the house and the sound of many. The leader of the dancers wanted to stop.

"Don't stop now; let's finish it," they started saying.

He went back and went out again. All right, we then set out on foot again, heading for the next house at the back of the village. The sound of the whistle stopped; the sound of many stopped. And while there at the front of the house we reached, the house at the back of the village, the one there said,

"You folks do this when the whistle sounds again: you folks shoot at the back of the house."

All right. Again the two Wolves went inside. The spirit singers started to Ts'i:qa: again. We were scared. Very very scared! The P'ishxi:nak, the fierce dancers, were worse, hitting everything. They were real ugly! They were like that because they, too, were scared. As soon as they were all inside the house the dancers stopped. Then it became more fierce. The whistle started very loud again from the outside. The people outside started shooting their guns off because they heard now how fierce the sound coming from the house was. It sounded very ugly.

Then we set out on foot for home. We went straight to our homes. We did not go back to where the Tlo:kwa:na ceremony was because now it was frightening. It had become very scary now. I stayed at the house. And then I started thinking about what I should do to the one who was doing things against us. I got an axe,[16] a small new one, and I got a crowbar. I also got some coal oil, one container full, a tin can full. I was thinking that as soon as they started digging under the wall boards all around the house, I would spring into action! My late mother was talking; she was praying for life. She was praying because it was now becoming very dangerous, sounding awful outside the house. It was dark, pitch dark at night. Our children were hiding. They were up at the platform near the ceiling. They were up there with their mothers; just us men were down below on the floor. We did not go to sleep. Just our Chief used to come from time to time. His name was H̱o:mʔis. He only came to the door.

"Are you folks all right?" he said to us.

He never came inside the house because he had barricaded our front door and nailed it tight. It was fearsome out there at the back of the house in the woods. A shrieking whistling sound was heard out there, a ceremonial whistle. We set fire to old blankets and threw them out back of the house. The blankets on fire produced an awful smell while burning. When daylight came the next day, my wife spoke to me and said,

"Say, go get your big canoe and pull it out to the water so we can move."

"Let us all go to the coastline location," the people were saying who were from different houses because, they say, it had become unbearably fearsome.

'It's very frightening!" they were all saying.

It was as if the weather was bad that day, as if it was dark at Nomaqimyis[17] even though the sun was hot. In spite of that it was dark for it was very very scary like a haunted atmosphere. It was like that now for three days. It was impossible for the dancers to perform. Whenever someone started to Ts'i:qa:, then the sound of the whistle would start outside all along the village of Nomaqimyis. It seemed to really annoy it whenever someone started to Ts'i:qa:.

All right, then they got ready, those three who had a very strong mind. They said they would go into the woods when night came to find out what it was that was bothering us. La:ma<u>ho</u>:s took a little hatchet, the other took a spear, and the third took along a gun, a rifle. Ho:m?is, the Chief, took a lantern along with him to light the way in the dark. He had it covered, for he had a blanket on; that is why the only spot of light showing was on the ground next to his feet which made it difficult to notice whether they had a light or not. They said they would go along slowly, listening as they went for whatever was making that shrieking whistling sound. They were gone for a long time, the three. The awful fearsome noise kept quiet. We, the people, were also quiet. It seemed as if no one was living there, we were so quiet. We were afraid because the awful noises would start when all started talking; that's why we tried very hard to keep quiet, all the people. The three men came back out of the woods and said that there was no sign of anything in the woods, just a lot of footprints made by people in the muddy areas but no evidence of wolf tracks. Then said the Chief, Ho:m?is,

"The oil of ?Owimy'is should be poured on the fire because the oil is cheap compared to the importance of completing the Tlo:kwa:na ceremony properly. That is what the doctor saw in her vision, that ?Owimy'is is angry that they did not pour his oil on the fire. Let us try that just in case. All right, you folks pour the oil in the fire."

Said the widow also, "All right, pour the oil on the fire."

The fire in the house got big where the Tlo:kwa:na ceremony was performed. Six huge flames flared up as the oil was poured on, the oil of the one called ?Owimy'is who had died that winter. The situation now became happier in the house as it got brighter. More oil was poured on the fire; it really got bright and happy in the house. The women started to Ts'i:qa: in support of the ceremony of pouring oil on the fire. Also those women who were just sitting there at home were doing Ts'i:qa: because they could not leave from where they were in the different houses since it was very fearsome outside. The awful shrieking noise could not be heard now. The oil was being poured on the fire, two men walking about on the floor. Poured on the fire was more oil that belonged to the late ?Owimy'is. Everyone was performing Ts'i:qa:, all the women, for that which had been happening was not happening now; the whistle did not sound again. The two men spread the news to all the houses the same day when daylight came. It was different now where it had been fearsome at night and very fearsome at daybreak. The whistling stopped when they all started to Ts'i:qa: as they poured oil on the fire, the oil which belonged to ?Owimy'is as the man was called. The dangerous situation stopped now. It was as if the "fire went out" just when they poured the oil on the fire.

We started walking about again, going to places where we had been unable to go; we started walking about freely again. The fearsome situation was gone, the people performing ceremonies which were started again. They began to go down to the beach again. The danger was over. The women were doing Ts'i:qa: again. All right, that is the only time I've heard of when the Tlo:kwa:na ceremony was interfered with. It had now become apparent that the medicine woman was telling the truth when she the reason ʔOwimy'is had gotten angry and used his supernatural powers was because they did not pour his oil on the fire. He had come to do us harm whenever we did Ts'i:qa: as long as we did not pour the oil of ʔOwimy'is on the fire. And just when they poured the oil, the noise from his power, the shrieking whistling noise, stopped all along the houses at Nomaqimyis. It stopped, the fearsome situation. That's what happened when the woman doctor told the real truth. What she said came true. She was named Chihinak, the one who saw that a spirit came to do harm.

114. Bone Game at Nitinat (La:maho:s)[1]

We went onto the steamboat *Tees*, we boarded. I was Tlatw'i:,[2] one accompanying a gift visit party. Tlapisim[3] was among those who came on the gift visit. Also H̲awi:hto?is came along. Tlapisim went to Tl'i:?ix̲im. He bought four boxes of Pilot bread. H̲awi:h̲to?is also bought four boxes of Pilot bread. We were a proud bunch. We went by Tlin?owis.[4] The sea was rough, the wind blowing hard that night. We got off at P'a:chi:na?a[5] at the place the White people lived at, and they gave us a place where we could sleep.

When daylight came we met and discussed things. Then we sent a telegraph message saying that we were now at P'a:chi:na?a. A message came back saying that we could open Tl'i:?ix̲im's house and that we should open the house of Tlawobe:y.[6] They also said there was lots of food there, dried dog salmon, and that we were to eat them. It was very stormy, snowing and windy. I spoke to our crew:

"You guys don't be like that. We will be invited to play bone game. You should think about the fact that we are the only ones here. There are no Ni:ti:na?ath̲ here at P'a:chi:na?a. The only thing we can do properly is pray, so let's bathe!" I said because those with us were good bone holders, Getters of many sticks.

Night came. It was very cold, snowing now. As soon as our crew went to sleep, I went outside and then set out on foot towards a distant place. Walking at night, I went to the middle of the beach. I took off my clothes and started bathing, knelt down at the spot where the waves were reaching and started to pray. In my prayer I said that I would beat my opponent when I played the bone game, that I would get a lot of tally sticks, that I would cause all of them to become confused, that I would cause everybody to forget, that my mind would take control over theirs.

"'He's the one who caused them to lose' they'd be saying of me," I said in my prayer that night.

While it was very cold and snowing I was in a position like you sit in a bone game, kneeling down; that's why I was half-submerged in the water as it came up the beach. I said in my prayer that I would cause all to watch, also cause to stare at me all the good pointers of the Ni:ti:na?ath̲, that I would beat the Ni:ti:na?ath̲. I repeated this prayer every time the waves came up to me. I was shaking my hands as if they missed me. I'd have my arms spread out, pretending they missed me. I had my bones for playing the bone game in my hand. I was counting how many times the waves came up, when it came up twenty and one times. Then I would scoop up the things that drifted in.

"All right, now I have beaten the Ni:ti:naʔath̲," I kept repeating.

Then I would start praying again. I was really praying ritually for playing the bone game. I was singing songs, the songs I would sing when playing the bone game. I was doing that and finished pretending to win four games, counting the incoming waves up the beach. Then I finished and put on my clothes after pretending to win four times. Then I went to sleep. I went home to find everyone was asleep although the fire was still burning in the stove. We were there for a long time. For four days I did that, bathing four nights, praying for bone game luck while it was extremely cold in the wintertime. We were there for five days. We slept there five times; that's why I had one night to sleep properly.

Then they came to get us. The weather got nice that morning so the one who came for us arrived. We set out then, went along in a launch and eventually arrived at W'a:yi,[8] our original destination. My, we saw many Ni:ti:naʔath̲ people! The Ni:ti:naʔath̲ came down the beach to met us, and we introduced ourselves. They took those who brought Pilot bread in their canoe up the beach. We were invited - we were invited by ʔO:ʔochisʔat.[9] Hey now, we went into the house, and the Ni:ti:naʔath̲ began coming into the house to sit and eat with us. They fed us dried dog salmon that's been soaked, and then we had tea. When we finished eating, everyone started having conversation with one another. The Ni:ti:naʔath̲ started saying,

"Hey! I wish they were bone game players, those strangers; we would have played bone game."

"Keep saying that please; we also came to play bone game," I said.

We then left the place where we were and went to this place where our guests stayed for two days, sleeping there twice. They began treating us as guests, all those of our crew, and they invited all the Ni:ti:naʔath̲ that night. All right, and then the Ni:ti:naʔath̲ came in as guests, all the people including children, and also women. It was evening as everyone came in. They must have had a meeting planning what they would do. We remained in there a long time. They met together a long time, the Ni:ti:naʔath̲ people. All right, we were taken inside the house, and not long after we entered there came the men and the women, the girls. They must have been getting dressed up in the other house. They were gone a long time. One person came in and said to the many people,

"The Ni:ti:naʔath people are getting ready. They are nicely dressed, ready to dance."

The man left, and then they were heating water for tea. They were going to eat what we had brought, the Pilot bread. One of the Ni:ti:naʔath came:

"Stoke up the fire. They are coming," he announced.

Then the fire flared up and it got really bright in the house where we were. They started to sing there at the doorway. They had us at the front of the house. We were anxious to watch. The dancers came into view. The men came in first. They had in their hands a branch held horizontally. Many came in. They were dancing, and the many Ni:ti:naʔath were singing. At this point the ladies came in, very pretty in their costumes. When all the ladies had come in, one of the Ni:ti:naʔath spoke up:

"Dance a little more, dance a little more, you are not quite doing it right!"

Then the villagers really started dancing, beginning to use the branch they were holding. It seemed as if they were one as they all moved right in time, as they did every move according to their leader in front. They all moved up and down as one as they went from one side of the house to the other. We were really watching, amazed. We'd never seen a dance like that before; it was the first time we saw anything like that. Then they ended the song. They were many, the people, and the big house was full. They sang again, and the dancers danced just where they stood. They sang twice while just standing there. Then one man went to the middle of the floor and said,

"You stop dancing now."

Next Shi:wish sang a song. Then the Ni:ti:naʔath gathered. They went to one side of the house, and then one said,

"Ho:y!"

And the others joined in. They did that four times:

"Ho:y! Ho:y! Ho:y! Ho:y!"

One of them started a song, and the rest joined in again like before. Then out came two young men wearing wolf masks. They sang four times and stopped. And then they gave a gift to Hawi:htoʔis, one dollar. They gave Tlapisim one dollar. They then gave the rest of us one dollar each.

"All right, there's another one," they said.

The same thing happened again: they danced. This time there were ladies wearing the wolf masks. After four times they stopped. They did the same to us again: gave us a gift of one dollar each. There were eight different ones who gave us gifts. Then they started to sing the song of our crew, directing it to us. They gave twenty-five dollars to Tlapisim in money and then two dollars to each of us that was with Tlapisim. Next they sang the song of the crew of Hawi:hto?is who was also receiving twenty-five dollars money and then each of his crew two dollars. Then they announced that they were finished.

"Now you may attend to the food," they said.

They took the Pilot bread and placed it in the middle of the floor. They then set tea cups in front of us. The people were talking excitedly, proud of the fact that now they would eat the gift visit food. The Ni:ti:na?ath were served and they ate. They finished eating, and everyone stopped talking. All right, it was at this time that I spoke.

"Be listening," the Ni:ti:na?ath said, "Be listening."

"All right, I guess that is how his mind is," I said. "Just to show that he has relatives here, still feels the same as how his forefathers felt who told him that it was his relatives who lived here when we went to gift visit - that is the reason that he came to visit his relatives. All right, I saw what you did, Ni:ti:na?ath, that you showed your support in singing your songs and using your wolf masks which you have for such an occasion like this, like we're doing now - that's why I am watching after your performances, watching what you are doing and how you are going about performing as your forefathers also did, you Ni:ti:na?ath. You are also descendants of a tribe called Ho:?i:?ath, those of you who are here - that is why they used to take along the remains of a mat when they go to Ni:ti:na?ath, those of us from our tribe, because we were at peace with one another for a long time.[10] All right, it is like this for all the Ni:ti:na?ath in the land of the place called Ho:?i:?ath[11] because of the fact that women so-called move about from tribe to tribe - that is why most of the Ni:ti:na?ath are at the land called Ho:?i:?ath. You are good, you are good, you tribe. I will take good news when I go home because I saw how you all are. All right, I will change the subject a little. Even though the Whiteman is trying to stop us from doing this, trying to stop us from having a meal with one another, it is good for us what we are doing now like this, laughing together here in this house as these many people because many of us are eating together."

All right, that's as far as I went. Now then Hin'a?om spoke. Hin'a?om gave a thank you speech. He said everything regarding appreciation of all that was done for us and all that was given to us. All right, he finished. Now spoke the Ni:ti:na?ath named

Tl'iloxwa?a.

"You said just what you should, what should be said. You said everything I would have said, too, if I was speaking, how I would have spoke. I would just like to thank you for the food you brought," said he to us. "You told the truth when you said that it was true that there were Ni:ti:na?ath in the land called Ho:?i:?ath. All right, it was likewise here, too, with Ho:?i:?ath in the land of the Ni:ti:na?ath."

Then he started thanking for the food, that we had done him a great favour, that he had had good food to eat. All right, he finished and walked away. We went out last. We found that there was a bunch of people at the front of the house outside, Ni:ti:na?ath young men.

"All right, should we not play bone game?" they said.

"All right, all right, let's play bone game," I said.

"Let's play bone game," we started saying, all of us.

I got cold because we were going to play the bone game. I got real cold all over because I was ready, having already prayed ritually for it. All right, we walked away towards where we were to play. We went inside and settled down. A lot of people gathered there, many of them. We placed our bets to the amount of twenty dollars and ten. We went against the Wa:ya:?ath.[12] We started playing then. It was not long before we beat them, and we took the money we won which was ours now. A man stood up on the opposite side and he called on the Tlo:?owis?ath.[13]

"Come all you people from Tlo:?ows, take our place on the opposing side," he said.

They placed their bet first, the Tlo:?owis?ath, their pot growing to be quite a large sum this time, a lot of money. And then we placed our bet, matching their amount. Hey then, we started playing! We were playing real hard now. There were more people on the other side, a lot of people watching. There were eight of us, eight on our team. I was glad that we were like this, just as I had said in my prayers when I was praying for the bone game. We played quite a while, but we beat the Tlo:?owis?ath too. We took the money, our winnings. Now then, someone stood up also from the Tlo:?owis?ath.

"All right, you people come," said the Chief of the P'a:chi:na?ath,[14] "Let us challenge them, those of us from P'a:chi:da?."

All right, the P'a:chi:na?ath placed their bet. Their pot exceeded the amount of the bet the Tlo:?owis?ath had had. We managed to match their bet again, how much they had. All the Ni:ti:na?ath bet against us. We started to play again. I was really playing! I was full of the bone game! I felt as if I had dove into a river, I was so soaked with sweat, moving around dancing, trying not to lose. It was close to daylight when we beat them again. We took the money again; we claimed our winnings. Three times we had won.

"Let's quit," said the Ni:ti:na?ath.

Then we all walked out; everyone went home. All right, that's how far we went. Then I said to our team mates,

"All right, you people, don't play bone game again for you might lose. I'm going home now."

Then I went home. I set out on foot towards Tsaxts'a:?a.[15] They must then have played bone game when I was not there. They lost. Three times they lost. All right, that is as far as this goes. That's how this bone game business is. It's hard to be a bone game player. It's hard to bathe ritually for it, trying to beat the bone game players of all the tribes, trying to get the pointer mixed up on the opposite side. If you are not prepared, not having done ?o:simch ritual training, when you are challenged to play bone game you will lose; you will not win. Then you will be very ashamed and embarassed; it's shameful. But if you have ritually bathed, you will keep on winning. This is the truth about this ?o:simch business.

115. How a Man Mishandled Power Given By the Beavers
(Sa:ya:ch'apis)

An old man was fishing for Sockeye salmon, but he wasn't really old. It was not far from the end of the Sockeye[2] season. The man went out to get fresh fish for boiling. He left in a canoe very early, at night when it was not yet daybreak. It got to be just a little bit light but it was still the middle of the night. He arrived at ʔO:qtl'as,[3] which was the name of the land. There were two young men standing there with ritual branches on their heads.

"Come ashore. Our Chief invites you," said the young men with the branches on their heads.

The man went ashore; his canoe was pulled up. They took the man along to a big house not far off. He went inside.

"Here he comes!" they said.

"Bring him here," said the Chief.

They put the man there at the rear of the house. He noticed that here inside was much blubber just like Humpback whale blubber. It had skin, the blubber, just like that of the Humpback.

"All right, you all cut up that blubber on the floor," said the Chief, "So the man sitting can have some."

The young men cut it up.

"Cut so there's lots," he said.

The women started boiling it; theirs was cooked up. There were lots of people in the house. The villagers were skilled at wood work. They were all adzing, always making all kinds of things: making bailers, making paddles. They were all wearing ritual branches on their heads.

"All right, call all the members of our household. Tell them to come and eat, Kw'a:lap'almiʔe."[4]

He called everyone that going around inside the big house, "Kw'a:lap'almiʔe:"! They all had one name, the name belonging to all of them. The villagers now came in as guests, sitting down starting from thr rear and going right around the house.

"Let's not eat for a while yet; let's first sing a song," said the villagers. "Let's have that man sitting there listen to us."

The villagers began singing their song.[5]

"Ha:ya::: niwa::: ha:ʔaya:shiwa ... ʔaʔaʔa... Ho:::wi howʔe."

They sang[6] their dinner song. Then the villagers stopped singing and started eating the blubber. The blubber was just like that of the Humpback whale; the oil was dripping like that of the Humpback whale.

"Give the man lots to eat!" said the Chief.

The man ate. The Kw'alap'almiʔa people ate. They finished eating. His leftovers were tied into a bundle as take-home-food.

"You people take it down the beach for him."

The young people took it down the beach. It was now evening at this time. The man went out of the house and set off in his canoe, going home. He landed at his house. He was the only one living there along with his wife and his little girl. The man went inside.

"Go and get my take-home-food from a feast. It's in the canoe."

The child went to get it. There was no blubber; the supposed blubber was not there. She hurried back.

"It's not here," she told her father.

"It's in the canoe," he said to his little girl.

She couldn't find it. There was only a bundle of wood in the bow of the canoe.

"Say! There is blubber in the canoe. Now you go get it," he said to his wife.

The wife went out. She could not find the blubber either; there was only the bundle of wood in the canoe. The wife took that and carried it inside the house. She was holding it like this, the bundle of wood.

"There's no blubber there. Only this alder wood."

The woman threw it down while she was at the middle of the floor. Alder appeared at the upper part of his body,[7] the cheeks, the eyes, and the belly; thus the alder came sticking through at several places. It must have been a beaver lodge that he had entered. As it turned out the alder's "blubber" was their food. The man did not get any Sockeye either.

"Call yourself an idiot, you fool, while you were at a house at ʔO:qtl'as, for there's no house there. You should be ashamed in your mind because there's no house there!"

The alder that he ate was sticking through because he went to[8] his house when he came in, because he saw[9] what his blubber take-home-food was, the blubber of the village where he had eaten. The alder sticks were coming through at different parts all over his body. He was the one who found out that alder was blubber to the beavers.

The man then started singing, making his wife listen. He sang the four songs[10] that belonged to the beavers. Then after he had finished singing the man died, for there was nothing but alder sticks in his stomach, puncturing it. The woman set out in the canoe, taking her little child along. She went to where there many houses at Ho:choqtlisʔath.

116. Sa:ya:ch'apis Meets a Storm (Sa:ya:ch'apis)

A gentle wind was blowing as we were out sealing one day. Every one of us got back on the schooner that evening. We had caught three, Si:xo:lmi:k and me. I was now steersman while he was the seal hunter, Si:xo:lmi:k.[2] The weather glass showed that the wind had started up. Our Captain wanted to go ashore. Santo was the one who didn't want to go ashore.

It happened when it got a bit late at night, at ten o'clock I think. Then it became stormy; the sea started to get big waves. Our Captain was called Louie.[3] ʔAlipe:k[4] was the name of the schooner we were riding.

Next day it was stormy. We could hear the ropes sounding like thunder as the wind blew through them. Our boat would be thrown out of the sea, then it would land upright again. Just like ʔI:h̲wanim Mountain,[5] that's how big the waves were. Louie shoved some caulking into a sack. Then he put oil on it, pouring on coal oil. He put two sacks like that out; that's why it caused the sea to calm down. The waves were broken up from what were now tied onto us at sea; that's how we got through till daylight. The young men would go out and look.

"We're already dead now," they'd say.

Then I thought I should get dressed up. I took my warm shirt and put it on. I put on my heavy thick vest. I put on my coat, a very thick one. I had paid five dollars for it at Hiko:l to Mr. Newcombe.[6] The Ts'isha:ʔath̲ were sleeping. I think we were half dead. One still had the voice to speak up, P'ishʔaktlim was his name. Then I got mad at those who were going out from time to time and just saying,

"We're already dead now."

"Nice things you all there are saying! Hey now, you guys quit saying that!" I said, speaking harshly to the young men. "We will live. 'Only the Ts'isha:ʔath̲ came ashore alive,' the tribes will be saying about us."

"Keep saying that, O you Chief!" said ʔA:m'a:qchik[7] to me. "Do something extraordinary, something supernatural, for you are powered by what's called Chiefly. Let me live. Take me ashore."

I went out. I had tied a long muffler on tightly around my head but as soon as I peeked out, it fell off my head because the blowing of the wind was so strong.

"You guys give me a string," I said to my shipmates.

I tied this little rope on, tied together under my chin. Then, like that, I went out again. The one called Tik followed me.

Now then two went forward to the mast there, but I went to the mast aft and stood on the deck beside it. Then I yelled, uttering what was the late Na:we:ʔi:k's spell to yell out when he got into a storm out whaling to make the storm abate. So then I put forth the spell. I spoke along in the speech of the mountains. I spoke of the head of Ts'o:maʔas,[9] telling what I had at sea with me.

"Let this cause you to calm down as I stand in this boat with good feeling towards you," I said, "Which always causes you to make it calm for me whenever I go this way in prayer to you, O Chief!"

I mentioned the name of my medicine power for making it calm that belonged to Na:we:ʔi:k, his calm weather medicine. Then I went to the stern when I was finished.

"Don't you weaken in your belief in what the Indians say," Louie said to me because he wanted to make it to shore.

"We are alive because of the fact that we are offshore. There's no shelter now towards the land," said our Captain to me. "We will all die if we miss the mouth of Alberni Canal; that's the only possible place to get in. I've come to tell you that we should not go ashore because that's how we're staying alive, because we didn't go ashore."

"Give me that raincoat. Bring the rainhat with it too," said Louie to the cook.

I stood alongside Louie holding the tiller, keeping our boat pointing the right way. We only wanted our stern to be facing away from the seas. I think it was about an hour after I finished praying: then, son of a gun, something happened to the sky! A greenish light came through the rain, right from where it was raining, and a strong shoreward wind was blowing. Hey, the bastard, green came through, breaking out straight above us!

Hey, then it bounced up at the bow again, like it was doing all the time because our schooner was underwater. Damn! The jib, which was tied up, became untied from the storm! The sailors sprang into action, the rascals. It was impossible for the jib boom to come out of the sea because our jib was full of water. They would be gone for a long time under the water, the Whitemen, when the bow went down. He turned the steering wheel, the rascal, at the right time. Hey, sure enough, that made the sailors come up out of the water. They tied up the jib as before, the sailors did. We were sailing along fair wind the length of the time the sailors took to tie it up. Then we

"Here, put it back in," he said to the young man.

The young man began to fill the container. Once again it was full. Meanwhile Kanop was singing because he had a song. Then he took his gunpowder again and did the same thing: spilled it into the fire. And the same thing happened as before: it was gone the same length of time, then poured back down again.

"Hish..." it said as it was dropping onto the mat.

He poured it back in again, and the container was once more full of gunpowder. As they watched the Tlaˀo:kwiˀath̲ were open-mouthed with amazement. His helping spirits began talking to him.

"Put all your blankets in the fire, as many as you own," they were saying to him.

The reason they were threatening him with his life was that he refused to burn his blankets. Then he gave in and burned his blankets, all of them, because they were telling him again:

"Burn them all up!"

He burned them all, all the blankets he had, because his new helping spirits were threatening him with his life if he didn't.

* * * *

The Tlaˀo:kwiˀath̲ were performing the Wolf Ritual, doing the biting ceremony down on the beach. One band, the Ma:lts'as, was getting ready. Just as they were going to start paddling off, one of them died! The Chief of the village died. My, the Tlaˀo:kwiˀath̲ sprang into action. They now gave all their attention to preparing the funeral because they could not do anything to revive him. He died all of a sudden for good. They did not know what caused his death: he just fell forward and died with blood pouring out of his mouth while all dressed up about to perform the M'a:kway'i:h̲. They buried the former Chief.

But then not long after, while the burial party was still away, another man died. Then not long after that, in the evening, another Tl'aˀo:kwiˀath̲ man died. He, too, died without apparent cause the same way as the others, just throwing up blood and dying. The people of Tl'aˀo:kwiˀath̲ started to really panic now because three men had died on the same day, a Chief in each case. And then while it still hadn't gotten too late at night yet another died! It was at this stage of events that they went to get Kanop, after four of the Tl'aˀo:kwiˀath̲ had died. Then they got Kanop.

Right away Kanop started making doctoring noises, taking death noticed that the jib boom, the bowsprit, had sprung out from where it sticks in the boat! Four fingerwidths it had sprung out, the end of the bowsprit, shifted out that far from the deck - sprung out four fingers, the rascal! Louie got all into an uproar about what had happened to his schooner.

"How are we now? Are we not abreast of our land?" I asked Louie.

The sun started shining, shining through the clouds. Louie took a fix on his chart.

"We are now at ... I see we are straight off Village Island,"[10] he said.

"All right, let's go to land taking advantage of the fact that, as you say, we are still off Village Island," I said.

"Hang up some male fur seals. Call them," he said to me.

I called them, all the crew,

"Make them four fat ones," he made me say.

Santo did not come out up on deck, he was so ashamed that it was his fault they didn't go ashore, that they would scold him. Everyone was scolding him, the entire crew. Hey, we set out sail! The topsail boom was stuck in against its bottom. Its head was lifted off the deck, just the top end. All the reefs were tied and the sail folded up. The jib and amidships sail were also reefed and folded up. Hey then, Louie started sailing his schooner towards the land! Then the Son-Of-A-Gun schooner started to sail! Our fur seals were suspended with long ropes, five fathoms I think being the length of the rope tied to two fat seals, two of them being tied on each side of the bow. We had tied on four fat fur seals. They belonged to Tich'i:nim,[11] and had had their skins taken off for the fur.

The schooner we were riding in started sailing. It was as if came alive, quivering as it began to sail hard. We would nearly turn and heel right over when we got onto a wave and surfed, the waves were so huge! The waves would break in half on account of the oil from the fur seals. We were not sailing for long. Hey then we saw land, recognizing that it was Ch'itokwaʔchisht![12] Hey, we saw land again, another one! We recognized it again, that it was Ts'isha: (Hawkins Island).

"Where shall we go in?" Louie, our Captain, asked me.

"Let's go in at Ts'isha:. It must be closed up by the waves, Village Island. I don't think there's a channel there now."

We saw in the rough seas that there were two schooners. We saw that one of them had three masts. They were at the point of Ch'ito:kwaʔchist. One of them must have had two masts. The other was a big three-masted ship. We found out later that they were both loaded with lumber. They were goners. They couldn't hoist their sails for they were drifting onto the rocks, nearly getting thrown into the breakers on shore. He looked through his glass at the schooner drifting in, the ship. Right away he saw that it had canoes on it, the schooner that was drifting ashore.

"You rascals go aloft! They must have a channel there! The schooner with the canoes aboard is going in. Get up the masts, you guys, and untie the sails!" the Captain said to his sailors, by golly.

Even then it was the two-masted one that unfurled its sails first. The ships, the scoundrels, started sailing, going along the breakers close to shore. It seemed as if it was very narrow there in between the rocks at Ts'isha:, as if there was foam across it. The Ho:m'o:w'a (Village Island) channel was breaking right across. The kelp in the bay was closed in by the breakers: there was no more channel because the storm got real bad. Hey, the scoundrels also came in where we came in, the two ships. It was now blowing onto the land so they could not tack along the shore. They went just one way drifting shoreward, sailing in towards way over there at ʔAtoʔyaqtlis[13] back of Hi:kwis, the ships did.

Our schooner anchored at Tl'atl'inqowis,[14] and the Ts'isha:ʔatẖ, launching their canoes, got off. We were the last to get off because our canoe was at the bottom. As soon as we came near Ch'ili:t we saw the big waves. Ch'ili:t was going underwater, the waves going right over even though it was high the storm was so bad, the ocean waves so huge! Si:xo:lmi:k looked back astern at me with a deep frown on his face for he got really frightened from the big waves where we were going along. That's how it was that I joked with my canoe mate:

"Keep going. Ch'i:naxt'a is in the canoe,"[15] I said in Nitinat, imitating Nitinat speech.

A Ni:ti:naʔatẖ said this while on a raiding party. One of them was showing the way who knew the place. Then just when they neared the rocks, something spoke as they were among the breakers.

"Hi:mt," it said, as if the land said that.

"You buggers back up: they're trying to swallow us!"[16] they said.

They thought the land was going to swallow them up. That's

when one of them said,

"Keep going. Ch'i:naxt'a is in the canoe."

They thought that the name belonged to their pilot, but the name Ch'i:naht'a belonged to where the Ni:ti:naˀath were going on a raiding party. That's what I imitated when I joked with Si:xo:lmi:k because he looked so afraid of the bad storm. We were out on the sea a little ways offshore at Ho:m'o:w'a, waiting for a chance to get into harbour. The canoes were all upsetting on the beach. They were going ashore, their canoes breaking up from the rough surf, the breakers on the beach.

"Don't you be worried," I said to Si:xo:lmi:k. "I own this ocean. I'll calm it down," I said to him just to give him hope, for how scared he was now, watching those canoes upsetting on the beach.

The breakers would come around the point and right to the beach at Ho:m'o:w'a. I was judging which one of the waves I would go to and follow along on. Hey now, I pronounced the spell! I used the spell belonging to Na:we:ˀi:k used for calming the sea. Then it was as if it was as flat as this floor. It got calm as we came to shore at Ho:m'o:w'a. We headed straight in to the shore, not even a drop of water splashing onto us, it was so calm!

The ?Aho:sˀath lifted up our canoe together with us in it. The surf was going up to where the ground was; that's why our canoe was put right up against our house. There were twenty canoes of ?Aho:sˀath on the schooner anchored off Tl'atlinqowis.

The sea became rough once more after we landed. There was no more chance to land again.

"It is now become clear that you are empowered with something, O Chief," said the ?Aho:sˀath to me. "Only your canoe calmed the ocean on this beach. All right, that showed your power. None of the other tribes have ever done that. Now you tell us."

"The ocean is rough out there on the open sea. I never saw anything like it," I said. "I'd be amazed if a schooner isn't wrecked."

The ?Aho:sˀath gasped together: "God, the Qiltsma?ath! Something's gone wrong for the Qiltsma?ath. Their schooner wasn't very seaworthy."[17]

As it turned out later, the Qiltsma?ath did die out there. This is as far as we went.

Next morning I made Si:xo:lmi:k invite the ?Aho:sˀath. I paid them for pulling up our canoe. I used to take things seriously, whatever was done to me by other tribes. On the vessel were the Chief from Hashsa:th and the former N'an'achp'iyok. The ?Aho:s?ath came as guests, walking over the island to the feast. There were forty, for there were forty on the schooner. A pot of rice was put on the fire. When it got cooked our pot tipped over and some of the rice spilled out but not much.

"Go and get Tik," I said to Si:xo:lmi:k because he was playing lahal down on the beach.[18]

Sure enough, he brought him into the house.

"You go and call the people. Run around fast! Invite all the Ts'isha:?ath people. Say to them, 'You are to go see him'," I said.

My, it was not long before all the Ts'isha:?ath came in! Hey, I sang my spirit song! Hey, the Ts'isha:?ath were yelling!

"He is ashamed because the pot spilled while a Princess had it on the fire," I made him say even though there was very little spilled.

Then we sang a song. I gave the Chief of Hashsa:th double, two together edgewise. Then I distributed one apiece. I gave twenty people one blanket each, one at a time. And again I gave twenty dollars to twenty people, one dollar for each. Not one of those upsetting on the beach did this; not one paid the ?Aho:s?ath though they were the ones who rescued them. For a long time the ?Aho:s?ath held me in high regard, saying that none of the other Chiefs of the tribes compared with me. That is what happened to us. We paid back for what was done to us.

117. Kanop the Shaman (Sa:ya:ch'apis)

Kanop was sitting down at the beach in the middle of the village of Hopits?ath.[2] He belonged to the ?Apw'in?as?ath[3] people. He was sitting not far from the little creek flowing out of the beach in the moonlight, the sky clear and the moon full. Then he heard what sounded like paddling, the sound of people paddling away. There round the point appeared a war party from Ma:lts'a:s,[4] paddling hard! My, it was like a rapid drumming because there were many paddling together, a big canoe full of men. It turned out to be a very big war party, their long canoe stretching from here to there, very large.[5] As soon as they came opposite where he was sitting on the beach, the war party said,

"Let's get some water. Let's get some water from this creek."

They stopped, lying to alongside the beach, and two young men got out, each with a water bucket. Then the Otter Spirit of the canoe started talking, as did its Wolf. It was as if the world split, they spoke so loudly! Yet none of the Tla?o:kwi?ath heard though it was so loud it was impossible not to hear the noise being made there. The ones who were fetching water were halfway up the beach when Kanop's legs failed; the poor bugger was staggering on the beach. The Angry Warrior in the canoe was yelling way over in the bow. Others were singing happy T'ama: songs there in their canoe. Singing a doctoring song was the Shaman of the canoe, and the Whaler was singing his ghost song. Also there was a Ya:tya:t singer, the Chief of the canoe who now went to the stern.

Kanop could not get closer to them because his legs were dead so that now he was crippled on the beach. The two young men now began to fill their buckets full of water. Kanop was powerless to do what has to be done in this situation, whenever you see such a thing: that you should take whatever you want to become. You could choose to become the Angry One if you so chose. You could take the Shaman in the canoe if you wanted to become a doctor. And you could choose to take the Chief in the canoe if you wished to become wealthy.

The young men went down the beach, their buckets now full of water. The Otter in the canoe was now speaking; the Wolf was also speaking. The Angry One in the canoe was yelling; the Wolf was speaking. The Sea Mammal Hunter was communicating with the spirits. The Singer of happy T'ama: songs was singing. The Doctor was singing his power songs. The Chief was performing his Ya:tya:t ceremony. He was singing his wealth songs, sung to show his riches, singing two kinds of songs. Those young men who went to fetch water got into the canoe. None of the Tla?o:kwi?ath were aware of all this even though it was impossible not to hear them proclaiming on the beach, the war party. The raiders started off, sounding a loud

"Ho! Ho! Ho!"

It sounded so loud because they were a great many paddling as they travelled along, heading towards the point. As soon as they had gone a ways off from the beach, Kanop started reviving. His legs weren't shaking on the beach anymore. He was cursing himself as he helplessly watched the war party leaving. Kanop ran down the beach crazy with excitement, the rascal! He dove into the water at the spot where the war party had been. Afterwards he went up the beach and entered his house. Next morning Kanop was sick all of a sudden.

He had gotten some sea foam when he dove into the water. It was just like sea foam only it was a bit harder, more solid. It was the foam caused by the paddling. Kanop became aware that they had put him in the canoe, the raiders he had seen. He was now dying, sick. There was a man on each side of him, holding him. He now saw that the war party was still out there on the water where it had been before. They started telling him that he should be speared through, that the spear should be poking through him. Only if he had that done would he get better. They told him to get it done at once by such as he saw.

"You will not get better if you don't have a spear through you," they told him.

So then someone went and got his friends, fellow warriors who now entered the house: Ts'axsats'os, Tlani'iqol, Hishnaq, Kanoxwi:ʔitl, Ch'o:ha, Ts'eʔinwa. These were the warriors of the Tlaʔo:kwiʔath.

"You are to spear me, that's what I want of you," he said. "You are to spear me and have the spear sticking through."

"Which one of us will throw the spear?" the friends began saying among themselves.

"Let Tlan'iqol do it," they said of Tlan'iqol.

He got ready, Tlan'iqol, taking hold of the spear. Now Tlan'iqol went close, intending to spear, but he got scared and hesitated whether he should spear or not. Hishnaq then took his turn, also going up to spear, but he, too, got scared, Hishnaq. He backed out, he said, because it was a hard thing to do for he might kill him.

Kanop began dying, going under for a long time, losing life. He really became lifeless, the man. They saw that those sitting on both sides of him who said he should be speared through when he was dead would do so at that time. At daybreak they saw that Kanop was almost dead. The brother-in-law got ready in the morning. It was Ts'axats'os who got ready. Twisting his spear in his hands, he was uttering something as he went in.

"ʔOy, ʔoy, ʔoy," he was saying as he went in, Ts'axsats'os.

Then he went close to where Kanop was. The sick one was now sitting up. That's how he was when he was speared in the belly, the spear going right through his body, the Head-Cut-Off One! Even then he took it back out a bit, this spear here. Ts'axsats'os backed out, too.

All at once Kanop took the spear and speared right in his own belly, which made a sucking sound. He speared there, a little under the navel. The spear was wide and tipped with iron, three fingers wide at the end made of sharpened iron. Suddenly Kanop, the rascal, struggled up to his feet. He stood up and yelled the warrior's yell with his guts flopping out. He took his knife and cut them next to the skin of his belly; cut off his guts, flung them towards the door and began rubbing his belly at the spot where the hole was. Then it happened as he had been told: sure enough, Kanop got well. He ran out the door, the rascal, leaving his entrails steaming there on the floor! He went out the side exit and into the woods, naked with not a stitch on, Kanop!

He was gone that evening, gone all night, still gone came dawn, and all the next day. He stayed in the woods four days, was gone for four days. Then on the fourth day they heard a strange noise. He had a song and was singing it as they heard him coming out of the woods. He entered the same way he went out, through the side door. He came in singing. The Tlaʔo:kwiʔath found out that Kanop had now come out of the woods. The Tlaʔo:kwiʔath rushed to his house to see him. They filled up the big house singing because Kanop was singing, this song:

Hiya ʔahiqya ehe: ʔahiya ʔanga:w hiye:
ʔangiye ʔahow hiye:
His has flown out of the body, our Wolf Ritual.
His is acting like the Otter, our Wolf Ritual.

Then from the wall he took his powder horn which was full of gunpowder and the rascal spilled the contents into the fire. The fire flared up as the gunpowder ignited.

"Give me a mat," he said to his wife. "Make that a white mat."

He spread it out right below the smokehole. Then the gunpowder poured down. The gunpowder there on the floor was not gone for long: there the powder was still in its original form, that which had been spilled into the fire. It was making a noise like "hish..." there on the mat.

out of the body. He came alive, the one who had died, as if he just woke up from a long sleep. It was like a H̲i:na supernatural crystal, what Kanop took out of him. Kanop now became known for his powers. Then another man died. Then the people of Tl'aʔo:kwiʔath̲ all started dying. Kanop began taking the death out of each man, catching them as they died. He didn't even have to go over; the dead began to revive on their own. There were only those three Chiefs who had died first that they had not gotten Kanop to revive. Then the rascal started to bring them back to life, too.

Now it became clear what his spirits had planned, why they told him to burn all the blankets he had, telling him he would get lots more from his doctoring. He now became wealthy, the rascal Kanop. They would give him all that they had, those he had brought back to life. We then heard he was like that. He became a respected man, held in the highest regard by his fellow tribesmen. It was just when they started to burn up all of those things that what they were doing made them die. Then the Tl'aʔo:kwiʔath̲ stopped dying. Kanop had now become a shaman. He became a great shaman doctor and used to revive those who were dead for a day and a night, bringing them back to life then.

I saw the one who was called Kanop. He was my grandfather through my father's father[6] for he is an ʔApw'inʔ̲asʔath̲. All right, I've reached the end; that's how long this story is.

118. Ch'it'oqwin'ak Becomes a Shaman (Sa:ya:ch'apis)

Ch'it'oqwin'ak used to go at night to get the shags that dwell on the cliffs. He was a Yo:loˀilˀath of the Ha:yopiy'ataqiml band, Ch'itoqwin'ak. His loins were girded up where he was sticking in the shags. At night the shags are asleep, which is how they take them, twisting their necks to kill them, those who go getting shags on the rocks. Hi:shmi:ˀa[2] it is called, and that is the name given to those who do so. Those who get just five are the unmanly ones; they make the shags wake up and run away down the cliff. But those who are properly trained with the ˀo:simch ritual bathing, the shags do not even know they are there even if they are right among them. The shags sleep perched on the steep cliff face. It's as if it's like the wall of a house when you are uninformed; you see it thus even though it's like a bed when you are properly trained having completed the full course of the ˀo:simch ritual, rubbing until you get to be as if you are on top of a bed. The steep cliff becomes level. You are rubbing with branches at the feet when doing ?o:simch for Hi:shmi:ˀa.

He had lying on the ground at a suitable distance from the cliff a bare slippery sapling. From there, strung over the slippery pole, was a twisted cedar bough rope. It was tied down to the tree on the ground. He had it rigged like when you make a swing: you just sat in the loop at the end of the rope. Then he would move the rope when he filled this belt of his, hooking the heads of the shags into it to hold them.

"Now pull me up," he would say.

His three assistants for the purpose would then pull, bringing him up for a while with his shags. Then he would slip down again until he reached where the shags were asleep and start killing them once more, wringing their necks. We say, us native people,

"Well, I'll be damned. I wonder what holds those things up, keeps them from falling down when they are asleep?" Thus we say when we are untrained.

Ch'it'oqwin'ak was a Getter-Of-One-Hundred when he went after the shags, getting a hundred at a time. But one didn't sleep for Ch'it'oqwin'ak, the one with Hi:xwa:, dentalium, inside. He used to find that one awake, the rascal; he would find it talking. Then there it would go, jumping into the sea! He stopped doing this Hi:shmi:ˀa hunting at the waning of the moon.[3]
Ch'it'oqwin'ak then said to his wife that he would try to do ˀo:simch ritual for getting the one with the Hi:xwa: inside. He started bathing from after that phase of the moon in March; as soon as the new moon began, he started to bathe. For four days he bathed at the beginning of the new moon. Then when it was

getting to be the full moon, he again began bathing. But he never bathed while the moon was waning; the people considered it taboo to bathe at the waning of the moon.

It is said that the Chief of the shags is the one with H̲i:xwa: inside it. Ch'it'oqwin'ak, saying that he would cause the one with H̲i:xwa: inside to sleep, bathed all summer long in preparation for when winter came. He moved up the inlet at the beginning of the fall when the Spring salmon move up the canal to Nam'int. The Yo:loʔilʔath̲ moved upriver when fall came. Ch'it'oqwin'ak got ready.

"Don't you worry about me: I'm going for a long walk and I'll be gone a long time," Ch'it'oqwin'ak told his wife. "I'm going to M'itlow'a."

There is a mountain at Nam'int called M'itlowa. Ch'it'oqwin'ak started poling his little canoe upstream. He arrived at the falls of the Nam'int River and tied up his canoe on this side, the same side we are on, the north. He had his small iron chisel stuck in his belt. He started walking towards the back of the falls along the little trail there and came to a small tributary of the main river. He emerged where the small stream flowed out on rocks, and lo - going about in the pool were White perch, Red perch, and a cod called ʔo:x̲. In colour they looked as if they were extremely hot. They would back out downstream into the little pool at the rocks, the ʔo:x̲ cod, Red perch, and the White. Then they would go upstream again. Standing there on the rocks Ch'it'oqwin'ak was working his mind as to which one he should take. My, he decided on the ʔo:x̲. As soon as they backed out again as they had been doing all along, backing down towards the shallows, the rascal Ch'it'oqwin'ak grabbed it! It was as if the White perch and the Red vanished: he didn't know where they went. It was as if they went right into the rocks.

He started walking toward the back of the falls, holding the ʔo:x̲ by the neck with both hands. The rascal now had that as he went up to M'itlow'a. He was up there when night came. Then, damn it, Ch'it'oqwin'ak heard it singing, what he was holding in his hands! It was as if there were many singing doctoring songs. He heard it whenever he went to sleep. He remained there on the ground, then began to see the shamans, the rascal! He would see that he was inside a house, a big one with many inside showing off their powers. Four days he remained at the place called M'itlow'a.

On the fourth day he walked down. The sun was low but not quite all the way down. Then it got dark before he was all the way down. Suddenly he became aware of something that appeared to be fire, bounding through the woods where he was going. Again it came back, looking like a ball of fire. Then it went up to the trees and while there it was as if it was thrown across the treetops way up high. He couldn't do anything because he was holding something in his hands. It happened four times and then disappeared. The trees must have been throwing the fireball at each other, showing off their doctoring powers. He dreamed, too, that it said,

"Guess you don't really want to become a shaman for you didn't try to take the fireball."

He went to sleep right there on the ground. He started making medicine of what he had, wrapping it with moss and pieces from his clothing. He ripped off the right edge of the blanket he had on. Then Ch'it'oqwin'ak tied up that which he had found. He forgot what he had been doing ʔo:simch for and started doing ritual for doctoring. He was thinking only of what he had just seen, forgetting that he had been doing ʔo:simch ritual for the shag with H̲i:xwa inside, and began imitating doctoring practices since he was among doctoring things. Ch'it'oqwin'ak was among doctoring things.

Ch'it'oqwin'ak was gone eight days, then came back downstream on the eighth. He used to make noises like a shaman.[4] He would never sleep and was going "Hai hai hai," making the sounds the shamans make when performing the Wolf Ritual.

The village was at a place called T'iqo:ʔis,[5] a site on the rocks up the river of Nam'int. There were ten families owning the village site. The T'iqo:ʔisʔath̲ had someone sick at a place just upstream from where Ch'it'oqwin'ak lived. Their sick person now became very ill. Ch'it'oqwin'ak went gathering firewood downstream on the Nam'int, then as soon as the tide came in he came back upstream loaded down with firewood. When he came home he found the villagers were in a sad state, the ones who had the sick person. He went into the house with his arms full of wood.

"What's this weeping I hear?" he asked his wife.

"Oh, it's for the sick one who died. You should be the one to bring their deceased back to life with whatever kind of spirit power you have. You always seem to have plenty of ways about you when you make Wolf Ritual sounds day after day causing me to stay awake," said his wife, adding ironically, "You're never bothersome."

"Haven't they buried it yet?" Ch'it'oqwin'ak asked.

"I guess not. Maybe they still have him in the house," replied the wife.

Ch'it'oqwin'ak walked over there, went in, and found that the coffin box was already tied up.

"Excuse me, excuse me, excuse me. Get out of my way," he was saying as he went along inside, Ch'it'oqwin'ak.

Right away he sat on the lid of the coffin, sat down on it and felt what it's like when a person just died. He felt some sign of life yet, so he did not sit there very long but got off again and stood up.

"You fellows untie it quick!" he said.

They did not untie it for him.

"Untie it, you folks!" he repeated.

Then one woman said, "Untie it, just in case ...."

Slowly they untied the coffin, then doubtfully removed the lid. My, he reached into the box, the rascal Ch'it'oqwin'ak, and felt the belly of the corpse!

"He," it said once as soon as he laid his hands on it.

My gosh, that bugger Ch'it'oqwin'ak took it and pulled it out! At the same instant the one who was dead sat up. He was scratching his head and rubbing his eyes with the other hand as he sat up. That son of a gun had something like what they always refer to as "Tsiqtskwi," a frog! They were just looking at each other in astonishment, all those who came to weep, for they were most surprized. They were as if struck dumb, those who had been weeping. The one who had been dead got out and stayed way over there. Ch'it'oqwin'ak was still girded up because he had just come in, his firewood still in the canoe. Hey then, they paid him, the rascal, giving him all that the dead man had. That's how it was revealed that Ch'it'oqwin'ak had become a shaman.

The news flew everywhere; all the tribes were talking about Ch'it'oqwin'ak. He would not go when they came after him to doctor someone who was sick and still alive. The only time he went was when they came for him to doctor someone who had been dead for a day. My, then he would go in a hurry! He became sought throughout all our tribes, Ch'it'oqwin'ak. When they came for him to doctor, he would ask,

"Is the person you want me for dead now?"

Ch'it'oqwin'ak became wealthy as all riches began coming to his house. The Ts'isha:ʔath came to a Ts'a:yiq doctoring ceremonial at Hinap'i:ʔis.[6] This was in the generation of my grandfather's father; that's how long ago this was. The Yo:loʔilʔath entered doing the Ts'a:yiq. Gosh, the scoundrel Ch'it'oqwin'ak showed up, leading the dancers as the Yo:loʔilʔath came in performing the Ts'a:yiq.

"The upper hand power of my M'inoqy'ak disease thrower will show even if you people let the shamans in first," his song said as Ch'it'oqwin'ak walked in.

He had tied at both ends what was called a Ch'ochmawtskwi, a Mountain Goat blanket about a fathom long wrapped up as he came in. As soon as he came close to the middle of the floor, his wrists made a motion. Then he put his hands behind it and broke what could not be broken because it was wrapped many times. He was dragging the long pieces of the remains of the break, holding them in view with shaking hands. He held up the broken pieces for a long time, showing them to the Ts'isha:ˀat<u>h</u>. Then he gathered the broken pieces into a bundle and, the son of a gun, blew into it while it was like that, and lo - it was a fathom long again the same as before. It was wonderful to behold sure enough. The Ts'isha:ˀat<u>h</u> who came to the Ts'a:yiq performance were truly amazed.

119. The Youth Who Followed a Shag (Sa:ya:ch'apis)

A youth was out shooting. He wounded a shag and was chasing the creature with his arrow stuck in it. He came to the river at Ho:choqtlis. The shag went up the river with the arrow in it and into the lake. It reached the creek coming into the lake at the other end. The youth was shooting along the way but kept missing. It went upstream again, up the headwater creek. He was folowing it, the youth, actually two in the canoe with his younger brother. They went up the headstream and got to a bluff. The shag jumped onto the rocky bank and went into a bunch of bracken ferns. The youth close behind jumped out, too. He parted the ferns and saw a way off down there a beautiful land! The youth went in. His arrow was thrown away. He saw that there were many winter Spring salmon in many small creeks[2] there. The tree branches were bent down to the ground from the many eagles.[3] There were many deer, many bears, many martins, many minks, many river otters, many raccoons, and many elk. The youth returned home to his house, saying to the brother,

"You'll not tell our father and mother, will you?"

He had a sister, the youth.

"I've seen a beautiful land. We'll go there," he said.

The youth took his sister along with him that night while the whole village was still asleep. The father didn't know where they went. No one saw them; the brother and sister were lost. They got two children, boys. They were gone a long time; four winters they were away.

"All right! You two will go and visit your Grandfather! He has lots of dried winter Spring salmon: 'Dried' it's called," said the young man. "Say, 'We are looking for our Grandfather that we heard about. We are the children of the one who was lost a long time ago'."

The boys went downstream, paddling through the lake.[4] They arrived at the village just as night fell. The children went up the beach and started looking around, peeking in from house to house. There at the doorway they would be. Then along came a young man who took them and asked,

"Who are you?"

"We are the children of the one who was lost a long time ago. Our Father has us looking for our Grandfather that we heard about."

"Then come with me," said the young man, "So you can get to it;

his house is way over there."

He took the children along.

"These children are looking for you. They say their father is the one who was lost long ago."

The old people got all excited.

"Come here, come here, come here!" said the old folks.

They took them onto their laps. The woman took the children, their grandchildren.

"We've brought lots of dried Spring salmon. You folks come and get what's in the canoe."

"They say there's lots of dried Spring salmon!" said the old folks.

They started to pack the salmon into the house, lots of dried winter Spring salmon. They invited the whole village, all of them. The H̲o:choqtlisˀath̲ became guests; all were guests. The whole village now ate! The village was satiated. Night came, another night, and all the people went to sleep. The children left in their canoe. No one was aware of what they were doing, not even the grandparents. When daylight came the children were gone. Far away again, they remained absent a long time. They were gone two years.

Then they came downstream again, this time the one who was lost long ago, together with his sister as a couple. He had bear meat and lots of bearskins. They were tied down in the canoe with a rope.[5] They landed at the village with the many people. The young man went up the beach, the husband first and the woman in the rear. One of the women from the many houses spoke:

"Step lively ...," she called out, "You who had your own brother..., the one walking there on the beach...."

The woman sang back to the one by whom she was addressed:

> I've got two hundred bearskins on my feet'
> That's why I'm stepping lively.[6]

The old man gave a feast again. The young woman became ashamed. Night came, and all the people went to sleep. The young man went off in his canoe. Again no one saw them go as they left that night. They both went home, the young woman and young man as a couple. They got lost for good, never returning.

120. A Runaway Slave Comes to the Chief of Wanin
(Sa:ya:ch'apis)

These three brothers who were Chiefs came from the other river flowing into the lake to get a moving canoe.[2] They had one father, one mother, and were the only ones in the village. They lived just at each end of the house.[3] They came downstream to where there were many people, and took along the moving canoe, the three riding in it. They started paddling to the lake and were going through it. They rounded the point. There on the rocks was a hair seal. The three men watched it as they paddled along. Suddenly out jumped a cougar! It clawed the seal on the head. One of the three saw that it was not a cougar. Two of them said,

"It's a cougar."

"It's not a cougar," said the one. "It has heads at both ends!"

"It's a cougar," said the two.

"No it's not."

They put the hair seal in the canoe. The head of the seal was bleeding; it was a little hair seal. They set out paddling and arrived at their house that evening. They told about how the cougar had clawed the seal.

"It was not a cougar," one of them said again as they were telling their wives.

"Say! You're a liar!" they were saying to each other.

The seal was now cooked. The slave grasped what the one was saying by 'It has heads at both ends'. The slave took note of the fact that the claw marks were at the head because only the creature called T'ot'ohtsaqts'o:, Head-On-Both-Ends, does that. He believed the one of the three.

"Come. Come, let's go out in the canoe," he said to his boy.

They went out that evening fishing with a gill net.[4] They were fishing for provisions for when they would be moving the next day. At midnight they went home and entered their house. The name of the slave was T'i:t'iqwin?a.[5] His boy was named Tlo:swi.[6]

"Wake up," said T'i:t'iqwin?a to his wife.

The woman was dead! He went to the next person, gave him a

shove, and found that he also was dead. He went to his Chief and
pushed him; here, too, he was dead. All the people in the house
were dead, women and children included, on account of their
having eaten[7] the hair seal that the T'ot'oh̲tsaqts'o: had clawed.
He opened up the boxes of goods belonging to the late Chief. He
threw away his sockeye and put in the goods in their place, the
valuables of his late Chief. Then he paddled downstream and
arrived at a place called N'ima.[8] When daylight came he pulled
the canoe into the bushes. They hid in the woods, staying there
all day.[9] Then in the evening he set out again. He went to a
place called ʔO:qwa:tis, arriving there at night. They landed at
a place named Tl'asimyis[10] near ʔO:qwa:tis. He hid his canoe and
was staying there when day came.

Ho:h̲inkwop[11] sat down on the beach to look about. It was still
very early as he was sitting, looking around. He was on the
beach at a place called Wanin. His boy called Tl'isʔachim[12] was
going about shooting small birds. His name was like that on
account of the Gray whale's belly being white, for his father was
hunting the Grays. The boy was out shooting for wrens and
sparrows. He went towards the place called Tl'asimyis; the boy
reached Tl'asimyis. Then someone attracted his attention by
whistling, drawing the breath in.[13] The boy looked.

"Come here."

There he was sitting in his canoe.[14]

"Is your father home? Go and tell him that I'm come to see
him. 'There's a man over there come to see you', you tell him,"
the boy was told.

The child went back. He shot an arrow. He took another arrow
and shot it towards where his father was on the beach.[15] He got
to where his father was.

"Dad, there are two persons on the ground over there," he said
to his father. "You are to go and get him. He said he is come
to see you."

Ho:h̲inkwop went up to his house without hesitation.

"You fellows come. They say there's a man over there," he said
to his younger brothers.

He set out together with all his younger brothers. They
reached where the two persons were. Ho:h̲inkwop took them, having
the father on this side and on that side the child. Taking by
the hand to his house, he put them in. The younger brothers took
the canoe and packed it up to the house of Ho:h̲inkwop, the Chief
[to be] of the Waninʔath̲.[16] No one took his prize from him, not
the ʔO:qwa:tisʔath̲ Chief, because the land belonged to Wanin;

that's why it was called Tl'asimyis?ath. My name is not really Waninˀath for it's Ma:ktl?i:ˀath. Ho:hinkwop gave an invitation to a feast, and the Chief of ˀO:qwa:tis came as guest. He went to the village called ?Asiml,[17] going as a guest, the Chief of ˀO:qwa:tis. Hohinkwop sang his spirit song:

> Mine, for my part, is what's for throwing away,
> The big coppers.
> Mine, for my part, is what's for throwing away,
> When I have two hundred of wealth.[18]

He gave things to the ˀO:qwa:tisˀath. Hohinkwop's song was properly sung. He gave coppers. The ˀO:qwa:tisˀath went home. The ˀO:qwa:tisˀath Chief was happy now. He gave him a stream which has Cohos in it in season, the stream which is called Wanin. They got to be different, another tribe. Ho:hinkwop got to go there regularly. He built his village at Wanin, and from then on they were called Waninˀath.

121. Wealth From a Shag (Sa:ya:ch'apis)

The young Chief from ?Ots'o:s was unmanly.[2] His father was a Getter of Humpback and Gray whales. His father was also Head Chief of the ?Ots'o:s?ath. His wife did not bear children; that is why his father was very angry at him. So his father 'threw him away' as you would any useless article. That is what our forefathers used to do: 'throw away' sons who were useless and unmanly. He was looked after by his uncle, his father's younger brother, who didn't throw away his nephew. He was just friendly to his nephew although he did not have him with him. That is who was counselling him about what he should do if he saw someone unnatural, telling him everything, including how and when to bathe ritually, counselling his nephew.

He obeyed, K'o:k'ots'itl'i:k, whatever he was told to do by his uncle. His father had named him K'o:k'ots'itl'i:k[3] because of the fact that he only went after small mussels; that's all he had as food, the young man. He would usually be gone for two days when he went for the small bay mussels though he sometimes would be gone longer, up to six days. There they bathed, trying very hard, the couple did. That is the reason they would be gone so long, because they were bathing ritually. The father would give him a piece of blubber whenever he got some. But he used to throw it away, didn't eat it, because he was looking as well for a way to become a 'man', saying that he was counselled by his uncle. He really hated his father.

Even so he was going home, the rascal, and then lo and behold: there was a great big shag on the beach. All at once he remembered what his uncle used to tell him. Right away he jumped out of the canoe and ran, for there was the shag walking. It was as if he saw it to be wingless although it had wings. But they were bare, without plumage. At once he took it.

"Give me what's inside you," he said.

"Give me what's inside you," he repeated.

"Please give me that which you have inside you," he pleaded.

After he asked four times, he saw that out of the shag's rear end came a Hi:xwa:, dentalium!

"All right. Give me another, make it man and wife!" he said.

Then and there another one came out making a mated pair. Then he released the shag, saying,

"All right, you can go."

The rascal K'o:k'ots'itl'i:k now had something! For a while, the span of a day, he attended to that which he had seen. Then he went home to his little abode. His small mussels were packed up the beach, what he had brought in his canoe and was fond of eating for which he was called by that name by his commoners. He tied up his box and put it in his canoe, the box which he usually kept at the head of his bed. That night he had in his canoe the thing he had found, what he now had. Daylight came and he unpacked it. He found that box half full of Hi:xwa:. The pair of Hi:xwa: kept on top pf the mass of stuff the two were spewing out of their rear ends. He divided the mass into three groups for they were of three groups of Hi:xwa:. That night he found that the same thing happened as before that morning: there he found the box half full again of Hi:xwa:. It was adding up very fast, he could hardly keep up dividing it up, the remains of the big ones were adding up to so many Hi:xwa:, the rascal! He put mats where he was keeping them on the floor and put up boards for partitions to make little rooms to store his Hi:xwa:. Nobody knew of what happened because no one ever came to visit K'o:k'ots'itl'i:k. Hey, now he had lots of Hi:xwa:, the rascal!

When summer came he was still storing and separating the Hi:xwa: on the floor into the big ones, the mid-size ones, and ones that were small. None knew of this, that he had lots of Hi:xwa:, that he was getting plenty. When it became summer some Tl'a:ʔasʔath[4] came along the coast on a Hi:xwa: buying trip in four canoes, looking for Hi:xwa: from tribe to tribe. They were full of goods to trade for Hi:xwa:.[6] They could not find any Hi:xwa: among those villages they had visited and began telling of their failure in getting them the Tl'a:ʔasʔath did.

"Ha! I guess we will not get any on this trip for these people have only a few Hi:xwa:."

"You fellows go to that single house there on the beach. He is the only one who has a house full of Hi:xwa:," someone said, speaking sarcastically to make fun of K'o:k'ots'itli:k.

"Is that so?" said the three canoes.

They sent one canoe to take a closer look and it went past the house to see. The three canoes didn't move. They found out that they were just making fun of him because K'o:k'ots'itli:k was unmanly.

"We are looking for Chiti:nok," said the Tl'a:ʔasʔath.

The Tl'a:ʔasʔath used to call Hi:xwa: 'Chiti:nok'.[6]

"Those from across the bay said you have lots of Chiti:nok," said the Tl'a:ʔasʔath, "That yours is full, those of you who live here, we heard."

"Oh. Take a look then. On the floor towards the door is what you're looking for," said K'o:k'ots'itli:k.

The Tl'a:ˀasˀath uncovered it. He got red in the face as he saw that there on the floor piled high in the partitioned room were many Hi:xwa:.

"There are more on the other side of the house. Push aside the cover again," said K'o:k'ots'itli:k. "There are still more at the head of the house. Pull the curtains aside. You'll see what you're looking for. I want to sell the small ones and the medium size for the same price."

The Tl'a:ˀasˀath canoe started buying. K'o:k'ots'itli:k was fair in his dealing: he was selling the Hi:xwa: for less than what it was worth so that the purchasers would feel good about buying. Pretty soon the Tl'a:ˀasˀath ran out of the wherewithal to buy. They went back over to their fellow canoe parties. They started telling them,

"It's true what they said, the house is really full of Hi:xwa:. We ran out of trade goods. He's not selling the Hi:xwa: for what it's really worth. He's not stingy."

The rest of the Tl'a:ˀasˀath, the three canoes, went across and began buying as well. In a little while they, too, ran out of goods to trade. Then the four canoes went home, all four. They arrived at their home at Ni:ya:.[7] The four canoes had a consultation in which they agreed to keep it all secret. They remained at their home two days, then started off for Kwinyo:tˀath,[8] all four canoes, intending also to reach the Kwi:na:yilˀath,[9] they who are called ˀI:ts'oqˀath, because that is where they used to sell Hi:xwa:, the reason for the Tl'a:ˀasˀath buying trips. For that's where Hi:xwa: was worth lots, the seaward side. The four Tl'a:ˀasˀath canoes then headed home all loaded down with wealth goods. They arrived at their home.

Again they got ready to go towards ˀOts'o:s, the four canoes. The people got suspicious of them, for they were about to travel in their canoes again, those who travelled by fours. One of the four canoes' crew told one of his friends, a relative. He said that even if all the tribes should land at the beach front there were so many Hi:xwa: they would not seem to get less, there being three varieties partitioned off. The Tl'a:ˀasˀath held council, those who were left behind. They, too, got ready and started off.

K'o:k'ots'itl'i:k got a measuring stick. That was their measure, the people of old: one string of Hi:xwa: was one fathom long strung out. Then strings of these were called "N'o:phta:yok". This is how K'o:k'ots'itli:k used to measure his

Hi:xwa:, that's what he went by. He pulled it out into the container as much as the measure would be; that's how he measured it easily when he sold it.

The Tl'a:ˀasˀath followed in ten more canoes. These canoes and the original four added up to fourteen canoes coming to buy Hi:xwa: from K'o:k'ots'itli:k. The whole fleet of canoes got to K'o:k'ots'itli:k's beach front, all fourteen of them! They landed bow first on the beach where K'o:k'ots'itli:k lived, the rascal! They started buying from the man: ten measures for a slave - some bought with slaves, those who wanted to, the Tl'a:ˀasˀath Chiefs - five measures for a slave boy the size of No:txasˀaqtli and Ma:ma:tli:ts.[10] The main villagers just watched from the other side. K'o:k'ots'itli:k got five slaves, two female and three male. He was buying everything, all the wealth possessions of our forefathers like mountain goat blankets. There were no trade blankets at that time. Some of the Tl'a:ˀasˀath had them on the back. All of the fourteen canoes were overloaded. There were also camas bulbs, steam cooked; that's what the Tl'a:ˀasˀath used for trade, too. They had twenty sacks of steamed camas, one hundred of dried blubber, also a sea lion bladder full of oil for his dried herring eggs. Those of the people of the village who had spoken sarcastically saying, 'He's the only one full of Hi:xwa:, the one over on the other side,' were now ashamed.

All this caused the Hi:xwa: piled up in the house to become a little less, about half the amount on the floor there. They ran out of things to trade with again, the Tl'a:ˀasˀath, so they went home. K'o:k'ots'itl'i:k got loaded down with wealth possessions. He invited the people from the other side to a camas feast, giving it at his father's house. He gave a feast of blubber twice, doing so there at his father's house.

The Ni:ti:naˀath[11] as well heard about this from the Tl'a:ˀasˀath on their way home full of Hi:xwa:, saying that even if all the tribes went to buy Hi:xwa: from him it wouldn't make a dent:

"We never even made it a wee bit less because there are so many."

Right away the Ni:ti:naˀath started off in twenty canoes. Round the point they came again. Ni:ti:naˀath. Oh my, but it looked like many canoes, the twenty! The Ni:ti:naˀath, too, brought many trade goods including mountain goat blankets. They, too, started to buy. Again they had slaves to barter for Hi:xwa:. K'o:k'ots'itli:k bought five more slaves. He also bought mountain goat blankets. Some of the Ni:ti:naˀath Chiefs had two. This time they bought all of the Hi:xwa:. The people from the other side were looking with envy at those trying to outbuy the others, they were just watching all the bartering.

For a while he had put away his H̲i:xwa: producing couple; they were not producing for a while.

He got a house for all his slaves. He didn't let them live in the same house with him but put them far away at the back of the village, his slaves. The tribe gave him two boards from each of his subjects, and he paid each person who gave him boards in H̲i:wxa:. Then he rested a while, having sold all his H̲i:xwa:! The H̲i:xwa: couple that defecates knows when they are not required to produce when they defecate; they just stop what they were doing. He would put them into a small bay mussel shell and tie it together when he made them stop defecating. The H̲i:xwa: couple would also know when they were required to give birth again. They would be put into a large box, and they would start giving birth in a hurry!

* * * *

Then K'o:k'ots'itli:k went to get small mussels, what he did all the time. He went again with his wife and started getting bay mussels because he held them in high regard as his best food. He worked till dark and was going home. then he saw a fire there on the rock point. The island by the shore had a sandy area at its neck. The fire was there at the little island separated from the shore by a strip of water. Hey, then he heard a baby cry!

"ʔA:h̲o:," said the Na:ni:qa mother.

Na:ni:qa it's called by the up-inlet people, but we call them Yaʔ̲i:, those of that kind. That last noise sounded, the one which makes us scared. K'o:k'ots'itli:k turned his canoe and went backwards. They say it's as if the earth trembles when it utters the last sound; that's what caused K'o:k'ots'itli:k to become weak in his bones. It was just as if a woman was saying 'ʔAh̲o:, ʔah̲o:' trying to stop its crying when her baby is crying. K'o:k'ots'itli:k's canoe hit the sandy beach stern first like a spear.

"All right, guy, jump out of the canoe," he said to his wife.

He used to jerk the canoe. 'All right, you rascal, jump out of the canoe,' he'd say.

K'o:k'ots'itli:k became crippled, his legs going dead. He was crippled and unable to walk.

"The rascal here in the canoe has done great!" said the wife.

Out jumped the wife and went at once to the one on the rocks holding the baby, the Na:ni:qa. Hey, she took the baby from her, K'o:k'ots'itli:k's wife did!

Give me my baby," it said. "For a belt it has a Hiˀitl'ik. Take that off. It has a Hihiqtoy'i:k for a belt. Take that off it, too. For a side pillow it has a Sea Otter on the right side of the face. For a side pillow on the left side of the face it has a Hair Seal."

After it said all that, she threw the baby behind her. The Na:ni:qa caught it. Its baby did not hit the ground. The fire went out, as if you closed your eyes. The channel had given up what it had for him.

He went towards Ma:n'o:ˀisˀath,[12] starting to make medicine of it. He didn't take the whole thing but took only half of each one. It is taboo to keep the whole thing: you're supposed to split it in two, take the right side and throw away the left. He put it onto a yew tree. It is the yew that knows how to look after medicine and the cedar, the slender ones still growing up, saplings. On the yew tree he placed the Hiˀitl'ik and the Hihi:qtoy'i:k, then on the cedar the Sea Otter and Hair Seal together. He stayed there praying and waiting ritually, was away four days, and while there he saw Wolves, ten of them. These must have been the great hunters of the Wolves. They gave him tree needle twigs from which they were empowered to be good hunters. He then added these to his medicines, the more reason to pray and wait.

On the eighth day he headed home, starting off at night. He reached a nice flat rock sloping slightly downward. From there came the sound of a hair seal squealing, so piercing it was as if the world burst! At once K'o:k'ots'itli:k went towards the shore, towards where the sound came from, and just then as he approached he heard the squealing start again. K'o:k'ots'itli:k got out and went up on the rocks. Suddenly he was looking down into a hole and saw things that looked like stars for a whole bunch of seals were looking up at him. Not doing anything, he went down the beach. Thinking that he had found something, he didn't even touch. He arrived at night at his little house.

"K'o:k'ots'itli:k must have some kind of sea mammal in his canoe; that's why he was gone," he heard them saying about him ironically.

He stayed home quite a while, about six days, then went back to where he would go to and stayed there overnight. He got out of his canoe and went to the secret cave. He took a mid-sized seal, not a real big one. He took it down from the rocks and put it into the canoe. He cut it on the side, making it look like it was wounded, and landed at the village on the other side.

"Hey now, this happened just in time to us poor folks! We have found a dead drift carcass. There's a hair seal here in the canoe. Come and see, guys, if it's the one that got away from you," said K'o:k'ots'itli:k.

The hunters went down the beach to look at the seal.

"I'm the one who speared it at this spot. It pulled out," said one the hunters.

"All right. All right, all right. Take it," said K'o:k'ots'itli:k.

My, the hunter took it out of the canoe and up the beach! Then the one who pretended to have gotten the seal gave a feast. The people at the feast began talking, being satiated, saying that K'o:k'ots'itli:k was very useful because he was always about doing something or going someplace.

"We would never have gotten this if it was not for K'o:k'ots'itli:k being always on the move," they said.

K'o:k'ots'itli:k stayed home for quite a while before going out again. He was gone for two days. Two nights he was away and then came home. He had taken a big seal, the biggest one, taken it down the beach and put it in his canoe. He had fixed it the same way: wounded, with guts sticking out.

"Now then we have met again, those of us who are orphans, always on the go," said K'o:k'ots'itli:k. "Come down the beach again, you hunters, and look at it to see which one speared it. Here in the canoe again is a hair seal."

Again one of them recognized it as the one, the big one he had speared. My, he took it up the beach and gave a feast again! They were glad that they were now having feasts often. They were thanking K'o:k'ots'itli:k, saying that it was he who was finding those seals that had gotten away from the hunters.

For a while K'o:k'ots'itli:k did not go out. Then after staying home eight days he went out again. He was away for two days again, then came home. This time he took two from his seal cave. He took one big seal and one medium sized. He put the seals in his canoe; now he had two in there. Again he fixed them with a cut on each in the side with the guts sticking out and went towards the village, paddling. My, once again the hunters came down the beach to meet him.

"You guys must be busy spearing seals. This time we are really in luck!" he said.

He told them where he got each of the seals, making the places far apart.

"That big one is mine. I'm the one who speared the big one," said one hunter.

Hey now, two hunters started arguing, each pretending to be the one who speared the big one! One of them had as a witness his steersman testifying that it was he indeed who speared the big one. The steersman was saying that it nearly upset the canoe for it was so big, pulling very hard! The two began to quarrel, each saying to the other that he, too, knew how to get big ones. Then one of them weakened and took the smaller one. K'o:k'ots'itli:k was secretly laughing at them for now he was getting even for the times they were making fun of him. K'o:k'ots'itli:k went home. The two hunters were often giving seal feasts while K'o:k'ots'itli:k was always left with nothing; that's why they believed him, for he kept only his paddle.

He called his uncle who had helped him. He asked him if he was not willing to go along the coast to find him a sealing spear.

"I am willing to go if you send me looking for it," said the uncle.

He left and went to Hishkwi:ʔath[13] looking for a sealing spear complete with the harpoon heads strung on because his nephew had said to look for a spear already strung with the harpoons and lines. No one knew that he went to buy a spear because he arrived at his nephew's place at night.

"Burn the bottom of your canoe," he told his uncle.[14]

Over four fathoms in length was his uncle's canoe. His uncle put the canoe on its side, drying it. Then he burned its bottom that evening. It was all ready, burned and burnished, the next morning. He pulled it out that evening when the sun went down, then went across to where his nephew lived. Hey, the rascal K'o:k'ots'itli:k came down the beach and, lo, there he was carrying a spear! Not many spoke in suspicion save two.

"So that's why he pretends to get drift seals each time. He's acting funny indeed for there he goes getting ready to go seal hunting," they said suspiciously. "He's in a big canoe for sealing, K'o:k'ots'itli:k; nevertheless, he'll fill it up no doubt," they continued, making fun of K'o:k'ots'itli:k.

He went towards the open sea with the spear sticking out on the bow, the rascal. As soon as he reached the open sea he stopped there and waited until dark. Then as soon as it got dark he went back inside and travelled at night towards where his seal cave was. He arrived there while the night was not too advanced, while it was not yet midnight. He got out of his canoe and tied it up. He started killing the seals, and his uncle was taking them down the rocks right away. He killed fifteen, selecting only big ones. He went and put the seals in the canoe, then looked to see how his canoe was loaded and found that it had lots of freeboard yet, still needed more. He went back up and got five more. My, again he took them down and put them in his canoe. My, this time it really sank lower into the sea! When he had put twenty seals in, they started off, still at night. He went towards the open sea where he had gone before and stopped out there. He was still there when daylight started coming. He was not out there long when daylight came, and waited until it got really light before starting off; that's why it was just at sunrise that he rounded the point, the rascal K'o:k'ots'itli:k! The whole village sprang into action, everyone running outside.

"Ko:k'ots'itli:k is loaded to the brim with seals!"

His sealing spear which he did not even use was still strung in the canoe in pretense of having been used. The people all ran down to where K'o:k'ots'itli:k lay alongside the shore; the whole village was down the beach to meet him. The hunters again came down to take the seals from him.

"Here he is again, the one from whom you're taking things," some of the people were saying. "Did he really bring in your seals? Come on down and take his seals like you've been doing before."

Those who used to pretend they speared the seals went inside in shame. K'o:k'ots'itli:k's canoe was now being unloaded. All the seals were wounded as if from his spear. He gave all he had in the canoe to his steersman, his uncle, all twenty seals. Then he cruised by the village in his empty canoe with no more seals inside. The slaves lifted up his canoe and beached it. These were the slaves he got from his H̲i:xwa:.

After ten days he went out again with the same person, his uncle. Again he went towards the open sea, pretending to go out there as always. As soon as it got dark he headed back to where he went before towards his seal cave. He arrived at night at his cave and started killing the seals. This time he changed things by taking not just big ones; he took the mid-sized ones. He began taking them down the shore in the night. That was done without too much effort because the rocks there below the cave were sloping down; it was easy to do by one man. Twenty-five seals were loaded onto the canoe. It sank down; the canoe got very low in the water. While it was still night he started off again, went past where he left from and back towards the open sea. He was not out there long before daylight broke. Again he came around the point early in the morning. My, my, it looked like K'o:k'ots'itli:k had seals again in his canoe, coming round the point with his spear sticking out of the bow! Hey, all the villagers ran down the beach to meet him! Oh my, this time it looked like there were even more seals than before on the beach, twenty-five! His uncle cut up the seals once more because he got all of them for being the steersman, all twenty-five seals. Then they heated stones, throwing them on the fire. There were many layers of wood over the fire. The ?Ots'o:s?ath sat down to a feast. Just as the people were eating K'o:k'ots'itli:k entered. His father gave him a name. He gave him a new name for the other time before when he came in with lots of seals and his uncle gave a seal feast.

"I don't want you all to call me anything else. Just keep calling me K'o:k'ots'itli:k," said K'o:k'ots'itli:k, "For I don't want to shame you because it was you who gave me this name when you disowned me."

After saying that he went out and headed home. Then he went out hunting again but this time he didn't get so many. He had just ten in the canoe for he was afraid they might get suspicious and start spying on him. It became winter and he was out hunting all the time. He would have up to ten in the canoe but didn't bring home many too often.

* * * *

Then while it was winter he began getting ready to go whale hunting. He bought a whaling harpoon shaft, also cedar withe rope, and started making the sealskin floats himself. He got everything ready. He put pitch on the blade of the harpoon head he bought from the Tl'a:ˀasˀath with his Hi:xwa:. He bought a whaling canoe. When summer came he had all his equipment ready; he had everything ready by the time the Gray whales started blowing.

The whalers of all the tribes started going out. The ˀOts'o:sˀath whalers went out, too. It was when all the whalers had gone out that K'o:k'ots'itli:k also went out. For crew he had his uncle as steersman and the rest were all slaves, four of his slaves, for there are six men in the canoe of those who go out whaling. There was no one at the middle of the canoe. That space was saved to store the coiled up cedar branch rope and the sealskin floats, for which reason there were men only at the ends, three at each end. They paddled out towards where the whalers were waiting and tied up to kelps on the sea. They were there not too long when, my gosh, the water started churning at the front of their canoe where they were tied up! There it blew at the right side of their bow, a Gray whale. They took but two strokes, the Gray was so close. Hey then, the rascal K'o:k'ots'itli:k speared, the shaft going in right up to the binding[15] it sank in so deep! His whale just shook a little and died at once. The other whalers came and only towed K'o:k'ots'itli:k's catch. They tied it on the beach in front of his father's house. He had them butcher the whale, had the whole tribe come to cut the blubber off for themselves, all the people.

His dorsal fin was taken up to his faher's house and suspended facing downward on a horizontal pole at the head of the house.

Next day K'o:k'ots'itli:k went out whaling again and had another one tied up on the beach. Again it had died at once because he was powered by the Ya?i: spirit he saw. He tied the Gray whale again in front of his father's house. He did the same as before: had all the people help themselves to the whale. Just the steersman, his uncle, would get his measure of blubber, four hands wide on each side at the mid-section, the wide part of the belly right around the girth. His dorsal fin went up the beach once more to where his father lived. There were now two dorsal fins suspended on rafters in the house of his father.

For four days he went out each day, caught four and then stayed home for a while. The villagers got lots of blubber because there were now four Gray whales on the beach. Then they cooked the dorsal fins for him, all four saddles which K'o:k'ots'itli:k had. The whole village had a feast when they cooked the four dorsal fins. Just those women who had stopped menstruating were allowed to come to the feast, not those who were still having their monthlies. When one gives a dorsal fin feast, the leftovers are not taken home; they stay right in the house. People used to go in there to finish eating cooked dorsal fin. K'o:k'ots'itli:k now spoke when everyone was there at the dorsal fin feast:

"You people are now sharing this feast with me, what I'm eating," he said. "These are the small mussels that I eat. You are now eating small mussels."

The people were all ashamed, those who used to delight in making fun of him, laughing at him for liking to eat small mussels. Then he went out again for four days, getting one whale a day. He had the same number of dorsal fins suspended on the rafters again.

"This is my own catch, what you're eating now," he said to his fellow tribesmen. "I did not use my grandfather's equipment, though my father is also a Getter of whales, for I don't know his ritual words."

His father wanted him to move into his house. K'o:k'ots'itli:k didn't have him have all the four Grays. They cut up the whales for him. Then he invited the other tribes to come buy his blubber. The Tla?o:kwi?ath came to buy blubber; also the Qiltsma?ath, ?A:ho:s?ath, Hishkwi:?ath, and Mowach'ath. The rascal K'o:k'ots'itli:k got wealthy; his house became full of riches. Then he went out again, went whaling once more, K'o:k'ots'itli:k. He only took two, got two more,[16] and then let it go for a while. That's as far as the story of K'o:k'ots'itli:k goes.

122. Tlatla:qokw'ap Sees the Thunderbird and Gets Power From a Sea Egg (William)

He went out, it is said, from Ts'isha:. He was whaling and went far offshore; all the small islands sank out of sight. He saw a Humpback whale, speared it, and then started fighting it. There were many whales and they all disappeared. The weather was nice as he started chasing after it. Then from far offshore came a cloud all bunched up. The whale he was after stopped coming up. It had been coming up and going down in a hurry. Then the dark rain came, passing right above. Uh, it got light! The whale came up and stayed on the surface. They must have known of it. He got scared. They must have seen the cloud long before. Then it thundered. He stopped and got alongside the other canoe with his younger brothers. The whale was headdown in the water but did not go under. It started to hail - big hailstones, hurting. He took the bow duckboard and laid it over his head. The whole crew covered themselves, all who were in the canoe.

It took his whale with its claws. He was the one who saw what it was like; he saw clearly that it was a man there with a mask on his head. It really picked up his whale with no trouble, lifting it by the head, then dropped it on the water. Then he could not see it because it was hailing again. It was doing the same as before, grabbing the whale with its claws, lifting it up by just the head, and letting it go again. It lifted it once more; for the fourth time the whale was seized by the talons and released. Then it went off to its land and was not seen any more.[2] They killed the whale there at the same place on the water. Tlatla:qokw'ap spoke:

"You guys be sure and say that you saw and remembered what the bird looked like. I will keep it," said he.

They tied the whale to the stern and started towing to Ts'isha:. Then he saw what the dorsal fins looked like: one was small and one was big. He'd never seen such before. He stayed home, not going home. His mind told him that he would make a valuable property of what he saw and that he would keep it.

Then he went out again. This time his younger brother speared, and they started capturing a whale once more. It wasn't a long struggle before it died, and they started towing. Now they saw what this one was like: it had a one-sided tail. It must have been what is referred to as "One-Behind." They towed it towards shore. As they were doing so the man fell asleep and while sleeping he heard this song about what they had got. It was singing a song he found out in his dream.

Then he went out again. He was out but didn't see anything; they were out all day and saw no whales. He went home, just came back ashore. When they came close to shore they saw a whale and speared it right away. It must have been what is called "Broken-Tail": its tail looked broken. They got ashore, went home and stayed there.

They cooked the dorsal fins from the three whales and gave feast inviting all the people including the children. Then he revealed what he had seen. He had it on a wide board: he had a Thunderbird on it because it had tried to take away his whale in its talons. He told his fellow villagers of what had happened to him. He made a family property of it to have to pass on to the future generations; that's where I got what I had at the time I[3] started to go after sea otters. They went out whaling again, reaching the place way offshore. They started capturing and got two, one apiece.

"Let's just look after this many," they said.

They towed the two in to shore. They stayed home for three days before going out again. They speared again. This time it was Nanatla:ʔop who speared, the youngest brother. They wanted him to capture this one; the older brothers just wanted to help. They could not kill it. After two days and two nights they got tired of trying and quit for a while. They rested a while before starting to try to kill it again. Evening came, and they had not killed it! The one who was trying to capture went to sleep. Then it spoke to him:

"I will not die. Stop tring to kill me," it said to him in his dream. "Sing to me. Only then will I come ashore."

"Wake up you guys," he said to his older brothers.

He got ready, putting on his regalia. He started singing and the whale went down. The whale started running; it swam! They gave up trying to kill it. It was swimming, diving as it went along. They simply hung on. It took them all the way to Ts'otsit, arriving just after noon. Then it died while still running just as it reached Ts'otsit. As soon as they reached Ts'isha: they began butchering. It must have been what is called "Liver-Inside."[4] In it were two liver-like organs and that must have been the reason it could not be killed. It had fat inside. It had a small dorsal fin.

He went out again and saw an island of shallow dry rock[5] not very far offshore. When he got close it was a supernatural thing. He stopped on the water and saw a big halibut there. They must have sen what they call Ch'oya:.[6]

"What should we do?" he asked his younger brothers.

"Let's spear it!" said the second oldest who wanted to.

"Let's not," said the oldest brother. "We can't. We might lose our equipment."

"Let's do it anyhow. Let's kill it!"

"All right!"

Then it came up shallow like a reef, not going deep. He speared, and the halibut went down and ran. He suddenly realized that all the floats had gone out of his canoe, the halibut ran so fast.[7] They were gone for quite a while, then floated up all together.[8] It must have come off. The halibut was soft and must have come off. The harpoon pulled out. They lost it entirely, not knowing where it had gone. Then they started looking for Humpback whales again. The older brother speared, and it died. They didn't fight it long; it died at once.

"Let's look after many," they said.

The middle brother speared, and his also was killed. They went closer and did the same again, tied the whales together. The other one speared, and the eldest brother killed it for him. Then the youngest brother speared. There were four of them, towing in four. They put in two nights and came ashore. For a time they stayed home, rested a while.

Then they went out again. They stayed out on the sea two days and went home without anything, the ones who never failed. He was sad because he wasn't used to failure. In the evning they went for a walk, going to the seaward side of Ts'isha:. He took his clothes off and started to bathe that night which was moonless and dark. He swam towards Ts'otsit. It's far offshore, Ts'otsit.[10] Then he saw something big that looked like a round trap. He dove down, going after whatever the thing was that looked like a round trap. When he grabbed hold it stuck right through his fingers.[11] It must have been that special sea egg spoken of.[12] He held on to it as he swam on to Ts'otsit where he stepped ashore at daylight. He set off to the top and made medicine of what he found. He discovered that inside it was nothing but fat. He left it hidden at the very top and stayed at the bottom until evening. As soon as it grew dark the younger brother set out looking for his elder. The younger brother didn't know whether he had gone that way and sat down on the rocks to look out on the sea. He clearly saw a man there who then appeared up out of the rocks. It had to be his older brother! He ran to meet him.

"Is that you?" he cried.

His teeth were rattling he was so cold, for he had been swimming a long time coming in from Ts'otsit. The older brother was helped up the rocks.

"I found something supernatural," he started telling the younger brother. "You go home now. I won't be going home for four days."

So the younger brother came out of the woods and went home. Four days went by. Four days he did not sleep, four days he did not eat. Then he came out of the woods. He didn't eat, he set the proper time of ten days before he ate. He stayed home ritually occupied.[13]

Four days went by, and he went out whaling. Just as he came to the seaward side of Ts'isha: he saw a whale and speared it, not taking long to land it. Then he went out to sea. The youngest brother had a canoe and he towed it in towards Ts'isha:. Then he came back out, making up his mind that he would look for his older brothers. He looked for them, met them out there, and found that they were already towing on their way to shore. Coming ashore at Ts'isha:, they went home. They caught three whales on the one trip. This was because of the fact that he got, as medicine power, the Tl'imy'aqtl[14] sea egg. He began to always be thus: getting two at a single outing. He started going after the fat ones. He was foremost among the three canoes because he now had good medicine. That is what used to happen whenever they found a supernatural thing; they alone got like that. But those didn't find it whose minds were not strong. Just the ones with strong minds got that sort of medicine power and the weak-minded didn't.

123. How the Nitinats Got the Thunderbird and Lightning Snake
(Captain Bill)

There was a flood, it is said, when the salt water came up above the normal sea level. The tide kept rising until all the land was gone. The whole land was flooded. There was only one spot that was not underwater, the mountain called Ka:ka:piya:[2] where Xitlxitl'iˀi landed on the rocks. He had a daughter called Chi:ˀilim.[3] For a long time the water was high. The land was flooded for four days, and they were in a canoe, a big canoe. They stayed for quite a while at Ka:ka:piya:. While they were up there the girl called Chi:ˀilim got pregnant, and she did not have a husband there on the mountain. She was the only one who knew who the father was, the father of her child. She realized that the father of her baby was the supernatural being called Yaˀi:. She had a baby boy. Her baby got big. They were not in a hurry to go home. The child was a boy and was now christened with the name Ha:wilxim. The one who gave it the name was the father, the Yaˀi:. Now the boy had gotten big, growing very fast because he was supernatural. They went home to their house,[4] descending from the mountain called Ka:ka:piya:.

Ha:wilxim became a young man and began going after Gray whales, started whaling, getting the whales to come right onto the beach.[5] The Grays would stop at the beach where he was after them. He caught as many as five in a single day. He kept hunting in this way for a long time. The place was near his house from which he would watch the whales as they stopped there. Then he would go out. A child was born to Xitlxitl'iˀi [Ha:wilxim].[6] His baby was a girl, and he named her Chi:ˀilim also. Another child was born to him, a boy this time. He now had two children, a boy and a girl.

The boy grew up. Tla:tla:qoksapshi:l[7] was his name. The father now told him that he had a mountain from the time of the flood, that he now owned the mountain Ka:ka:piya:. The youth received knowledge of it from what was said to him by his father. He did not tell his father that he was going to go up the mountain, that Tla:tla:qoksapshi:l. Then he started walking, Tla:tla:qoksapshi:l did, going towards the peak one whole day and arriving there in the evening. He now stayed there for four days on top of the mountain. Then at night it started raining. The youth went to sleep. At daybreak he saw there on the rocks an immense bird which had to be the Thunderbird. It must have landed during the night having flown to the rocks. Meanwhile the rain was still coming down. He went near to make sure of how it looked, what its head looked like. He just left it thus undisturbed on the rocks for fear that if it flew he would die, it was so big! The youth now headed home, coming out of the woods. He went to his house.

The sister of Tla:tla:qoksapshi:l started menstruating. She

moved to the far end of the house behind a screen.[8] He put a design on the puberty right screen of the kind of bird he had seen, the Thunderbird. For eight days she remained there all alone.[9] At this time the girl saw that there was what is called a H̲iˀitl'ik, the Lightning Snake, giving birth to young. The one at puberty had a supernatural experience seeing the H̲iˀitl'ik there on the floor, a young lady giving birth.

The father, Xitlxitl'iˀi, made medicine of it. He received a name from it, Wa:lti:lamaˀoq, and started making the H̲iˀitl'ik, the image of it, on the board. Also he made a representation of how its head is. He made a headmask just like my headmask, this copy of it.[10] Xitlxitl'iˀi designed it. It was Tla:tla:qoksapshi:l, the son, who started making this with his father on the middle of its chest: he designed a Thunderbird. He also started making a house. On the side of the house he made a design of what she saw. The girl menstruating at puberty saw it there, and they made a family privilege of it. Xitlxitl'iˀi started the Wolf Ritual dance in honour of Tla:tla:qoksapshi:l, had him do the H̲iˀitl'ik dance, and told about what the girl saw. It was the father who was telling this. She now received a name and was called Wa:lti:lamaˀoq.[11]

124. A H̲iko:l?ath̲ Sees Thunderbird and the Aurora Women
(William)

He thought it over and said to her that he should go for a walk for a while.

"Say," he said to his wife, "Make me some lunch, I'm going for a walk. I'll set out in the morning before the people wake up."

His wife bundled up his lunch putting four strips of dried blubber inside. He set out walking. He started to bathe, bathing all day, rubbing himself ritually. Just four bites of food would he take so he wouldn't run out of lunch because he knew he would be gone a long time and that he would be walking all over the place bathing at night. He scrubbed himself ritually, then at daybreak made his fire and ate again. For four days he would bathe. Bathing and rubbing during the day, he would go right past the evening and start making his fire when dawn came. He would want to warm up by the fire and start eating. He wanted to put in four days and nights bathing; he wanted to stop smelling bad.[2] On the fourth day he stopped bathing ritually. He went to sleep. He was very sleepy because he never slept for four days.

Something grabbed him from the back, right here at the shoulder joint on the right side.

"Wake up! Hurry! Why do you sleep? Don't you want to see me?" it said to him.

He opened his eyes, woke up in a hurry! Whoever it was was nowhere there. He sat up. His mind started working. He became aware that he had seen something while half asleep and half awake.[3] He started bathing again. Then he stopped bathing, stopping just about midday. He set out walking again. Now he heard something squealing but didn't know where it was coming from. Looking for it he stopped and sat down on a rock. He wanted to see it but could not find it. He stood up and started looking again. He didn't see anything. He looked up and spotted it way off yonder - there in the sky he saw something twirling and twisting coming down. It came closer to where he was standing on the rocks, watching as it approached, and when it landed the man went over. There it was not far off, a large feather. He took it. The man passed out from grabbing the feather. It spoke:

"You will see something," said the feather to him.

He was dreaming. It said to him that he would see something. He woke up, came back to life. All right he still had ahold of the feather; he did not let it go, did not hide it. After one day there was thunder. The feather that he found must have belonged to a Thunderbird. He sat down and listened to the thundering sound coming from afar, gradually coming nearer. It came into view. It started to hail hard, hailing on the tree tops. The man was afraid to look. Then he saw there on the rocks a fire. And also on the rocks was what had to be a Lightning Snake which must have been the coiled thing that dropped away from the Thunderbird. the hail got really strong now. Then the man saw there, flown onto the rocks, a bird. The man keeled over, his limbs all going dead. He was conscious but could not get near it. He could only use his eyes to watch. He saw clearly what the bird looked like, how it was dressed. He saw how the Lightning Snake looked. He really observed it well, what its appearance was. Then he could not se the bird anymore as it had lifted off. The man revived, his limbs coming back to life. For four days he stayed there on the rocks where he saw the supernatural thing.

He set out walking the wrong way, not going home for a while. He was afraid because he had seen the supernatural thing. Then he saw people, ten of them. The man stopped where he saw something, saw some people. That evening he was still there. Then he saw when evening came that there was a fire. There were ten beings there. The fire flared up really high! It was as if it had become daylight the way the fire flared up. It must have been what is called the N'a:n'a:st'o:.[4] The man remained on the rocks as he watched this unusual thing which made it seem like daylight. Then he saw that there were women there. The ten he saw must have been women, those people he saw. There they were, pouring something on the fire. These must have been the Ts'i:tlts'i:yaˀotltaqiml.[5] The weather got nice. He finished getting an year's worth of experience.[6] Now he was powered by two supernatural things. He started walking towards his home. When he arrived, he went in.

"Come here," he said to his younger brother.

he started discussing things, telling his younger brother of what he saw, that he had seen a great big bird. He told him he knew what it was and that he also saw what's called N'a:n'a:st'o:, that he saw those two things.

"We will make this our family topa:ti right," he said.

He said so because the bird had said to him that he gave him lots of names. He knew how many names he had received from it. And it was what he started painting on a board, a wide board. He had two figures on it. He put on the bird just as he had seen it. Then he put on the Lightning Snake, also exactly as he had seen, and a feather of the kind he saw. He painted the feather just as it had been, red on top with black at its main stem. That's how the painting was. He placed it there at the head of the house, set up on edge on the floor. It now became his topa:ti right. It got to be his story, his legend. Now he had it put away for future use. He kept it for the time his girl reached the age of puberty when he would give a puberty rite ceremonial.

At that time he told his fellow villagers how it happened that he got a Thunderbird. He finished telling them, he finished telling them about that. It was now evening. Then he began showing what he saw, that he had seen another thing, the N'a:n'a:st'o: or Northern Lights. He started showing those that evening. All this he was doing at his house. His fellow villagers were watching, amazed. No one knew what he was doing because they had never seen anything like that before. He was doing this for the full traditional period of four days because he had been told in his supernatural experience that it was a full four day ceremony when showing it. When he finished he started telling of how he got these things. He told everything. Then he named his girl Ts'i:tlts'i:yaʔotl or Ts'e:tlʔis for short, N'a:n'a:swiʔis,[7] N'a:n'a:sat'aqs[8] and N'a:n'a:y'alok.[9] He got the names from the bears.[10] His name now was Hihi:qtoʔa,[11] his name became Yaya:tspiy'a,[12] his name became Hihiwitoʔa,[13] his name became Hihiwahsoʔa,[14] His name became Mi:xtachi:k.[15] Thus many names he got. That's how I got to come into possession of the Thunderbird right.

125. A M'o:ho:lʔath Youth Visits the Thunderbird (Tyee Bob)

An individual was very unmanly, unable to do anything; he had not been properly taught. The youth began thinking that he should begin looking for a place where he could bathe ritually. He set out on foot from his home to the falls of Tl'a:sʔaʔa:l.[2] It was summer. He began bathing, rubbing himself. He had ten different things for rubbing; he rubbed himself. The first time he stayed away for four days, rubbing himself ritually. It was his sole occupation to rub ritually from morning till evening, all day from end to end. He went to sleep. Then daylight came and again he was rubbing from morning till night, scrubbing himself. After three days of rubbing his skin became raw. Then he was using the finer, softer needles for one more day. On the fourth day he went home, and the next four days he remained at home allowing his skin to heal. Then he set out walking again, and continued bathing and rubbing with his leaf rubbers in the same order of use as before. In the evening he again went to sleep. He would stay in the woods and sleep there. For two days he rubbed himself again morning till night, from dawn to dusk. He would rub himself in the morning, than again at evening. For four more days he rubbed himself.[3] Then he went home and stayed in again for four days. Again he set out to bathe and rub. Four times he went on a four day bathing and rubbing trip. Then he went to sleep and dreamed:

"Let's go," an old man was saying to him. "Go to where the Thunderbird lives."

He woke up and stored away in his mind what he was dreaming of. He went and told[4] his mother, saying that he would go walking in the woods.

"Don't think that I died. I'll be gone ten days," he said to his mother. "If I don't come back in fourteen days, then consider me dead and say, 'I guess he died'."

The youth set out for the place he dreamt he was supposed to go to, and began to rub[5] himself again on the way to the Thunderbird's house. He was climbing a mountain for four days, the mountain called To:ta:.[6] He would bathe ritually whenever he came to a creek, then he would walk on again. His skin became hard and tough after he was walking for four days. Then he arrived where there was no trail. It was sheer cliff way up all around: he could not climb any more. He turned home and came down, taking a day to descend. He now stayed home, having been gone for eight days. Then he told his mother,

"I went," he said, "To the house of the Thunderbird."

He knew now that the Thunderbird's house was at a mountain

called To:ta:. His mother started counselling him.

"Bathe ritually for a long time. Don't have intercourse with anyone," the mother said to her son.

She counselled him for a long time, the mother did. She did not tell her husband what their son was about because he never really did counsel his son. Then she finished talking to the youth, and he went into the woods again. Before he left he told his mother that he would be gone ten days. He began bathing ritually again. This time he really tried in earnest,[7] now adding four more bundles of tree needles. He went to sleep. Day came. He bathed ritually that morning. This time he had ten bundles of needles and four extra. Another night came. He bathed ritually for a long time and prayed that he might have a way, a trail to where he wanted to go. He was saying just that, only that when he bathed, asking for a trail. In the morning, in the evening, all the time he was saying only that, asking that a trail be given him. After ten days he went home. He had now reached ten days just as his mother told him to do when she taught him. He arrived that night and let his mother know that he had come home. His competitor found out, the one who was a Getter of hair seals. He stayed home again for four days; none of the other people ever saw him. His mother was teaching him all the time now. Then he went into the woods to start to bathe ritually once more.

There is a little creek in the woods straight back from Tl'a:sʔ̲aˀa:l called Maʔ̲itqnit.[8] The little creek got dried up all along it on account of his ritual bathing.[9] He bathed for two more days out there in the woods at Maʔ̲itqnit at evening, asking that he might have a good trail to go to where he was going. He was now praying to the "Chief" on high, that he would take pity on him and give him a trail. He started saying this all the time, that he be given a trail so that he would be able to walk up there at the steep cliff where he was unable to proceed any farther the last time.

Daylight came on the sixth day. This time he tried extra hard speaking, and the words now came easily.[10] It was as if someone told him, 'Say so.'[11] For two days he stayed at the cliff, then set out on foot. Again he began bathing and found a bird. He found the bird in the river where he bathed. He took the bird. It was dry.[12] Where it came from, the little bird, he didn't know. He took it. The little bird was pretty; it had a pretty head, the little bird. He bathed that evening, and when he finished he went home to his mother.

"I'm going to the place I went to, Mom."

Next day he arrived at the foot of the mountain. He had some shredded cedarbark, lots of cedarbark. He set out and went up, travelled four days and arrived at the cliff. This time there was a trail there, a good trail; he found a good trail. The cliff disappeared. Now he had gotten past the ugly place on his way. He saw a house and went in; he went inside the Thunderbird's house.

"Sit down over there," he was told.

There were lots of Hiʔitl'ik Lightning Snakes. They were afraid of the shredded cedarbark. The chamberpot called out:

"He's come into your house...!"

The chamberpot was the one who called out. Then the chamberpot called out again:

"He's come into your house... a human being!"

Again the chamberpot called out:

"He's come into your house...!"

Four times it called out.

"Ho::::"

Thunder sounded from afar.

It thundered again: this time he heard it distinctly. Again it sounded, really clearly now as it was nearer. It thundered once more from afar. The chamberpot now spoke:

"Go hide over there."

The man went and hid. Then he gave his cedarbark headdress to the chamberpot.

"Ho::::"

It thundered again outside. A man came inside.

"I lost my head. There's a human there on the floor," said the chamberpot.

The man took off his clothing and put it there near the door close to the Hiʔitl'ik, that's where he put his blanket. The man sat down. His legs were very thick. He was a huge man.

"Come on out," the man who was hiding was told.

He came out and sat down on the floor. There was afire in the fireplace.

"You will eat."

The huge man went out. He was not gone long, then came in with blubber, the man did, with a big piece of blubber. He took his box, a big one. Two rocks were at the fire, rocks which were hot all the time. Now he put water in the box and put in a rock with tongs.[13] As the broth pot began bubbling, the blubber was put in. With the big tongs he took out the rock. The other rock was tonged in, and the water began to boil. The broth pot was covered, the blubber inside. He waited until the rock cooled, took it out, took his other rock, put it in with the tongs, and it began boiling again. He had two rocks. He waited a while, and it got cooked.

"You've done well," said the Thunderbird as the man brought the cedarbark and gave it to him.

"I am always in a poor state. My father thinks I'm no good. I want to improve myself and that's why I came to you, O Chief! I am not a Getter of bears," he told the Thunderbird.

The Thunderbird man didn't say anything, didn't speak. He took his blubber, took it out of the pot.[14] His blubber was cooked now.[15] The man received and ate the blubber. The man was not afraid to eat. He ate a big chunk of blubber and finished eating. The Thunderbird man spoke:

"I am going to give you the old[16] <u>H</u>iʔitl'ik."

The man accepted the <u>H</u>iʔitl'ik the Thunderbird gave him. The Thunderbird also stated,

"I am always looking for the remains of cedarbark when people move. All right, you will go home now."

He went out of the house, and there outside was a Humpback whale!

"You will take this with you."

"All right!" said the man.

He took his knife, a black knife which might have been of stone. The man began cutting the Thunderbird's whale. His knife was sharp; he split the whale in two.[17] The Thunderbird cut a hole in it and lifted up a half of the blubber.

"It's light now," said the Thunderbird, taking it up with his little finger.

The man did not speak, afraid that it might be too heavy. Then the Thunderbird cut the piece of blubber in twain and again took up a part.

"It's light now, see?" he said to the man.

The man still did not take it, saying it was too heavy.

"Your piece might be too small. Very well, I'll take it in my teeth although your piece of blubber might be too small."

The Thunderbird man went into the house. He was gone inside a while getting ready, getting dressed in his flying outfit. He came out of the house as a bird.

"You will be here," the man was told, meaning under the armpit of the Thunderbird. "You keep your eyes closed. Don't open your eyes or we will die."

He took hold of the man and put him under his arm.

"All right! Close your eyes!"

The man closed his eyes. It was as if thunder was sounding from afar, not loud: the man could hardly hear it. It was not doing what the birds do to fly but only making a slight rocking motion through the air, flying seesawing. Now he stayed steady. He came down at Tl'a:s?a?a:l. The man got on the ground. He was told by the Thunderbird not to open his eyes for a long time.

"I might die," the Thunderbird said before he left to fly home.

It left the blubber at the place called Nanimxsh.18 The man did not go home to his mother. He stayed in the woods four days. Then he went home at night to his father and started telling him that he had gone to the Thunderbird.

"He has blubber for me on the ground at Nanimxsh."

"We are still eating," said the father. "You have something supernatural."

Early next morning they set out on foot to where the blubber was. The father inspected the blubber: he didn't know what it was, had never seen anything like it before. The father made medicine of it, gathering the baleen and making spirit medicine. Then they went home. He told his wife, but she already knew since she was the one who made her son do that to make a man of him. Then the news went out that the unmanly youth was alive, for they thought he had died after not seeing him for a long time.

Three old persons wanted him to give a feast of bear meat to them.[19] He went bear hunting to a lake.[20] He came in, came home with two bears in his canoe. They cut up and started cooking the bears. He gave a feast, and the people came as guests, all of them. They started eating the bear meat. They finished eating and went home, the people.

The hair seal hunter began competing with him. He did not go to the feast but went instead down the beach to the saltwater. The man came home with three hair seals. He gave a feast also, and all the people came again as guests. The many people ate the three seals. The whole bunch went home. The one who went to the Thunderbird did not do anything for a long time. Then he went bear hunting and got two bears. He got ten bears in two days, butchered them and dried the ten bearskins. He invited all the men, women and children to a feast. At the time he was inviting[21] the bear hunter went home with two more bears and was cooking them a way over there on the ground outside. The great quantity of cooked bear meat was brought into the house. The guests were served and the many people ate. The father told them that there were ten bears altogether. And then, it is said, he fed his father a lot of bear meat and also much fat, bear fat. He was taking revenge because he was not good to him. The father ate that night.

"You will eat all," said the young man to his father." "I might not get anymore if you do not eat all of it."

He got full just as the dish which had been full got empty.[22] He just fell over and died.[23] It was not known that he had died from overeating. He wrapped up his late father with two bearskins. He buried him at a place below the falls. Then they found out that the father died of the one who went to see the Thunderbird. The one whose father died did not do anything now. But the Ts'o:maʔasʔath seal hunter went hunting and came in with four seals. He gave a feast of the four seals when he came in.

The one whose father died did not do anything for a long time. Then he went to Nanimxsh where the whale was. He put leaves over it and went home. It was rotten now, having been left there for a long time. It was my late father who knew of those which must have been the vertebrae at Nanimxsh. And then he distributed sixteen bearskins. Inside he had six vertebrae to show the people when he gave out things. He went about the village inviting. He was prepared to do the dance of the Thunderbird which he saw, one year later. Then he distributed his things. All were his guests there at Tl'a:sʔaʔa:l. He sat there on the rocks at Tl'a:sʔaʔa:l. He had a likeness of the Thunderbird in cedarbark made into a headmask. He copied the appearance of the head of that which he saw, the Thunderbird. Nobody knew what his "thing" was. He finished, then went inside into the house. He distributed bearskins to the Ts'o:maʔasʔath and the Ho:pach'asʔath. The one who did this was the youth who went to the Thunderbird. His sister received a name, and the name was

To:ti:s?a?ato?aqs.[24] There were many names coming out of this affair. The youth's name became Sintsit. The name Wi:wimta?i:k[25] came about, a name he made for himself. He finished again, having distributed more goods. Then the seal hunter came in with ten seals and also gave a feast. He gave a lot of uncooked Cha:?o food.[26] At that time when my father used to go, there must have been lots of rubbing leaves. He became a Getter-of-Many from the rubbing leaves from one who went to get the Thunderbird. That's from where I know how to hunt bears without too much effort. It is on account of the four kinds of ritual rubbing leaves which were obtained at the time he went to the Thunderbird.

NOTES TO NARRATIVES, TALES OF EXTRAORDINARY EXPERIENCE

113. Shamans and Ghosts

1 Told by Dick La:maho:s to Alex Thomas, ms. 50dd:76-122. Previously no. 114 together with next account.
2 "Seeing into the future".
3 She was dancing.
4 I.e., mean.
5 I.e., parent.
6 *Tl'a:ʔasʔath* could be freely translated as "Coastline people", meaning those living far off on the outer coast, and was used to refer to the so-called "Makah" (from Klallam for alien) of Cape Flattery, actually the *Qw'idishchiʔath* or "Cape people" as mentioned elsewhere. Like other tribal names, Tl'a:ʔasʔath is here used to refer to the locality of Neah Bay, *Di:ya:*, their principal village on the Juan de Fuca Strait side of the cape.
7 Principal people of the east side of Barkley Sound who were joined by three war-reduced tribes: the *Ki:xʔinʔath* and *Ch'imataqsoʔath* around Cape Beale, and the *ʔAnaqtl'aʔath* of so-called Pachena Bay (misidentification of *ʔAnaqtl'a*).
8 Ozette.
9 Population shrank from disease and emigration to Neah Bay.
10 Quilleute, a Salishan people south of Ozette who adopted many Nootkan features like whaling and the Wolf Ritual.
11 *ʔOse:ʔlaʔtx* in Nitinat and Makah.
12 Ms. "n".
13 With a rope.
14 The Wolves took the children away as novices to be initiated into their secret society.
15 Clownish supernatural figures in the Tlo:kwa:na.
16 A hatchet.
17 Nomaqimyis, Nomaqami:s, "Taboo-Beach"; Sarita Bay (St. Claire 1991:91, 86 Map 8 #25).
18 .30/30 Winchester lever action Model 96. (John Thomas)

114. Lahal at Nitinat

1 As for no. 113.
2 A ceremonial paddler when going by canoe.
3 Raccoon.
4 *Tlo:ʔo:ws*, "Camping Place", in Nitinat (Arima et al. 1991:262, 271 Map j.). Commonly "Clo-oose".
5 *P'a:chi:daʔ* in Nitinat, "Sea Foam" (Op. cit.:266, 267 Map i). Commonly "Pacheena". Port Renfrew, also Port San Juan from Spanish Puerto de Juan.
6 Jimmy Thompson.
7 *Di:ti:dʔa:ʔtx* in Nitinat.

8 *Wa:ya:ʔaq* in Nitinat (Op. cit.:263, 271 Map j). Refering to a high site, often fortified, this place name recurs several times along the West Coast. Variously spelled in English, e.g., "Whyack".
9 Joe Shaw.
10 Territorial dispute is longstanding between the two sides, yet war is not specifically recalled today, there being just a tradition of a jump-off across a ravine by two champions (Op. cit.:232).
11 Tribal name as place name.
12 People of Wa:ya:ʔaq.
13 *Tlo:ʔo:wsa:ʔtx̱*. Separate village into 1960's.
14 *P'a:chi:da:ʔtx̱*. Once numerous ally of the Di:ti:dʔa:ʔatx̱.
15 Bamfield.

115. How a Man Mishandled Power Given By the Beavers

1 Dictated by Tom Sa:ya:ch'apis to Edward Sapir 16 Nov 1913, bk. XIV:34-41; a H̱o:choqtlisʔath̲ family history.
2 Sockeye when it comes in is *hisit*; when old, *meʔ̲a:t*.
3 "Body-Of-Water-Under-The-Ground".
4 "You walking around on the beach with branches on your backs".
5 A Yatyak song. Tom forgot three others belonging to this one.
6 *yatshitl*, "to make a feint at, pretend to do and leave off". Seems to refer to the character of the Yatyak songs which are rather short, ending when one expects more to come. Always begin with rapid beating.
7 It was growing out of his body or, rather, sticking out.
8 He should have stayed out in the woods for four days and thus retained his power. Hence his wife's remark: he should have known there was no village there and that they were not human.
9 I.e., he should not have looked at it in his house.
10 See note 5.

116. Sa:ya:ch'apis Meets a Storm

1 Told by Sa:ya:ch'apis to Alex Thomas, received 28 April 1916 at the Division of Anthropology, Geological Survey, ms. 50v:154-67, titled "Tom encounters a big storm on a sealing schooner and uses nawêʔik's spell to calm the waves".
2 Douglas, son of narrator and Alex's father.
3 A trader.
4 Identifiable perhaps.
5 ʔI:h̲wanim, "Big-In-Middle", the mountain right across from Port Alberni (St. Claire 1991:197, 192 Map 19 #96).
6 A trader.
7 An old T'okw'a:ʔath̲.

8 Dick.
9 Alberni Canal or Inlet (Cf. account 87 n. 18).
10 Ho:m'o:w'a (Op. cit.:148, 129 Map 12 #97). The English name Village Island fits the Captain's dialogue, but Ho:m'o:w'a is also known as Effingham Island today just as Ts'isha: which has been Hawkin's Island for years is also Benson's Island for some government official on recent maps at least.
11 William.
12 Ch'itokwa:chisht, "Where-One-Catches-Fur-Seal", an outermost islet about 3 mis. southeast of Ts'isha: off Ya:ˀaqtl'a or Howell Island (Op. cit.:146, 129 Map 12 #88). In English, Cree Island.
13 ʔAtoˀyaqtlis, "Deer-In-Cove", back of Hi:kwis. (Not in St. Claire but he notes Hi:kwis and for Lyall Point to its west gives ˀA:toshap, "Standing-Deer-Point", and the latter's north side does reach a mile and a half into a cove behind the old Ts'isha:ˀath winter village site. Op. cit.:134-6, 129 Map 12 #25, #31)
14 Tl'atl'inqowis, Effingham Bay on north side of Ho:m'o:w'a where canoes landed when too rough at main village location (Op. cit.:147, 129 Map 12 #93).
15 Sa:ya:ch'apis's imitation is partial of the Nitinat, "Wa:lak'aˀb ya:ˀa:xsaˀ Ch'i:daxt'a."
16 In Nitinat, "To:shiyo: kwa:chitl'its be:ˀitl'tid."
17 The West Coast Agency Agent's Report for 1886 says that 20 Qiltsmaʔath died, leaving behind 18 widows and 41 children (Canada Dept. Indian Affairs 1887,1:108). The disaster so reduced the already small tribe of Vargas Island that the remnant was absorbed into the ʔAho:s'ath.
18 Sounds like Dick La:maho:s.

117. Kanop the Shaman

1 Told by Sa:ya:ch'apis to Alex, received 28 April 1916, ms. 50v:91-103, "Story of kanup who became a shaman he was a Laˀôkwiˀath."
2 Hopitsˀath, major Tlaˀo:kwiˀath village; commonly written "Opitsat". Also referred to as Tlaˀo:kwiˀath, written "Clayoquot" and pronounced "Kla:kwot".
3 "Middle-Of-The-Village-People".
4 Ma:lts'a:s, "House-Against-Hill", a village at the left side of Tlaˀo:kwiˀath with a house built right against a hill.
5 War canoes could be up to 50-60 ft. long, though around 45 ft. seems more usual. Before guns they had a high wide bow as a shield when landing but its form is not known with certainty.
6 In the grandparental generation all consanguines are *ts'ani:qs*, "grandparent".

118. Ch'it'oqwin'ak Becomes a Shaman

1 Told by Sa:ya:ch'apis to Alex, received 28 April 1916, ms. 50v:240-51, "tc!it!uqi'nak imitating tc!it!ôł". John Thomas translates the name as "War-club Dancer"; Morris Swadesh in his texts list as "Sword Dancer".
2 To go around at night killing cormorants by wringing their necks.
3 Last quarter of the moon in March.
4 *n'an'ach'in* is when a shaman while doctoring is going "Hia hia hia." Or when one is dancing Ts'a:yiq they utter this: "Hai hai hai hai."
5 "Rock-At-Point-Of-Beach". (Different from T'iqo:ˀis on Somass River listed in St. Claire 1991:186).
6 Hinap'i:ˀis, "Beaches-On-Both-Sides", winter village place; Spring Cove with the Ucluelet lifesaving station (Op. cit.:172, 168 Map 14 #24).

119. The Youth Who Followed a Shag

1 Dictated by Sa:ya:ch'apis to Sapir 15-16 Nov 1913, bk. XIV:28-34; a H̲o:choqtlisˀath̲ account.
2 So:h̲a come from the underground world of ghosts where they run in little creeks. Once when a T'okw'a:ˀath̲ Chief was about to die, he said that he would test the belief by sending up So:h̲a the next run; he told them to watch next season if there was an unusually heavy run. This happened when Aleck was young. The *good* place in the underground world is where they eat So:h̲a. In the *bad* place they eat lice.
3 In stories they often say about a "good country" that eagles weigh down its branches. (Alex Thomas)
4 Henderson Lake. (Cf. St. Claire 1991:117-18, 116 Map 10 #12-18. No lake name given but specifiable as such, *ʔ̲awʔokok*, of Henderson River.)
5 Because there was so much in the canoe that otherwise it would have fallen out.
6 Prose form: "ˀOˀoqh̲tamah̲ chachashx̲h̲ta h̲a:yoq motsmoh̲aq yayaqh̲toyi:s chachashx̲h̲ta." "I have on my feet walking quickly two hundred bearskins (is) what I have on my feet walking quickly."
The "walking quickly" phrase means "what I have on my feet that makes me go fast is ..." For the number of bearskins *h̲ayo:q* is translated as "ten" by John Thomas; however, the figure given in the original is retained.

120. A Runaway Slave Comes to the Chief of Wanin

1 Dictated by Sa:ya:ch'apis to Sapir 16-17 Nov 1913, bk.

XIV:41-49; a Ho:choqtlisˀath and Waninˀath account.
2 A Shi:tlats is about forty feet long, six fathoms bottom.
3 I.e., they only occupied, slept in, the front and rear sections, not the sides, one family divided between front and back.
4 Drift gill nets, *mityo:*, caught all kinds of salmon. Dip nets, *ts'ima*, were used only for herrings when they spawn. Herring rakes, *chochy'ak*, were used only in deep sea fishing.
5 "Sitting-In-The-Middle-Of-A-Rock". (John Thomas: "Sitting-Midstream-On-The-Rocks".)
6 "Young Herrings".
7 Better: *haˀokwitqa* (Alex).
8 N'ima, "Nipple".
9 He was afraid someone might kill him as a runaway slave and take away his *p'atqok* or goods.
10 Tl'asimyis, small stream at east end of Tseshaht I.R. no. 8 where stood the Tl'asimyisˀath house until they moved to Hi:kwis since at low tide canoes had to be dragged over too much beach (Op. cit.:134, 129 Map 12 #24).
11 He was Waninˀath, but originally was Ma:ktlʔi:ˀath becoming the Waninˀath Chief in the course of these happenings.
12 "White-In-The-Belly".
13 Pursing lips, Schnazlaut.
14 Better: *ch'apats* (Alex).
15 To avoid attracting attention by hastening with message.
16 See 10 above.
17 ʔAsiml, "Adzed-All-Around", islet by northeast Hand Is. (Op. cit.:136, 129 Map 12 #32 ʔA:simil).
18 At this time Ho:hinkwop was still Ma:ktlʔi:ˀath, not Waninˀath. The song verse is given in prose form.

121. Wealth From a Shag

1 Told by Sa:ya:ch'apis to Alex, received 28 April 1916, ms. 50v:211-40, "The ˀots'ôsˀatH young man who became rich by a shag."
2 The ʔOts'o:sˀath or "Otsosat" of Flores Is. and the inlets behind were destroyed by the ʔA:ho:sˀath in the early 19th century.
3 "Getter-Of-Small-Mussels".
4 "Outside coast people", meaning Qw'idishchˀaˀtx or "Makah".
5 Dentalium was a money-like form of wealth traditionally, given lengths of the slender shells strung together, e.g., cubit, having certain values.
6 *chiti:dkw* in their speech.
7 *Di:ya:* in Makah; "Neah Bay".
8 Quilleute, Chimakuan speakers past Ozette at LaPush.
9 Quinault, Salishans to south again toward Grays Harbor.
10 Boys of Watty Watt aged six and seven.
11 *Di:ti:dˀa:ˀtx* in Nitinat but Nootkan of narrator retained.
12 Manhousat on Sidney Inlet.

13 Of Hesquiat Harbour.
14 To remove drag producing slivers. Then the hull is rubbed smooth with old matting. The burning also helps preserve the cedar.
15 The wrapping at the scarf of a harpoon shaft is usually several feet from the tip.
16 For a total of ten making him a Getter-Of-Ten in a season.

122. Tlatla:qokw'ap Sees the Thunderbird and Gets Power From a Sea Egg

1 Dictated by William to Sapir 6 Jan 1914, bk. XXI:1-13; a Ts'isha:ʔath̲ story.
2 Old fashioned; does not mean "he didn't see the land."
3 I.e., my ancestors. In family legends one often speaks of one's ancestors as oneself.
4 Refers to two long liver-like masses of fat all along inside of the body, like in a dogfish, not real liver. Oil is made from these organs which few whales have. The native people knew of Tochichw'in, "Teeth-In-Middle", i.e., Sperm whale, but didn't try to get them. They were too big and dangerous to attack; moreover, their meat is too fat for food. They are supposed to come from lakes into the sea by underground passages, a sea-land connection more often cited with seals.
5 Wih̲ʔa:ʔa is a rocky island of which the bottom can be seen in the water. No real rock is referred to in the account.
6 "Passing-By-On-Its-Way-To-Someplace". This Ch'oya: always follows Gray whales on its way north. Said to be a halibut of great size, it has bones as big as those of a whale. It can only be caught with the whaling spear and is good eating. Not often seen, it gives no power and is merely a strange thing like the four preceding types of whales.
7 I.e., before they had time to notice it, all the floats had been quickly dragged out of their canoe.
8 The floats stayed under for only a short time.
9 *wikʔaktli*, "come with nothing behind; also "having no buttocks".
10 Ts'otsi:t, English Sail Rock, is a good quarter mile from Qapch'aqtl'aʔa or "Blowing-Sound-Beach" on the southwest side where the trail from the village emerged (St. Claire 1991:142, 129 Map 12 #66, #65). The cold water and currents should be taken into account. Ts'otsi:t marks the southwest corner of the Ts'isha:ʔath̲ islands in Barkley Sound and thus is most out to sea.
11 Refers to the sharp spines of the sea urchin.
12 Not the ordinary kind but supernatural.
13 *ts'e:ʔiyil*, "to stay in house and observe *noma:k*" [taboo]. They do so for four days after coming from the woods after finding *ch'ih̲a:* [spirit].
14 *Tl'imyaqtl*, "Fat-Inside", is used for any "power" that one finds that is fat inside. Then the hunter has good luck in

getting fat game. West Coasters are avid for fat to go with the high protein diet since short on vegetable carbohydrates.

123. How Nitinats Got Thunderbird and Lightning Snake.

1 Dictated by Captain Bill to Sapir 30 Dec 1913, bk. XVIII:18-23.
2 Ka:ka:piya:, "Sticking-Up-Above-All-Else", mountain 10 miles up Nitinat Lake on east side; Mt. Rosander (Arima et al. 1991:274, 273 Map k).
3 "Pulling-In-The-House".
4 They stayed long with the father in the woods on the mountain before leaving for the mother's home.
5 This shows he was a supernatural hunter as one does not very often see a Gray whale coming on to a sandy beach.
6 He now had his grandfather's name.
7 Not the one of the Ts'isha:ʔath legend.
8 Even at the time this text was recorded the Ts'isha:ʔath did not let the newly menstruant girl out of the house for four days and let them eat only dried food.
9 I.e., she was the only one back of the board. After, the board is moved from the rear of the house to a corner.
10 Supposed to be used only by the girl.
11 "Always-Gliding-Out-Of-Corner-Of-House".

124. A Hiko:lʔath Sees the Thunderbird and the Aurora Women

1 Dictated by William to Sapir 6-7 Jan 1914; a Hiko:lʔath story refering to an ancestor who discovered the Alberni Canal.
2 I.e., wanted to take away human scent from himself.
3 *n'achink* is to see when sleep and being awake come together.
4 Northern Lights.
5 "Pouring-Women-Family", another name for Ya?i: Women.
6 After getting an experience in the woods when you receive power, you are sure to get another "blessing": thereafter, maybe a few days later or an year or several years later. As soon as you get the complementary experience, you are said to be *ho:henksap'at*. The first experience you get is equivalent to half an year, the second finishes your "year" of supernatural experience. If you get many powers, you are said to *ho:henksap'shi:lʔatok*.
7 "Saying-'Day'".
8 "Sliding-Down-From-Day".
9 "Looking-After-Day".
10 Ya?i: spirits.
11 "Gliding-Over-Rocky-Ridge-After-Rocky-Ridge".
12 "Stepping-From-Rock-To-Rock".
13 "Glided-Over-one's-Head-On-The-Rocks".
14 "Several-Gliding-Out-From-The-Rocks".
15 "Mi:xtach-On-His-Head".

125. A M'o:ho:lʔath̲ Youth Visits the Thunderbird

1 Dictated by Tyee Bob to Sapir 1-2 Jan 1914, bk. XIX:8-28; a M'o:ho:lʔath̲ story.

2 "Always-Sliding-Down", an old Ho:pach'asʔath̲ village that was in use when Alex Thomas (b. 1895) was a boy (St. Claire 1991:185, 183 Map 18 #42). There were no Ts'o:maʔ̲asʔath̲ even then except for Mrs. William. Alex claimed that as far as he had heard, the Hach'a:ʔath̲ got as far up as Y'aqis to T'iqo:ʔis as their *hisʔo:kt* (conquest); the Ts'isha:ʔath̲ got the country down from Y'aqis; the Hiko:lʔath̲ were last and were at the head of the Canal and at Tlichnit. Wi:tsah̲, the wife of Tom (Sa:ya:ch'apis), has right (her family only) to clover digging at ChaʔaK, the island at the head of the Canal; Johnson Is. (Cf. St. Claire 1991:185-7, 183 Map 18 #42, #46, #48; 193, 192 Map 19 #77)

3 In every *ʔo:simch* (bathing ritual), whenever you go out you begin with a *ti:chʔimch* "prayer for life". Words are:

N'ach̲ʔ̲a:ʔatoʔis *H̲aw'e:l* *lakso:qstoʔis*
Look down on me, O Chief, have pity on me,

ti:ch'apis. *Hoʔatsaʔapchip'is* *ʔo:shh̲ʔatqo:s*
cause me to be alive. Cause mine to go back, to be sent back, whatever I am by someone done to

ʔo:shwa:ʔat *p'ishwa:ʔat* *ʔo:kwaʔamach'apikqas*
said about me by someone something bad said, may I cause him to have his evil prayers take effect on himself,

qa:hʔayimch'atqo:s *ʔo:shh̲ap'is* *ʔokwats'oqsapikqas.*
at whatever time one does ʔo:simch by someone may I cause him to swallow his own (bad words)

Wi:ksha h̲ap'is *H̲aw'e:l.* *Qa:tsi:ʔatl'is*
Cause me to be without affliction, O Chief. Grant me

h̲aw'ilmisowʔitqak *H̲aw'e:l ...*
your wealth, O Chief ...

This is the general style. The actual words may be different, generally longer. The reference to wealth is made only when you ʔo:simch for wealth; correspondingly for other purposes. (Alex)

4 Better: *wa:ltaqshiʔatl*, "he said before leaving" (Alex).

5 The idea of rubbing is to take away the distinctly human odour, which other beings dislike. Also it is good for strength per se.

6 To:ta:, "Thundering"; Thunder Mountain on the north side of Great Central Lake (Op. cit.:180, 179 Map 17 #14).

7 In rubbing they actually rub skin off in many cases, of the hands, arms, back, legs. Palm skin is rubbed off when rubbing, *kwi:qa*, with *kw'a:lok* branches. A sore part is rubbed with medicine so that it heals quickly. *Nashyʔi* "strength medicine" is used, which is also drunk.

8 *mama:ʔ̲eyo*, "Bullheads", like codfish only smaller.

9 Better: *tich'imtskwiʔi*, the thrown away rubbers.

10 If in praying you come to a halt or begin to stutter, it is a sign that someone is listening, which nullifies effect. It is good luck to have the words come easily. (Alex)

11 I.e., was prompter.

12 Though in water. It was *ch'ih̲a:*, supernatural.

13 If a child would play with tongs and always split it through, it was a sign that it would always lose wives or husbands.

14 Bob was thinking of pot. Should be *hilakwist'ah̲sʔap'atl*.

15 Used also for "ripe".

16 I.e., long used as a belt and rather worn out, but good enough for a human being.

17 There was a girl at Clayoquot (or Nootka) whom Galick used to be after when young. She would have none of them. She said a bear and thunder were after her, but she preferred the latter. As soon as she said this, she died and it thundered very loud, nearly knocking down the houses. Her body disappeared next morning after they went to look for it in the burial box in a tree. Her mother, whenever it thundered, would *ts'i:qa*. So now they say he has a wife (only one).

18 In woods from Falls (not towards Sproat Lake).

19 If one wants, he or several banded together, can go into someone's house and *haw'ah̲sa*, "ask to eat so and so". It must be given to him in great quantity, and he must eat all he possibly can. These *haw'ah̲sa* are sometimes announced long beforehand. Thus, Ta:yi:ʔ̲a recently (as of Jan. 1-2, 1914) announced here (Alberni) that he wanted to *haw'ah̲sa* for salmonberries of the H̲o:choqlisʔath̲; they are supposed to get wind of it and act accordingly. In 1912 the Ts'isha:ʔath̲ were invited by the Qiltsmaʔath̲ to come to potlatch. As report had gotten around that the Ts'isha:ʔath̲ were *haw'ah̲sa* for devilfish, the Ts'isha:ʔath̲ on being invited, warned the Qiltsmaʔath people that they would go for the potlatch and not *haw'ah̲sa*. It is customary for the invited tribe to pay *chichichi* "teeth" money to the host before starting to eat when food is set down before them. The Ts'isha:ʔath̲ did not do so, and the Qiltsmaʔath̲ (or rather ʔ̲A:h̲o:sʔath̲) later unjustly criticized the Ts'isha:ʔath̲ people.

Once Cultus Bob asked Tom for *mix̲tim* "salmon roe" as *haw'ah̲sa* at the time they were drying salmon. Then Tom gave a feast to the Ho:pach'asʔath̲ and Ts'isha:ʔath̲ and gave Bob several sacks of apples. He ate all he could, and could take the balance home as *m'a:mot* (leftovers). The one who eats the most gets a prize (in older days blankets). Food is always set down four times.

When the Clayoquots are here next winter (1914-15), young fellows banded together as a H̲o:choqtlisˀath̲ fraternity expect to give a feast to the Qwinistaqiml as announced at a recent potlatch by Mrs. Jackson.

20 ˀ̲Awˀokok Tliko:t, "Lake Tliko:t", lake of Sproat River, i.e., Sproat Lake (Op. cit.: 178, 184, 179 Map 17 #3, #35).

21 I.e., he was out hunting again and came with two while his people were inviting to a feast.

22 I.e., it got empty just when he was so full that he could not have eaten any more.

23 Alex considers this getting even with his father for not encouraging him and teaching him hunting lore is quite typical of olden days.

24 "Carrying-Thunder-Going-Down".

25 "Always-Potlatching".

26 So they can take it home and prepare as they like. Chinook "chow".

TEXTS

113. Shamans and Ghosts *(La:maho:s via Alex Thomas)*[1]

Cho: ʔo:n'ak'oh̲ʔatlah̲ N'a:chn'a:cha[2] ʔo:n'ak'oh̲shitlma t'a:tn'eʔis N'a:chn'a:cheʔi. Ya: ʔo:n'ak'oh̲shitlma ʔaya t'a:tn'eʔis N'a:chn'a:cheʔi ʔo:n'ak'oh̲shitla ʔoshtaqyoʔi N'a:chn'a:cha ʔanich sokwiʔath̲weʔin t'a:tn'eʔisʔi ʔoh̲ʔat ho:ʔaktskwiʔi qah̲shitl qo:ʔas ch'ih̲a:ʔatlʔi, wa:ʔatlma ya:l N'a:chn'a:cheʔi ʔoyi sokwiʔatqo qwam'e:ʔitq t'a:tn'eʔisʔi qwaʔini:n'akʔoh̲shitlʔitq. Sokwiʔatlmaya:l t'a:t'aln'anakʔisʔi wala:k'ap'atl hilh̲ʔi:tq N'a:chn'a:cheʔi ʔotsay'ap'atl.[3] Hixwalolʔatlma ya:l N'a:chn'a:cheʔi ! ʔI:h̲ʔatlma ʔo:shmaqak'atl Wawatso:poʔotl ʔokla:ma N'a:chn'a:cheʔi lo:ts.sma. Wawa:ʔtlma ya:l N'a:chn'a:cheʔi ʔanich ʔo:shmaqak'atl pipi:sath̲atlh̲weʔin ch'ih̲a: ʔo:ts'inʔak'atl so:m'inh̲ʔatl'atʔi ya:l t'a:tn'eʔis ts'awa:kma w'asna ya:l t'an'eʔisʔi meʔitlqats ʔokla:ma ya: w'asneʔi Chapiqtlil. Sokwiʔatl'matla ya:l meʔitlqatsʔi w'asneʔi. ʔOh̲ʔatl'atla: ʔomʔi:qsakʔi wawa:ʔatl'at,

"ʔA:no:kw'alsatleʔits, h̲achatak'atlma hiyilʔatl qwam'i:n'ak'oh̲shiʔatitq t'a:tn'eʔis."

Wik ya: meʔitlqatsʔi wasna. Hini:ʔasʔatlqo: ya:l N'a:chn'a:cheʔi ʔotsachiʔatlqo: hita:qtl'asʔi hilst'iʔ̲asʔi ʔayaqh̲ʔatlma na:ʔokshi:l cha:kopi:h̲ʔi ʔo:sh lo:ts.sa:mi:h̲ʔi. Hoʔatsachiʔatlqo: machinoʔatl ʔo:shmaqak'atl lo:ts.smeʔi ya:l machqo:lʔatl ʔoqo:lʔatl ts'ak'omts ʔo:no:tl ʔani ts'osts'os.shqa ya:l ts'ak'omtsʔi. Wa:ʔatl.tla: ya:l N'a:chn'a:cheʔi,

"ʔO:shtsokw'atlma sokwitltso:meʔitso: yaqo:kw'alʔitq

meˀitlqatsˀi," wa:ˀatl.tla:, **"Hiy'aqtl'ap'atl'atma m'oksy'iˀi ˀi:h̲ mah̲t'i:ˀakˀi ch'ih̲e:ˀi,"** wa:ˀatlmatla: ˀo:shtaqyoˀi N'a:chn'a:cha, **"Sokwitlts.so: ˀ̲ats'ilats.so:, so:ˀatl'atokma qoˀalsma ch'ih̲e:ˀi ˀoh̲ˀat,"** wa:ˀatl.tla:.

ˀAh̲ˀa:ˀatlma sokwitl'asˀatl ˀatlachinkatl lo:ts.sa:mi:h̲ ˀom'iqsoˀi ˀish neˀi:qsoˀi ˀatlachink'atl sokwitlasˀatlat.tla: Chapiqtli:l. Hinasiˀatlat.tla: hi:lˀitq meˀitlqatsˀi.

"ˀA:no:kw'alsatleˀits kwa:tlitl, wi:makshiˀatleˀits," wa:ˀatlat.

Tsiqshiˀatl ya:lˀi: meˀitlqatsˀi.

"Qwa:ˀaˀatla:ˀaˀasap'at'a:h̲chas," wa:ˀatl.

P'iyachiˀatl[4] lo:chsa:mi:h̲ˀi ˀatla hi:nits.sotlshiˀatl sokwiˀatlat meˀitlqatsˀi hi:hishtsiw'anoˀatl'at tlakishsapmaˀi:qstop'atl'at tla:kishsapshiˀatlat. Wawa:ˀatl meˀitlqatsˀi ya: ˀani wikqa: !

"Qwa:qtl'a:ˀasap'at'a:h̲chas," wa:ˀatl.tla:.

ˀI:qh̲wa: wi:ˀakshitl lo:ts.smeˀi ˀatla ya:l tsitsiˀ̲inchiˀatl. ˀAni:silatl ˀatleˀi wawi:chiˀatl ˀani ˀi:h̲qa: wikˀay'aqtlqa, wikˀayaqtly'ih̲atlhakqo: wawi:chiˀatlat. Ya:ts.shiˀatl hoˀatsachiˀatl ya:l ˀatleˀi lo:ts.sa:mi:h̲ ˀi:qh̲okw'atl ˀani w'asnaqa.

"ˀI:h̲ma: w'asna, nasakshitlin, w'asnaqaqma p'ishy'i:h̲eˀi wikˀay'aqtly'ih̲a."

Cho: ya:ts.shiʔatl ʔo:shtaqyoʔi N'a:chn'a:cheʔi k'ak'am'inqhchik'atl wik'i:thʔatlin kamat'ap wama:yi tsi:qtsi:qa ʔani kwi:shiyatskw'atlqa ʔoʔokwink'atl chiha:. N'aʔo:kw'atlma hachatak'atl t'a:tn'eʔisʔi ʔohʔatl'at hini:ts.sʔat yatyo:qwatsʔitq ʔo:tsoʔokw'atl ya:l ʔi:hʔi: m'oksy'i t'iʔa:ʔa maht'i:ʔakch'a ch'iha: hiyilokw'ap'ati:ch qoʔatsmam'inh t'a:tn'eʔisʔi ʔohʔat ch'iha:.

Hinasiʔatl to:shqapaʔoʔatl hachatak'atl qwam'e:ʔitq naʔok. Ts'os.shiʔatl lo:ts.smeʔi ʔo:shtaqyo ʔokwiqhʔatl hitinʔatspeʔeʔi ʔoʔomhiyap ʔana: ts'osyaqshitl ʔahnahʔatʔitq t'ohts'iti, ʔoʔomhat hitaqtl'otl t'ohts'itstʔi hitaqtl'oʔatl'atqo: t'ohts'iti. Qwa:qhʔatlqo: ʔahʔa: tsi:skchi:skatl,

"Kwa:tl'ik !" wawa:ʔatlqo:, ʔimtʔimt.shiʔatlqo: yaya:qleʔitq ya:l t'a:tn'eʔisʔi ʔahʔa:ʔatlqo: tl'ik'aqtl'iʔatl sokwiʔatlqo: ʔimt.shiʔatlqo: ya:ʔitlʔitq sokwitl yaqle:ʔitq t'an'eʔis ma:. ʔAhʔa:ʔatlma ʔah wa:ʔatlqo: hini:ʔatl yaqwatsʔitq[5] t'an'eʔis. Sokwiʔatlqo: yaqwatsʔitq t'an'eʔis,

"Kwa:tl'itl so:kwiʔatlah so:til," wa:ʔatlqo: yaqwatsʔitq t'an'eʔis, qwa:ʔama ha:chatil qwam'e:ʔitq t'a:tn'eʔis.

"Cho: ʔa:naqtl'aʔasatlma Chapiqtlil," wa:ʔatlmatla: ʔo:shtaqyoʔi lo:ts.sma.

"Hisʔap'a:hʔatlah ʔani wik'i:tqa hinat.shitl."

Hiy cho: ya:ts.shiʔatl ʔotsachiʔatl hiy'athʔitq ʔo:shtaqyoʔi lo:ts.sma hi:kwalma ʔiha:qatl ʔomʔi:qsoʔi ʔish neʔi:qsak Chapiqtlil ʔoʔo:yokw'atlma ʔanich ʔa:naqtl'aʔasatlhweʔin ʔani wa:ʔatlqa ya:l ʔo:shtaqyoʔi.

Hi:sap'i:ksatlma ʔoh̲ walʔ̲aqatl ʔomʔi:qsoʔi ʔish neʔi:qsoʔi ʔani ʔi:h̲ʔatlqa ya:ʔak'atl'at limaqsti ʔanich ʔa:naqtl'aʔasatlokʔal t'an'a.

Chitakshiʔatlma ʔoh̲ ya:l yatya:qwatsʔitq t'a:tn'eʔis ʔo:sa:h̲atl ʔani hini:p'atl'atoqa ʔoh̲ʔat ʔo:shtaqyoʔi ʔani hoʔa:nakshiʔatlqa ʔ̲a:ʔ̲a:tiqshiʔatl'atma ya:l ʔo:shtaqyoʔi ʔoh̲ʔatl'at qwam'e:ʔitq t'a:t'atn'anakʔi. Tsiqshiʔatlma ya:l ʔo:shtaqyoʔi

"H̲i:sili:y'apshitlsa:h̲ah̲ ya:l w'asneʔi Chapiqtlil," wa:ʔatl, **"So:ʔatl'atma chamih̲tat ch'ih̲e:ʔi ʔoh̲ʔat machi:lʔap'atl'atma."**

Cho: h̲a:h̲o:pshiʔatlma ʔo:shtaqyoʔi ʔo:kwilʔatl ya: t'a:t'atn'anakʔisʔi, h̲a:h̲o:pshiʔatl.

"Hat'i:sʔap'ichim," wa:ʔatl, **"ʔah̲ʔa:ʔatlso qwah̲imy'o:p'atl,"** wa:ʔatl.tla:. **"Tasith̲ʔapatlso:tla: ʔ̲oy'i,"** wa:ʔatl.

Chi:qts'inaqshiʔatlma qwam'e:ʔitq lo:ts.sma:mi:h̲ ʔokwi. Ya:ʔak'atl'at lim'aqsti ʔo:kwil ya: qwa:qtl'a:ʔasiʔi Chapiqtlil. Cho: hi:stm'a:notlma ʔah̲ʔa: wawa:lyatl ʔayeʔi lo:ts.sa:mih̲ ʔani ʔo:shsilamatakqa ʔe:ʔe:ʔisha ʔanich so:ʔatl'at ch'ih̲a: ʔoh̲ʔat wawa:lyatlma hopta:qh̲ʔatl tata:kinkwilʔatl ʔani ʔo:shsilamatakqa. ʔI:h̲ʔatlʔal ʔoya:ts.so:qtl, hi:kwalʔatlma ʔih̲aki:tl n'ow'i:qsak ʔomʔi:qsak neʔi:qsak Chapiqtlil. ʔAteʔish ti:ch wiktaqshitl teʔil qoʔi:chitl. ʔAyaqaʔ̲atlok t'a:tn'a tlah̲ʔoyi. ʔ̲I:la:wopshi:l ʔokla:ʔatl wiky'o: teʔil ʔanits'atli: qo:ʔas.

* * * *

ʔOtsachitlitin Tl'a:ʔasʔat<u>h</u>⁶ ho:ʔak ʔoyi ʔoʔoqwa<u>h</u> yaqiti
Ho:kw'a:xin ʔokla Ho:<u>ʔ</u>i:ʔat<u>h</u>⁷ <u>h</u>achy'a:k Ho:kw'a:xin
ʔotsachitlin ʔOsi:l⁸ ʔokla:ma ʔokwi kwispe:ʔi Ni:ya:.
Hilokwin ch'apats Ni:ya: hil<u>h</u>ʔatlin ʔa<u>h</u>ʔa: ya:ts.shiʔatl
yatsa:qtatlin ʔotsachiʔatl ʔOsi:l ʔokwinkshitlin
ʔoʔoqshiʔatlin ʔo:shtaqyiʔi Nopots'iqxaʔa ʔo:shtaqyoʔi
Tl'a:ʔasʔat<u>h</u> ʔow'a:tma ʔo<u>h</u> Ho:kw'axin. Qishʔaqtlima
ʔo:shtaqyoʔi, ʔi:<u>h</u> ʔoshtaqyo. Hist'a<u>h</u>siʔatl'atin kwispi:sʔi
Ni:ya: ʔoyi:qshiʔatlin p'inw'al tli<u>h</u>shiʔatl tla<u>h</u>ʔatl
ʔotsachiʔatl ʔOsi:l.

Hitasaʔatlin ʔOsi:l. Hitinqsaʔatlma qo:ʔasm'in<u>h</u> ʔokla:ʔakma
n'ow'i:qso ʔAshk'iʔi: yawqʔi:qin <u>h</u>a:w'ilatl ʔi:q<u>h</u>okwatlin
ʔanin ʔo:ty'a:pqin Xaxashk'ok mo:qomlchi tl'a<u>h</u>iqs. Wa:ʔatlma
ya:l ʔAshk'iʔi:m'itʔi ʔoyi ʔatlqimlchiqity'apqon ʔoʔi:
lo:chm'o:pokʔi. Hi:y hinoschisʔap'atl'atin ha:<u>ʔ</u>inʔatl'at.
ʔA<u>h</u>ʔa:ʔatlma ʔa:t<u>h</u>shiʔatl weʔichoʔatlin. N'a:s.shiʔatlma
ʔa<u>h</u>ʔa:ʔatl ha:<u>ʔ</u>inʔatl'atintla: tlaʔo:q<u>h</u>ʔat.
ʔA:t<u>h</u>shiʔatlmatla:.

Cho: ʔa<u>h</u>ʔa:ʔatlmatla: n'a:sshiʔatltla:. Wa:ʔatl'atin
ʔanich'in ʔo:ʔa:q<u>h</u>liʔa:qtl'atl'at. Kam'a:ʔat<u>h</u>ʔisma
ʔatlpoqach'a cha:kopi:<u>h</u>.⁹ To:pshiʔatlma ʔa<u>h</u>ʔa:ʔatl
ha:<u>ʔ</u>inʔatl'atin ʔa<u>h</u>ʔa:ʔat waqʔoqpiʔatlin. ʔInxi:chiʔatl
naʔa:ʔat maʔasʔi. Hiy hininʔatl hi:lsʔatinoʔatl no:ʔiʔatlma
hi:lsʔatoq<u>h</u>ʔatl ts'a:yiqy'akokma no:k ya:<u>ʔ</u>itlʔitq no:ʔitl
machinoʔatlma. ʔO:wi:tsma ma:tli:ts t'oxyo:, ch'aʔo:shʔi
t'oxyo:. <u>H</u>achatakma ʔo:ʔo:wi:ts qwam'a:chinkʔitq
lo:tssa:mi:<u>h</u>ʔi cha:kopi:<u>h</u>ʔi, t'oxyo:ʔi ch'aʔo:sh <u>h</u>a:yi:ʔitl.
ʔAtlpimtqach'a lo:tssa:mi:<u>h</u>. Ya:ʔalʔatlin ya:ʔalʔatlma
y'o:qwa: ʔo:shtaqyakqin N'opots'aqxeʔiʔi. Wi:nappiʔatl
noʔatap'atl ts'ayiqi:ʔitlʔi tsiqshiʔatlma ʔo:shtaqyoʔi
lo:tssma ʔi:ch'im Kwinyo:t'aqsop.¹⁰

"Ma:nokwitlʔa:qtl'atlah̲ hischa:tlo:sis ʔo:shtaqyo," wa:ma tsiqshitl.

Han'ah̲toʔatlma nisha:nʔakʔi hawi:ʔatlma m'och'ich. No:ʔiʔatlma ʔah̲ʔa:ʔatl ʔo:tssaseʔi no:k ʔo:shtaqyoʔi lo:tssma. Halh̲aqawiʔatl. ʔO:ʔitlme tl'ah̲iqstskwi ʔaʔatlink ʔani:ts'ol X̲ax̲ashk'ok'wastskwiʔi tl'ah̲iqstskwi. ʔI:h̲ʔatlma tlo:kwa:ni:chiʔatl ts'axts'axmilʔapma tl'ah̲iqstskwiʔi wawa:ʔatlweʔin tsi:qtsi:qa tsitsiqink ʔoyi ti:tsachitlokqo: ʔoyi tl'ah̲iqstskwiʔi toh̲to:h̲n'ok'watlma tl'o:lapi chimtsa:sʔalʔi kwikwinkso ts'axts'axmilʔap'atl ʔoh̲ qatsa:sʔi kwikwinkso tl'ah̲iqstskwiʔi qi:chitlma qwa: wiklm'a:ʔak ti:chachitl. Cho: hawi:ʔatlma ʔan̲ʔa: lotssmeʔi noʔatap'atl.

Cho: tlaʔo:ʔi ʔo:shtaqyo ʔohi:chiʔatlma lo:tssma:tlmatla: no:ʔiʔatl y'o:qwa: ʔo:kwi:ts'iʔatltla y'o:qwa: no:k tlachity'ak nashokkw'atlma tlah̲ʔatl lo:tssmeʔi tlo:kwa:naqaʔatlma ʔo:shalyoqaʔatlma qwa:mitʔitq yaqwi:qh̲ʔitq ts'axts'axmilʔap'atlma tl'ah̲iqstskwiʔi toh̲to:h̲nokw'atl hina:tokw'atl ʔi:h̲ʔatl tlo:kwa:na nasqa:ʔatlma ya:lʔi nasqilimʔi nono:kw'atl.

Cho: pisat.shiʔatlokma lo:tssmeʔi ʔo:shtaqyo ya:l tl'ah̲iqstskwiʔi pisat.shiʔatlma tl'ah̲iqstskwiʔi hi:kwalma ʔo:xpi:lik pisat.shiʔatl ya:ts.shiʔatl ʔoʔo:kwaqh̲shiʔatl ts'axts'axmil ! Ya:ts.shiʔatl sayeʔiʔatlqo: wa:tlqo:tla: hoʔatsachiʔatltla: ʔoʔo:kwaqh̲ʔatl qwa:ʔap wik'i:th̲ʔatl'at so:ʔat ʔoh̲ʔatl ti:ch'ap ʔo:shtaqyoʔi toh̲to:h̲n'okw'atl ʔa:nah̲atl wi:napapilqh̲ʔatl ʔah̲ʔa:ʔatlma noʔatap'atl. Tsiqshiʔatlma ʔo:shtaqyoʔi.

"Wik'i:ch natalts'il," waʔatl'atin ni:h̲ilʔat, "Pipi:sath̲atlma ch'ih̲a:, ʔaya:tlma ch'ih̲a: hilst'oʔasʔi ʔah̲n'i: hi:lʔitqso:," waʔatl'atin.

ʔO:shmaqak'atlma ch'ihe:ʔi pipi:sathatlma. Saya:htachitlilʔatlin hawi:ʔatlin natalts'il. Naʔa:min wa:ʔatqin. Hilma: pi:tsksy'iqow'as ʔah hininqasʔi tlawa: ʔa:ni qwitsitsaʔatolqin yaqwintlqin ʔa:ni t'a:qa:k wa:ʔatqin ʔo:shtaqyoʔi t'a:qa:k wa:ʔatqin ʔo:shtaqyoʔi no:ʔiʔatlmatla: ʔiqsilatlmatla: tlo:kwa:ni:chitl. Wik'atlma ʔo:hw'al tl'ahiqstskwakʔi ʔa:nahisatlma nono:kw'atl cho: noʔatap'atl. Cho: ʔahʔa:yiyatl'atah hilʔi: Ho:kw'a:xinʔi wa:ʔatl'atah,

"Ma:nokwitl ʔahn'i: ʔo:shtaqyakqin kamatsap'a:ni chamihta qwiqo:si chiha:ch'a hinimlok ʔani to:hokw'atlqin, ʔanis ʔi:hʔatl to:hokw'atl," wa:ʔatlah Ho:kw'axin.

"Cho:," wa:ʔatlah N'opots'iqxaʔa, siy'a:ʔatl ma:nokwitlʔa:qtlweʔintsok.

"Cho:," ʔaniwa: ʔo:tsahtaksa N'opots'iqxaʔa ʔi:naxi:chitl sokwitlma ni:sa:kʔisokʔi ʔa:qshitl sokwitlma ma:tli:tsimʔakʔi t'ohyo:ʔakʔi tl'i:yaʔat'oʔisokʔi tl'i:yaʔat'oʔisokwita ʔeʔinhʔis hishtsoʔas. Han'ahtotlma tlitlihʔaqtlokʔi Qwahashotlma qwaqwahw'anop qa:ty'apt'atʔi qwaho:tlhtla:. Cho: no:ʔiʔatlma ʔahʔa:ʔatl wa:ʔakma no:k ʔanich hilʔathweʔin kwikwinkso hi:tapoleʔi kwispe:ʔi.

"Kwispa:ʔatah kwinkwinkso ʔo:no:tl ʔanis ʔo:shtaqyo," wa:ʔakma no:k Toshe:kʔi N'opots'iqxaʔa tlo:kwa:ni:chitlskapolʔatlma tlo:kwa:ni:chiʔatlma.

ʔOtsachiʔatlma ʔappiqtlilʔi. ʔO:shmaqshiʔatlma nono:kw'atlin hopi:ʔatl qwam'istaqin hachy'a:k. Ya:ʔalʔatlma ya:l ʔOsi:lʔathʔi ya:ʔalʔatl t'iqwi:lʔatl. ʔAhʔa:ʔatlma hini:ʔasʔatl ʔo:shtaqyakqin.

"Tlawasʔich ! Tlawasʔich !"

wa:ˀatlma ˀOsi:lˀath̲ˀswinh̲i ˀo:shp'alatlma ˀani hini:ˀasqa ˀanin ˀanich ˀaya:tlh̲weˀin ch'ih̲a: hilst'oˀ̲iˀatlma takst'oˀ̲iˀatl ˀotsachiˀatlma hilˀitq ˀayeˀi pi:tsksy'i. ˀAh̲ˀa:ˀatl kwisi:y'iˀatl naˀa:ˀat ˀo:shtaqyakqin nono:kqchik'atl hitakwalme::: qi:kwa:l ˀah̲ˀa:ˀatlma hininˀatl naˀa:ˀat. Histˀ̲atlˀ̲atlma no:ˀiˀatl naˀa:ˀat hi:lsˀatoˀi ho:ya:lˀatlma no:ksasatlokma. Wik'atlma ˀo:shtaqyoy'akok. Ma:chintlshiˀatlma ho:liˀitlshiˀatl no:nokshiˀatlintla: wikˀ̲atlilˀatlma ya:lˀi ˀOsi:lˀath̲ˀi.

Cho: hawi:ˀatlma noˀatap'atl ˀa:th̲iy'o tom'aqtlˀi ˀath̲i: m'itle:ˀi. Tsiqshiˀatlma ˀo:shtaqyoˀi N'opots'iqxaˀa.

"Wikma: ch'ih̲a:," wa:ˀatlma, **"Wikma: ch'ih̲a: tilti:chma qo:ˀassa k'ak'am'inma ˀaya ˀotspa:qh̲ma ˀah̲ko:,"** wa:ˀatlma.

Hishischil qwitspe:ˀitq Kwinyo:t'ath̲.

"Hashi:chitlˀa:qtlin ˀam'i:tlik ˀoyi we: ˀoyiqomtla: tlaˀokwilik hashi:chitl qwi:ts'imˀako:si ˀi:h̲ k'ak'am'in," wa:ˀatlma N'opots'aqxaˀa.

Cho: hi:stm'intlma ˀah̲ˀa: hawi:ˀatl.

Cho: ˀah̲ˀa:ˀatlin yoxtsiˀatl n'a:sshiˀatlˀitq. Hina:chiˀatlin walshiˀatl ˀotsachiˀatlintla: Ni:ya:. ˀI:qh̲okw'atlin hilh̲ˀatl ˀah̲ˀa: qwa:ˀa:nitqin ˀah̲ˀa:ˀatlma ˀam'i:chiˀatl. Hininˀatlma histaqshiˀatl ˀOsi:l qo:ˀas ts'awa:k wa:ˀatlok ˀoyaqh̲mis ˀanich hilqh̲we:ˀin ho:n'i: ˀi:h̲to:p hil kwispi:sˀi ˀOsi:l ˀatlchi:lshiˀatlh̲weˀin hil ch'iya: hilˀatlh̲waˀin ˀayaqaˀ̲atl qo:ˀas tlah̲ˀoyi ˀOsi:l Kwinyo:t'ath̲ˀatl ˀayeˀi qo:ˀas ch'iya:. Chitakshiˀatlma ˀah̲ˀa: N'opots'aqxaˀa ˀani ˀoh̲qa: t'aqokstotl qwiyiˀitq N'a:chn'a:cheˀitq wa:mitqa ˀam'i:qhˀa:qtlin hashi:chitl qwi:ts'inaqako:si ʔayeʔi k'ak'am'in wa:mitqa wikma: ch'ih̲a: ʔayeʔi k'ak'am'in qo:ʔassama wa:mitqa qwiyʔitq N'a:chn'a:cha. ʔI:h̲ʔatlni ʔo:shp'ala ʔani ʔa:niqa t'aqoqstotl. Cho: qwa:n'ak'oh̲itah̲ ʔah̲ʔa: si:y'aqsa n'a:tssa.

* * * *

Cho:, qah̲shitlma qo:ʔas ʔ̲ay'i:chh̲ʔi ʔoyi, ʔo:ts n'ow'i:qso Qwintin'ox, qah̲shitlʔi qo:ʔas ʔokla: ʔOwimy'is.[12] Kapschitlma qah̲shitl. Wikma: qi: teʔil k'achʔisma tl'it'oqshiʔalma tl'ah̲iqschinop'at. Chi:potl[13] hi:staqshitlsa hi:lh̲ʔitq qah̲shitl, wiktaqshiʔatma hini:tssoʔat. Milshitlma k'i:tqʔ̲atl k'i:tqy'ak qwiyiʔitq ʔich'achiʔatl chi:potl t'aqswi:sts'a. K'i:tʔ̲aqtlma hi:ni:tssoʔat hita:ʔ̲ato hilst'oʔ̲asʔi hita:ʔ̲ato ʔostʔi:tl hi:taqtl'itl k'i:tʔ̲aqtlqchik wala:k ʔotsay'ap'ol saye:ʔi. Cho: hawi:ʔatl k'i:tʔ̲aqtl wi:nap'iʔatlʔitq hopchiʔatl'atʔitq pi:tsksy'iʔi. Cho: wah̲shiʔatl'atokma qwiqwinakitoʔitq h̲a:chatilʔatlʔ̲atok wah̲shiʔat qwiqwinakitʔitq qo:ʔasitʔi qah̲shitl wah̲shiʔatok hiyiqtop ʔa:nachilsatokma wik'atok wah̲shitl tlaqmisokwitʔi ʔ̲oqwatschiʔi tlaqmis ʔo:tsi:chitlma lo:chmalʔi. Cho:, qwisma: ʔah̲ʔa:.

ʔAh̲ʔa:ʔatlma ch'oʔichh̲shiʔatl ʔah̲ʔa:ʔatlma Tlo:kwa:ni:chiʔatl wi:ʔotsmalʔi, n'ow'i:qsakit *Ko:tin*, Tlo:kwa:ni:chiʔatl, m'e:ʔiʔatokma t'an'eʔis[14] m'e:ʔiʔatma ya: qaqi:ʔakshitlʔi Qwintin'ox, qah̲shitlokwitʔi n'ow'i:qso ʔ̲ay'i:chh̲ʔitq ʔoyi. ʔA:yi:ʔatma m'e:ʔiʔat t'a:tn'eʔis tlatlaʔo:. Cho: ʔah̲ʔa:ʔatlma m'a:kway'i:h̲shiʔat m'e:ʔitl'inm'inh̲itʔi ʔoh̲ma: hi:ya:l La:mah̲o:s ʔish *Otto Taylor* n'ow'iqsakitʔi ʔish n'axswa qachts'amaʔal ch'apats ʔoyi:q. Tloshinqak ʔatla ʔaya:tlma qo:ʔas. Ya:ʔalʔatl ya:l ho:ya:lʔi m'a:kway'i:h̲iya. Ya:ʔatl ho:lʔi m'a:kwa'i:h̲iya. Wawa:ʔakma no:k ʔanich yatsachistosh̲weʔin top'alʔi ʔo:no:tl no:k yatsachishtoʔatlma top'alʔi ʔokwiqh saya:ts'atoʔi. Ho:ya:lʔatlma qachts'eʔi. ʔO:shp'alatlin ʔani yatsachishtqhqa ho:ya:l top'alʔi.

Cho:, hini:p'atlma: ʔahʔa: m'a:y'ip'atl m'a:kway'i:hitʔi. Cho: machinoʔatlma hini:tssʔatl'at kw'a:kw'a:li:ts'atl. Ha:ʔinchiʔatl'atma hachatak ʔanasa chakopi:hʔi. Cho: lalakw'in ʔatl'atma ts'i:tts'i:qmaʔokʔi ts'i:qshitl'asʔatlma ts'i:qshiʔatlma ʔahʔa:ʔatl ts'i:qshiʔatl,

"Wik'i:tma ʔo:shmis qwiqo:si."

Wik'a:tishitlma tsi:qa:mitʔi hini:sts'opiʔatl'atma ya:l qaqi:ʔakshitlʔi Qwintin'ox.

"ʔOyoʔalweʔin hilʔi: n'ow'i:qsakitʔi, hi:litʔi ʔahko: Haw'il ʔah maht'i:ʔi," wa:ʔatl Ha:ya:lʔim, **"Wa:ʔatweʔin hilʔi: ha:kwa:tlʔi ʔohʔat n'ow'i:qsakitʔi ʔink'atl maht'i:ʔi ts'iʔa:ʔatl tlaqmis. Cho: ʔa:ʔaniwatweʔin ʔahʔa:,"** wa:ʔatl.

Cho: ts'i:qshiʔatltla, ts'i:qa:saqh wikʔatlshiʔatl.

"Wikʔatlshiʔich," wa:ʔatl ts'i:qa:saqh ts'i:ʔaqeʔi.

Neʔi:chiʔatlin ʔahʔa:ʔatl hachatak k'i:tʔatlʔi k'i:tqy'ak. Qwamin haya:ʔakqon hista: tako:si. Qwa:ma: hi:simlapiqo: ʔi:hʔi: hasa:tok. ʔAhʔa:ʔatlma hista:tokw'atl ʔi:hʔatl ʔaya:tok hilst'oʔasʔi. ʔAhʔa:ʔatlin pokwiʔatl po:ya:sʔatl, hachatak qwam'e:ʔitq qo:ʔas po:ya:sʔatl ʔoʔo:tsachitlin hiyilokqin wa:walyo hachatak qwame:ʔilq qo:ʔas Ho:ʔi:ʔath. Wa:ʔatlma ya:lʔi ma:maqtlakqin ʔanich ʔi:hʔatlit ʔo:shmaqak, ʔanich hi:kwalʔatlsit kw'a:yi:ʔitlminh t'ashi:m'inhi ʔo:no:tl ʔi:h pipi:sathi ch'iha: !

Wikʔa:tlshiʔatlma k'i:tqa:mitʔi ʔaya:tok. ʔAhʔa:ʔatlma hininʔatl ʔatla qo:ʔas.

"ʔOtsachiʔich ya:tsshiʔatl hilʔi:tq Tlo:kwa:neʔi. ʔE:ʔe:ʔisha !" wa:ʔatin.

Wala:k'atlin. Wa:ma ʔanich,

"P'ishxi:n'ak'sho:tlqhweʔini," wa:ʔatlma.

Hine:ʔiʔatl qo:ʔas. ʔOhwe:ʔin wi:ʔaqstotl ʔahni: qahshitlitʔi ʔay'i:ch ʔoyi, ʔohwe:ʔin wi:ʔaqstotl ʔoʔo:yokshitlweʔin ʔanich wikokw'ap'at ts'iʔa:ʔa tlaqmisokwitʔi. ʔOhitweʔin weʔich Ch'ihin'ak, ʔohitweʔin weʔich. Wa:ma ʔoʔokwilʔat ʔi:hʔi: ʔo:shtaqyo ʔohwe:ʔin n'a:tssi:chitl weʔichh n'a:tssi:chitl ʔanich wi:ʔaqstotlhweʔin ya: qahshitlitʔi ʔoʔo:yokshitl ʔani wikokw'ap'atqa ts'iʔa:ʔa tlaqmisokwitʔi ʔoqmo:tchi.

"Wawa:ma ʔah ch'ihin'ak," wa:ma: ʔi:qhokʔi.

Cho: ʔahʔa:ʔatlma hamatsap'atl qo:ʔas ʔani ch'iha:qhhʔalqa wikqa: Q'a:n'a:tl'aqhʔal wi:na:t. Cho: ʔi:naxi:chiʔatl qo:ʔas qwam'e:ʔitq kw'a:li:tsoʔatl P'ishxi:n'akw'it'asʔatl ʔi:na:xi:chiʔatl ha:w'i:hatl hatha:n'ahtoʔatl ha:w'i:hatl tli:tlihʔaqtlokʔi wi:napʔich'atl ʔa:nachil tlishtliqy'akokʔi. Tasitoʔatl hismis ʔokwitoʔatl tasawiʔatl hismis hi:n'ahi:chiʔatl ʔahʔa: ʔinxe:ʔi. ʔOkwi:lshiʔatl hichma ʔoʔakwatitlma sitkwachitl loʔok ʔeʔi:hʔi. ʔAʔa:ʔatlowama:ʔatlma hini:tss ya: hichmam'inhʔi ʔono:tl ʔani ʔeʔi:h y'aqsqa: ʔi:hm'inh kwa:kwaty'ik. Mo:ma hichmeʔi.

Cho: wa:ʔatlma t'apat.shitl ʔoyi ʔatlaqo: ma:chi:no:l

ʔatlaqo: hicha: hi:ʔissa hita:sʔi. Hi:lsʔatoʔi
hi:n'aḥi:chiʔatlma Ch'i:ʔaktlim ʔatla lo:tssa:mi:ḥ wik
ḥa:tḥa:kwatl ʔeʔi:ch'im lo:tssa:mi:ḥʔi. ʔAtla takwa:ʔatlma
ʔo:tssoʔatl ya: P'ishxi:n'akw'it'asʔi - hisy'ak, ts'axy'ak.
ʔO:shʔatl po: ʔo:tssʔatl. ʔAtlama ya:lʔi ʔokw'ich motsmoḥak
ʔokoxs Sa:n'akoxsim. Cho: ʔaḥʔa:ʔatlma ya:tsshiʔatl.

"Ya:tsshiʔatl'i," wa:ʔatlma, "Hinasiʔatlin maḥt'i:ʔi:
tla:ʔo:."

Hilsʔatinoʔatl ts'i:qshiʔatlma ts'i:ʔatlinʔi ʔowi:ʔatl.
Cho: ʔaḥʔa:ʔatlma pisat.shiʔatl Sa:n'akʔi ʔatla
hitats'opiʔatl pisat.shiʔatl hitats'opiʔatl y'o:qwa:
P'ishxi:n'akʔi ha:w'i:ḥatl ḥatḥa:n'aḥ. Minkshitl maḥt'i:ʔi
hini:ʔas. Wik'i:t ʔo:shmis wikp'iqin wikin naʔa:p'iqo:s.
Histi:ʔitlin Hilst'oʔas ʔokle:ʔi maḥt'i: ʔi:ḥ ya:tsshiʔatlin
ʔotsachiʔatlin Saya:ch'a ʔokle:ʔi maḥt'i: hi:lsʔatanoʔatlin.
ʔIqsilamatla qwa:ʔapʔitq, machinoʔatltla Sa:n'akʔi ʔatla
ʔowi:ḥta sa:ch'ink machinoʔatl y'o:qwa P'ishxi:n'akʔi
minkshitl maḥt'i:ʔi hini:ʔas, wiki:t ʔo:shmis.
Ya:tsshitlnitla: wala:k'atlin T'akaqtl'as ʔokle:ʔi maḥt'i:
machintlintla: ʔaḥʔa: ʔiqsila qwa:ʔapʔitq ʔo:shi:n'akʔi.

ʔAḥʔa:ʔatlin hilḥʔatl ʔaḥʔa: tlaḥʔatl neʔi:chiʔatl
k'itʔatl'atlmatla: histʔatl hilst'oʔasʔi ʔaya:ktokshiʔatl
hawi:tlmaʔi:qstoʔatlma yaqwi:ḥtilʔitq.

"Wik'i: hawi:tl, ḥayi:ʔiʔin," wawa:lyo:chiʔatlma.

Ho:ʔatsachiʔatlma ʔaḥʔa:ʔatl hoʔi:ʔasʔatl.

Cho: ʔaḥʔa:ʔatlin ya:tsshiʔatltla ʔotsachtl'asʔatlin
tlaʔo:ʔi maḥt'i: hilst'oʔasʔi hil. Wikʔa:tlshiʔatlma ya:l
k'i:tqy'akʔi ʔaya:tokwit wikʔa:tlshiʔatl. Hi:lsʔatoqḥʔatlma

ʔah̲ʔa: hinasiʔatlqin hilst'oʔ̲asʔi maʔas wa:ʔatlma ya:lʔi.

"ʔOya:tl'ichim hitaʔatl'atlqo:tla: k'i:tqy'akʔi tl'ichiʔatl'ichim ʔotsay'ap hilst'oʔasʔi."

Cho: ʔah̲ʔa:ʔatlmatla: hine:ʔiʔatltla: Sa:n'akʔi. Tsi:qshiʔatltla: tsi:ʔ̲aktlim'inh̲ʔi to:h̲okw'atlin, ʔi:h̲ʔatlin to:h̲okw'atl ! ʔO:shalyatlma P'ishxi:n'akʔi, hi:si:satlma hiyiqtopʔi, ʔi:h̲ʔatl p'ishaʔatl ! ʔO:no:ʔatl qwa: ʔani to:h̲okqhʔatlqa. ʔEʔimshtima h̲a:yi:ʔitl'asʔatlʔitq wi:napoʔatl ʔo:shi:n'akitʔi. H̲a:h̲aneʔa:lshitlsatl ʔi:h̲ ʔo:shmaqak ʔi:h̲ʔatltla: hina:tokshitl k'i:tqy'ak hita:sʔi. Tl'i:tstl'i:yatl hita:sʔi po: ʔo:no:tl ʔani naʔatah̲ʔatlqa qwa:ʔatlʔitq ʔi:h̲ʔatl ʔo:shmaqak.

ʔAh̲ʔa:ʔatlin ya:tsshiʔatl walshiʔatl wa:lʔ̲aqasamin ʔoy'o:tsachitlin hiyi:ʔyath̲qin wik'atlin ʔotsachitl Tlo:kwa:neʔi ʔo:no:tl ʔi:h̲ʔatlqa h̲a:h̲anaʔa:lsatl ʔo:shmaqak. Hinasiʔatlin walyo:ʔakqin. Wa:ʔatlma ʔanich h̲a:h̲anaʔa:lsatl ʔi:h̲ʔatl ʔo:shmaqak'atl. Wi:nappiʔatlah̲. ʔAh̲ʔa:ʔatl t'apat'aqtlpiʔatlah̲ qwa:qh̲tso:wo:sis ʔo:shsilap. Y'o:qwa yaʔatqin hini:chʔasʔat. ʔOna:kshitlah̲ hisy'ak[16] ʔeʔinh̲ʔisʔi ts'oshok ʔona:kshitlah̲ kimty'ak tsikimin, ʔona:kshitlah̲ *ko:lʔa:yin* n'opts'iq tsoma: kw'ich'itaqiml. Wa:y'aqtlah̲ ʔanis ʔeʔimshtipʔa:qtlqas ts'osshiʔi:kqo: ch'itme:ʔi ʔa:nachtsaqimlʔitq mah̲t'i:ʔi!

Tsi:qtsi:qatlma ya: ʔomʔi:qsakitqas tsi:qtsi:qatlma titi:ch'inʔatlma, tsitsiqink'atlma ʔo:no:tl ʔani ʔo:shmaqak'atlqa ki:ka:ʔatl hita:sʔi hilst'oʔ̲asʔi tom'aqtlʔi ch'it'e:ʔi ʔath̲i:. Hopta:ʔatlma t'a:tn'eʔisokqin, hila:sʔatlma hitaqtl'asts'eʔi hilʔi lo:pi. ʔO:pa:lʔatlma hil ʔah̲ʔa: ʔoʔomʔiqsakʔi ʔa:nasatlin cha:kopi:h̲qin ʔostʔilʔi hil. Wik'atlin weʔichoʔatl. ʔA:nasama hi:ninʔa:l ya:l hil. Wik'atlin weˀichoˀatl. ˀA:nasama hi:ninˀa:l ya:l Cha:mat'akitqin Ho:mˀis ˀokla:mitˀi hi:lsˀat'akitqin ˀani:silat.

"Chachimhihaso:qa: ?"

wa:ˀatl'atqon, wik'atlqo: hine:ˀitl ˀo:no:tl ˀanin lilma:tlok t'ashi: tlap'iqyatlok. ˀO:shmaqak'atlma hilst'oˀasˀi hita:qtl'asˀi k'i:tqa:ˀatlma naˀa:ˀat k'i:tqy'ak. ˀInkhˀap'atlqon t'i:ya:s hilst'oˀasˀi hisi:ˀasˀap ˀinkqhˀap k'atshaqtskwiˀi hiˀi:shˀatlqo: ˀahˀa: ˀink'atl machp'alˀatl hilst'oˀasˀi. N'a:sshiˀatlma ˀahˀa:ˀatl wa:ˀatl'atah lo:tssma:kqo:s,

"Ne: sokwiˀatlchi chi:y'a:p'atlchi p'inw'alokqin shi:tlokw'a:ni."

"ˀOts'achiˀa:ni hilwi:ˀisˀi,"

wawa:m'inhˀatlma qoqwa:sˀi hiyi:staqshiˀatl tlatlo:ˀi ma:maht'i ˀanich ˀi:hˀatlit ˀoˀo:shsohtatl.

"ˀI:hˀatlita ˀo:shmaqak !" wawa:lyatlma.

Qwa:ma: wi:wi:qokqo: n'a:s qwa:ma: toto:mokqo: Nomaqimyis[17] ya:lˀatqo: tl'opa: hopalˀi, ˀatikha ˀahˀa: qwa toto:mokqo: ˀo:no:tl ˀi:h ˀo:shmaqak ˀoˀo:shsohta qwa:ma: ˀahˀa: qachtsachilshitlma ˀahˀa: qwa y'imolok ˀo:shi:n'akshitl. Wik'ahˀatlqo: tsi:qshiˀatlqo: ˀo:sh, hiy hitaˀatl'atlqo: k'i:tqy'ak hita:sˀi ˀanach'asˀitq Nomaqimyis! ˀOhok yaya:ts'a ˀoyi ts'i:qˀatlnak'a:hˀatlqo: ˀoyi.

Cho:, ˀahˀa:ˀatlma ˀi:naxi:chiˀatl qachts'eˀi nashokm'inhˀatˀi limaqsti. Wa:ma ˀanich qwiqh̲ˀato:sin wilwitach'at. ˀO:tssotlma hisy'ak ˀanah̲ˀis hisy'ak La:mah̲o:s, ˀo:tssotlma ts'axy'ak tlaˀo: ˀo:tssotlma po: t'a:ktli:yol[18] H̲o:mˀis Cha:mat'imtˀi ˀoh̲ˀatlma ˀo:tssotlma ˀinkts'o: hichi:sy'ak. Hopsaqtlma ˀani ˀokw'ichqa k'atsh̲aq yaqimtlˀitq ˀa:nasa n'eˀitlak ˀostˀasˀi tlishtlinˀatˀi wik h̲amat ˀoyi hichi:sqo: ˀoyi.

Ya:tsshiˀatlma hita:qtl'iˀatl hisi:kshitlma t'ay'asˀisˀi. Wa:ma ˀanich tlo:ltlo:la:qtl nanaˀatah̲ˀi:h̲qh̲chik qwiqo:si, qwi:toko:si k'i:tqe:ˀi k'i:tqy'ak. Hitakwal qi:kwa:l qachts'eˀi. Wika:tokw'atlma ki:kichi:lˀi. Wikˀ̲atl'atlin y'o:qwa:ˀatl qo:ˀasqin qwa:ˀatlin wik'ath̲qon ˀoyi ˀo:no:tl wikˀ̲a:tl'atl. To:h̲okw'atlin ˀani ˀo:yichi:lqa ki:kki:k wa:wichi:l ˀoyi k'ak'aminchiˀatlqon yaqwa:no:ˀatlqin ˀi:h̲ˀatl wi:kˀ̲atlsinh̲i qwam'e:ˀitq qo:ˀas.

Hininˀatlma ˀah̲ˀa:ˀatl qachts'eˀi hitah̲t'asˀatlma ˀi:qh̲shiˀatlma ˀanich wik'i:t qwiqo:si hita:qtl'asˀi ˀa:natskwisa ˀaya yatstskwi: qoˀatsi:ts ts'i:ts'i:lxˀasˀi, wiki:t Q'a:natl'aqi:ts yatstskwi:. ˀAh̲ˀa:ˀatlma wa:ˀatl H̲aw'ilˀi H̲o:mˀis,

"Ts'iˀo:tltso:ˀatlma tlaqmisokwit ˀOwimy'isit ˀani wikqa: ˀi:h̲ h̲a:h̲anaˀa:lsa ˀo:shstop tlaqmisˀi ˀo:piqa ˀoshstop, h̲a:h̲a:shto:qsap'atqon Tlo:kwa:na. ˀAni wa:qa n'a:tsi:chitlˀi, ˀanich ˀoˀo:yok ˀOwimy'isit wi:ˀ̲aqtl ˀanich wikokw'ap'at ts'iˀa:ˀa tlaqmis. Ma:nokwiˀatl'in hi:lˀih̲sa. Cho: tsak'o:p'atl'ich."

Wa:ˀatlma lo:chmaltskwiˀi,

"Cho: tsak'o:p'atl'ich," wa:ˀatlma.

ˀInkw'achiˀatl mah̲t'i:ˀi ˀi:h̲ hi:lh̲ˀitq Tlo:kwa:meˀi,

n'opoqoml ʔeʔi:h̲ ʔink, ʔinkw'achitl tsak'o:p'atl'at tlaqmisʔi ʔo:tstskwi:ʔi ʔOwimy'is ʔokla:mitʔi ʔoyiʔi qah̲shitl ʔ̲ay'i:chh̲itʔi. ʔO:ʔo:qokshiʔatl mah̲t'i:ʔi n'eʔitlshiʔatl, tsak'o:ʔatl tlaqmisʔi n'eʔitlshiʔatl ʔo:ʔo:qokshiʔatl mah̲t'i:ʔi ts'i:qshitlaʔ̲aqatlma lo:tssa:mi:h̲ʔi ʔoya:tl ʔani tsak'a:ʔatlqa tlaqmisʔi, ʔoh̲ʔo:h̲satl tsi:qshitl hi:yi:y'alh̲seʔi lo:tssa:mi:h̲ ʔo:no:tl h̲is m'inh̲ʔa:h̲ʔatlqa histaqshitlik tlatlo:ʔi ma:tma:s ʔo:no:tl ʔani ʔi:h̲ʔatlqa ʔo:shmaqak'atl.

Wik'atlma hitaʔ̲atl'atl k'i:tqy'ak, wikʔ̲atl'at, ts'iʔa:ʔatl tlaqmisʔi. ʔAtlachink'atlma yatsme:ʔiʔatl qoqwa:s. Tsak'o:ʔatlma tlaqmisʔi tlaqmisokwit ʔOwimy'isit. Ts'i:ʔ̲aqatlita lo:tssa:mih̲ yaqi: wiksilatl qwa:ʔamitʔitq wik'atlma hitaʔ̲atl k'i:tqy'ak. Wawa:ʔatlma ʔatleʔi qoqwa:s ʔiʔi:yaqh̲masʔatl qwam'e:ʔitq ma:tma:s. ʔI:qiyasama n'a:sshiʔatlʔitq kwisilatl qwa:mitʔitq ʔani ʔath̲yi:mtqa ʔi:h̲ ʔo:shmaqak n'a:sʔatlqo: ʔoyi. ʔO:yisatl hawi: ki:kʔ̲in ki:ky'ak ʔoyi ts'i:qʔ̲atl'atlqo: qwiy'iʔitq tsak'o:ʔatlʔitq tlaqmisʔi tlaqmisokwitʔi ʔOwimyis ʔokla:natʔi qo:ʔas. Wik'i:chiʔatl ʔo:shmaqakitʔi. Qwa:ma: ts'oxh̲achitlqo: ʔo:yisa qwiyiʔitq tsak'o:ʔatl tlaqmisʔi. Yaya:tspanachshiʔatlni ʔoy'o:tsachiʔatl yaqwilʔatlitqin wi:y'am'inh̲ʔatl ʔotsachitl yaya:tspanachshiʔatlni. Wik'i:chiʔatl ʔo:shmaqak wiwi:ksoh̲tanoʔatl ʔoshi:n'akshiʔatl ʔo:shi:n'akminh̲ʔi. Hi:tinqsi:schiʔatl wik'i:chiʔatl ʔo:shmis ts'i:qchi:lshiʔatl lo:tssa:mi:h̲ʔi.

Cho: ʔa:niyasatlah̲ ʔah̲ʔa: ʔoyoʔal y'imʔakwachitl Tlo:kwa:na. T'aqoqstoʔatl ya: n'a:tssi:chitlitʔi ʔo:shtaqyo lo:tssma ʔani wa:mitqa ʔanich ʔoʔo:yokshitlh̲weʔin wi:ʔ̲aqstotl ch'ih̲a:ʔatlʔi ʔOwimyis ʔani wikokw'ap'atqa tsak'a:ʔa tlaqmisokwitʔi. ʔAninʔanitsshiʔatlatqin wilwitach'at ch'ih̲a: ts'i:qʔ̲atlnak'atlqon ʔanitsʔitq wik tsak'o:tl tlaqmisokwitʔi ʔOwimyisitʔi tsak'o:p'atl'at ʔah̲ʔa: tlaqmisʔi tsak'o:tl tlaqmisokwitˀi ˀOwimyisitˀi tsak'o:p'atl'at ˀah̲ˀa: tlaqmisˀi wik'i:tshitl ˀo:tsah̲taksa kiki:kyimtˀiˀa:la ˀanach'asˀitq Nomaqimyis. Hawi:tl qwa:mitˀitq ˀo:shmaqak qwisita ˀah̲ˀa: ˀi:h̲ t'a:qoqh̲li:chitl yaqiti: ˀo:shtaqyo lo:tssma Ch'ih̲in'ak ˀokla: n'a:tssi:chitl ˀani wi:naqa ˀoh̲ ch'ih̲a:.

114. Lahal at Nitinat (La:maho:s via Alex Thomas)[1]

Hina:sitlin tsaxtqi: *Ti:s* ʔokwi:sitlin. Tlatw'i:mah̲.[2] ʔOksy'aqstakin Tlapisim[3] ʔatltaqimlin h̲achy'a:k, ʔoh̲ma:tla: H̲awi:h̲toʔis ʔoh̲ma:tla: ʔoʔi:ma H̲awi:h̲toʔis h̲achy'a:k tlaʔo: ʔanama Tlapisim ʔoʔi: Tl'i:ʔix̲im. ʔO:ty'a:pma Tlapisim mo:qomlchi tl'ah̲iqs X̲ax̲ashk'okw y'o:qwa:ma h̲awi:h̲toʔis ʔo:tya:p mo:qimlchi tlah̲iqs X̲ax̲ashk'ok ts'ama:knalin cha:kopi:h̲. Hitapomin Tlinʔowis[4] ts'aʔolama wi:qsi: ʔath̲i:. Hisoltatlin P'a:chi:naʔa ʔokwintlin Mamaln'iʔath̲ʔi. ʔoh̲ʔatin ʔona:ksapat hilʔa:h̲in weʔich.

N'a:sshiʔatlma ʔah̲ʔa:ʔatl tsiqshiʔatlin ʔah̲ʔa:ʔatl ts'i:sapiqshiʔatl ʔi:qh̲okw'atlin ʔanin hilʔatlqin P'a:chi:naʔa hoʔatsachiʔatlma tsiqy'ak wa:ʔatlma ʔoyi kow'itapqon maʔasok Tl'i:ʔix̲im, wa:ʔatlma ʔoyi kow'itapqon maʔasok Tlawobe:y. Wa:ʔatlma ʔani hilqa: ʔaya haʔom hink'o:ʔasasht ʔani haʔokwitlqin. Wi:qsi:ʔatlma kw'isa:ʔatlma wi:qsi:ʔatl. Wa:ʔatlah̲ ya:l ya:ya:qpalqin,

"Wik'i:ch qwa: ʔah̲n'i:," wa:ʔatlah̲, **"Hali:lʔa:qtl'atin Ha:naʔa tl'o:ʔi:ch chamolokqin qwa:qon ʔanin ʔa:nasaqin ʔah̲ ʔokwi wik'i:tqa hil Ni:ti:naʔath̲ P'a:chi:naʔa ʔa:nasaqin chamih̲ta hil kwi:lkwi:leʔin hat'i:sʔin !"** wawa:mah̲ ʔono:tl ʔo:h̲qa naʔo:k ha:tha:naʔaqtlminh̲ʔi.

ʔA:th̲shiʔatlma ʔah̲ʔa:ʔatl, m'alokw'atlma kw'isa:ʔatl. ʔEʔimshtimah̲ ho:ʔichotl ya:ya:qpalqin hini:ʔasʔatlsi, ʔah̲ʔa:ʔatl ya:tsshiʔatlah̲ ʔotsachiʔatlah̲ yi: saye:ʔi ʔopw'inʔisʔi saye:ʔi ʔotsachitlah̲ yi: saye:ʔi ʔopw'inʔisʔi saye:ʔi ʔotsachitlah̲ ya:tsshitl ʔath̲i:ʔi. H̲an'ah̲toʔatlah̲ ha:t'inqshiʔatlah̲. ʔOʔi:ʔisah̲ katsatl qwi:ma:p'aʔa:lʔitq ts'eʔi:ʔisʔi. Kwi:lkwi:lshiʔatlah̲ wawa:ʔatlah̲ kwi:kwi:la ʔanitli:s hiteʔitapitlqas Ha:neʔi:kqo:s, h̲atoʔaqtlikqas wikˀayaqstopitlqas k'ome:ˀi, hayim h̲iy'apitlqas, ˀoksp'intlokwitlqas lim'aqsti.

"ˀOˀashtweˀin hitaˀitap'wa:ˀatikqas,"

wawa:mah̲ kwi:lkwi:la ˀath̲iˀi m'alokwaˀatlˀi kw'i:sa:ˀatlˀi qweˀishˀatlah̲ qweˀish̲ˀatˀitqˀa:la Ha:naˀatl'atqo: ˀoyi kanish̲ˀatlah̲ yaqwintlqas ˀa:ph̲ta:y'ochsis ts'eˀi:saˀatlqo: ˀoyi. Wawa:ˀatlah̲ kwi:lkwi:la ˀanis ya:ˀalsapˀa:qtlqas, p'ax̲sa:pitlqas ˀah̲n'i: k'otk'om'aqtlok Ni:ti:naˀath̲ ya:ˀalsapitlqas Ha:neˀi:kqo:s hiteˀitapitlqas Ni:ti:naˀath̲ wawa:ˀatlah̲ ho:ˀaschikw'a:lˀatl qwam'a:pilˀitq ts'eˀi:satl. Toh̲to:h̲n'okwatlqo:s liˀa:qath̲ tl'i:kapatlqo:s toh̲to:h̲n'ok liˀa:qath̲ so:ˀatlsi so:y'akokqas Ha:naˀaqy'ak hoksa:ˀatlah̲ qwam'a:p'itˀitq ts'eˀi:satl, ts'aqi:tsp'ichiˀatlqo: ˀish ts'awa:k ts'eˀi:satl, ts'aqi:tsp'ichiˀatlqo: ˀish ts'awa:k ts'eˀi:satl, ˀah̲ˀa:ˀatlqo:s ch'inˀiˀatl ya: ta:tssisatltskwiˀi hishok.

"Cho, hiteˀitap'atlah̲ Ni:ti:naˀath̲," wa:ˀatlqo:s.

ˀAh̲ˀa:ˀatlqo:s kwi:lkwi:lshiˀatl ˀi:h̲ˀatlsi ˀo:simch'atl Ha:naˀaqsimch nono:kw'atlah̲ no:k ˀoˀoyaqh̲ ˀatlah̲ yayaqwiyaqh̲ˀa:qtlqas Ha:neˀi:kqo:s qwa:ˀamah̲ ˀah̲ˀa: h̲asi:k mo:p'ichitlqath̲ah̲ hiteˀitaphoksa: ˀokwil ts'e:ˀisi:sˀi. Hawi:ˀatlah̲ ˀah̲ˀa: m'och'ichoˀatlah̲ mo:p'ichiˀatlqas hiteˀitapqath̲. Weˀichoˀatlah̲ ˀah̲ˀa:ˀatl ˀoˀiˀatlah̲ ˀani ho:ˀich'atlqa ˀinqh̲ ˀi:qh̲i: to:pˀi hilin ˀah̲ˀa: qi:. Mo:chi:lshitlah̲ qwaqwa: hat'i:s mo: ˀath̲i:, Ha:naˀaqsimch qwa:yi:ˀatl ˀi:h̲ˀatlˀi m'alok ts'oˀichh̲ˀi ˀokwimin ˀah̲ˀa: soch'achil. Soch'ap'itin weˀich hil yaqwintlqas ts'awa:k'atlok chamih̲ta weˀich.

ˀAh̲ˀa:ˀatlin sokwiˀatl'at ˀoqomh̲ichiˀatl koˀal himinˀatl

yaʔatqin sokwitl'asʔat. Tlihshiʔatlin ʔahʔa:ʔatl
hini:tssoʔatl'at Tl'otl'omoʔin ʔoyi:qshiʔatlni hinasiʔatlin
W'a:yi[8] qwi:tsoʔokqin tlahʔatl. Hiy n'achoʔalʔatlin ʔaya
qo:ʔas Ni:ti:naʔath̲ ! Hitinqsaʔatl Ni:ti:naʔath̲
hinalts'atl'alin. ʔI:qhokw'atlin yaya:qʔi:qin hinoschisʔop'at
X̲ax̲ashk'okw'ah̲sm'inh̲ʔi ha:ʔinʔatinʔoh̲ʔatin ha:ʔinʔat
ʔO:ʔochisʔat.[9] Hiy machintlin hi:neʔitlshiʔatlma
Ni:ti:naʔath̲m'inh̲ ʔo:qts'o:w'it'asʔatl. ʔOʔi:sʔap'atin
hink'o:ʔasasht t'ila:k. ʔAh̲ʔa:ʔatlin ti:ʔisshiʔatl.
Haw'a:tomin ʔah̲ʔa: tsi:tsi:qts'in'aqpiʔatl ʔah̲ʔa:
wawa:lyo:chiʔatlma Ni:ti:naʔath̲m'inh̲ʔi.

"Hiy ha:tha:naʔaqtl'amitqo:ni ya. tla.saⁿakʔi
Ha:naʔap'i:kitnish !" wawa:lyatlma Ni:ti:naʔath̲m'inh̲ʔi.

"Wa:wasatl'ichim ʔah̲n'i: la:kshil, ʔo:ʔipsaqinqa:
Ha:naʔaʔas," wa:ʔatlah̲ tsiqshitl.

ʔAh̲ʔa:ʔatlin w'aqʔoqʔatatl. ʔOtsachiʔatlin yaqʔi:qin
histo:sqin ʔatlchi:lin ʔokwi ʔatlp'itin weʔich wa:tlin
ʔotsa:qshiʔatl'at chocho:kwaʔin masnakshiʔatlma yaya:qwʔi:qin
ha:chat'iʔatl qwam'e:ʔitq Ni:ti:naʔath̲ to:pshitlʔi. Cho:
ʔah̲ʔa:ʔatlma w'a:qʔoqshiʔatl Ni:ti:naʔath̲ hachatak'atl
qwam'e:ʔitq qo:ʔas t'a:tn'eʔisʔi lo:tssa:mi:h̲itla: ʔoyi
to:pshitl hachati:ʔitl. ʔAh̲ʔa:ʔatlqach'a tsi:qts'inaqshiʔatl
qwa:ʔa:qtlʔitq qi:ʔilin hi:l. Qi:ma: hishiml maʔasʔi
Ni:ti:naʔath̲. Cho: ʔah̲ʔa:ʔatlin sokwiʔatl'at machinoʔatlin
ʔah̲ʔa:ʔatl wik'ap'atin qi:ʔil hinʔat.shiʔatl ʔah̲ʔa:
ha:w'i:h̲atlʔi lo:tssa:mi:h̲itla: ha:tha:kwatl hilh̲ʔatlqach'a
ʔi:naxi:chiʔatl tlaʔo:ʔi maʔas. Hitakwalma qi:kwa:l
hine:ʔiʔatlma qo:ʔas ts'awa:k wa:ʔatlma ʔo:kwil ʔayeʔi
qo:ʔas.

"ʔInxa:ʔatlma Ni:ti:naʔath̲," wa:ʔatlma qo:ʔasʔi,

"Tlolˀatlma ˀi:naxyo ho:ya:lw'it'asma," wa:ˀatlma.

Hitakwalshiˀatlma ˀa<u>h</u>ˀa:ˀatl tl'o:m'a<u>h</u>siˀatlma ch'aˀakˀi, *ti:ˀi:*. ˀOˀi:sw'it'asˀatl'atma yaqwi:t'yapqin <u>X</u>a<u>x</u>ashk'ok. Hininˀatlmatla: Ni:ti:naˀat<u>h</u> ts'awa:k.

"N'eˀitlsap'atl'i ˀinkˀi: hinchiˀatlma," wa:ˀatlma.

ˀA<u>h</u>ˀa:ˀatlma ˀinkw'achiˀatl ˀinkˀi: ˀi:<u>h</u>ˀatl n'eˀitlshitl ma<u>h</u>t'i:ˀi hi:lqin. No:ˀiˀatlma hil<u>h</u>ˀatl hi:lsˀatoˀi. Hi:lˀap'atin hi:lsˀatoˀi ya:ˀaln'a<u>h</u>atlin. Katl<u>h</u>shiˀatlma ho:ya:l ˀowi:<u>h</u>tilma <u>h</u>a:w'ilatl ˀo:y'aqtln'okmaˀoqtln'okma sipto:p. Hinˀitlma ˀaya ho:ya:lˀatl nono:kw'atl ˀayeˀi qo:ˀas Ni:ti:naˀat<u>h</u>. Katl<u>h</u>shiˀatlma <u>h</u>a:t<u>h</u>a:kwatl tlolˀatlma ˀi:ˀi:naxyo. <u>H</u>achati:ˀitlma qwam'e:ˀitq <u>h</u>a:t<u>h</u>a:kwatl tsiqshiˀatlma ts'awa:k<u>h</u>ˀatl ˀi:ch'im qo:ˀas Ni:ti:naˀat<u>h</u>,

"Ho:ya:ltsk'inˀe: ho:ya:ltsk'inˀi, hisimmeˀe:ts !" wa:ˀatl.

Ho:lshiˀatlma maˀasˀi hi:na<u>h</u>w'inkshiˀatlma yaˀaqtln'okˀitq sipto:p. Qwa:ˀatlma ts'awa:kq<u>h</u>qo: qwa:ˀop milmilshˀatlma qwis ˀo:ktisˀatl'at yaqw'i:<u>h</u>tilˀitq qwa:ˀatlma ts'awa:kq<u>h</u>qo: lo<u>h</u>lo<u>h</u>sh kwi:si:tts'inl maˀasˀi. ˀO:shp'alatlin wiky'o:qin qwa:yoˀal hiya:l ˀeˀimqin qwa:n'ak'o<u>h</u>. ˀO<u>h</u>ˀa:ˀatlma noˀatap'atl. ˀAya:tlma qo:ˀas tsoma:ˀatlma ˀi:<u>h</u>ˀi: ma<u>h</u>t'i:. No:ˀiˀatlmatla: ho:lshiˀatl wi:napil<u>h</u>ˀatlma, ˀatlp'itma no:ˀitl wi:napil<u>h</u>. ˀA<u>h</u>ˀa:ˀatlma hitats'opiˀatl ts'awa:k qo:ˀas wa:ˀatlma,

"Hawi:ˀatl'i ho:ya:l."

No:ˀitlˀa:qtlma no:k Shi:wish.

Hiy hishimy'o:l Ni:ti:naˀat<u>h</u> ˀoˀi:yapilma hi:lts'aqilˀi ˀah̲ˀa:ˀatlma,

"Ho:y !" wa:ˀatl ts'awa:kqh̲.

ˀAh̲ˀa:ˀatlma h̲achatˀ̲atlinyatl mo:p'ichitlma wa: ˀah̲ˀa:ˀatlma no:ˀiˀatl tsawa:k ˀah̲ˀa:ˀatl nono:kshiˀatl qwa:ˀapˀitq. Hitatatssoh̲tatl h̲a:w'i:h̲atl ˀatla hi:hinki:ts. Mo:p'it.shitlma no:ˀ̲itl ˀah̲ˀa:ˀatlma hawi:ˀatl. ˀAh̲ˀa:ˀatlma p'achiˀatl'at H̲awi:h̲toˀis n'opqiml ta:na. P'achiˀatl'at Tlapisim n'opqiml n'on'o:pqimlayi:ˀatl'atin qwam'istaqin.

"Cho:," wa:ˀatlmatla:, **"ˀAnich tlaˀo:tla:."**

ˀIqsilatlmatla: ˀah̲ˀa: ho:ya:lshiˀatltla: h̲a:th̲a:kwatl'atlma hi:h̲inki:ts'atl. Hawi:tltla: ˀah̲ˀa: mo:pit. ˀIqsilatl'atin p'a:tlp'i:chiˀat n'o:n'o:pqimlatl'atintla: ˀatlakwalh̲shiˀatin p'a:tlp'a:yat. ˀAh̲ˀa:ˀatlma no:ˀiˀatl yaqwˀi:qin ˀah̲ˀa:ˀatl'atin ˀo:y'ah̲sitap'atin tsaqi:tsqimlayi:ˀatma Tlapisim ˀish soch'aqiml ta:na: ˀah̲ˀa:ˀatlin ˀa:ˀa:tlqimlayi:ˀa:lˀatl'at qwam'a:qin ˀokwiˀal Tlapisim. ˀAh̲ˀa:ˀatlma no:ˀiˀatl yaqwˀi:ˀitq H̲awi:h̲toˀis ˀo:y'ah̲sitap'at y'oqwa: tsaqi:tsqimlayi:ˀatma ˀish sochaqiml ta:na. ˀAh̲ˀa:ˀatlma ˀa:ˀatlqimlatl'at qwam'isteˀitqˀal. Cho: ˀah̲ˀa:ˀatlma wa:ˀatl ˀanich hawi:ˀatl,

"Chachimh̲iy'ap'atl'i haˀomˀi," wa:ˀatlma sokwiˀatl'atma X̲ax̲ashk'okˀi ˀotsay'apatl'at ˀoppiqtlilˀi.

Hina:h̲awiˀatlma ˀah̲ˀa:ˀatl hina:h̲aniˀatl *ti:*ˀi:sy'ak. K'ak'am'inˀatlma chitak'atlma ˀani haˀokw'it'asˀatlqa waˀasˀi. Hina:h̲awiˀatl'ma haˀokshiˀatl Ni:ti:naˀath̲. Haw'a:tatl hi:y wiwi:kˀ̲atlmalapoˀatlma.

Cho: ˀah̲ˀa:yiyatlah̲ tsiqshiˀatl.

"Nana:ˀatah̲malapiˀim," wa:ˀatlma Ni:ti:naˀath̲, "Nana:ˀalah̲malapiˀim," wa:ˀatlma.

"Cho:, ˀah̲ˀa: qwa:ˀatqach'a lim'aqsti," wa:ˀatlah̲, "Kamatmaʔ̲i:qtl'ap hilokqa ˀo:ˀow'at'in ˀah̲ko:, ˀi:qh̲i:ˀap qwa:ˀakitˀitq yaqwa:tstskwiˀitq yaʔ̲a:nitˀitq wawa:ˀat ˀani ˀoh̲okqa ˀoˀo:ˀow'at'in ˀah̲ko: yaqw'i:ˀatlqin, qwa:no:ˀatlˀitq hinat.shiˀatl n'a:chpanachatl ˀo:ˀow'at'inˀakˀi. Cho:, n'a:tssa:tlah̲ qwa:ˀatlˀitqak, Ni:ti:naˀe:th̲, ˀanik wiwi:kchilˀatlokh̲sok no:kno:kokˀitqak hinki:tsimˀakˀitqak ˀoy'akokˀitqak hinki:tsimˀakˀitqak ˀoy'akokˀitqak ˀah̲ qwaqwa:ˀatlqin ya:qinlqas n'an'a:chay'al n'a:tssa:tlsi ˀa:na:tl ˀo:n'ak'oh̲ˀatlsi qwe:ˀi:tqak pisatokw'atl qwa:ˀatlqo:weˀin ˀah̲ko: yatya:qwatstskwiˀitqak y'o:qwa:, Ni:ti:naˀe:th̲, ˀanik takwa:qh̲sok y'o:qwa: hista:l ya: Ho:ʔ̲i:ˀath̲ ˀoklˀe:ˀi hiyilˀitqak ˀah̲ko:, qwa:no:tliti:chˀa:la ˀotsachiˀatlqo: Ni:ti:naˀath̲ ya: qwiˀath̲qin, ˀo:no:tl qi:ˀatl qwa tlolst'al.[10] Cho: qwa:no:tl y'oqwa: ˀah̲ko: ta:kwamis Ni:ti:naˀath̲ hiˀi:s ya: Ho:ʔ̲i:ˀath̲[11] ˀokle:ˀi, ˀo:no:tl qwe:ˀi:tq ˀani pipi:sal hiqa ˀokle:ˀi h̲a:kwa:tl, qwano:tlˀitq takwamis Ni:ti:naˀath̲ hiˀi:s ya: Ho:ʔ̲i:ˀath̲ ˀokle:ˀi. Tlolˀatleˀits tlolˀatleˀits maˀe:s tlolˀa:qtl'atlokwah̲ ˀiyaqh̲mis walshiˀi:kqo:s ˀoyi n'a:tssa:tlsi ˀo:n'ak'oh̲ˀatl ˀah̲ qwe:ˀi:tqak.

Cho:, kwikwiswa:qtl'atlah̲ taka: ˀateˀish qwa:ˀakwaˀap Mamaln'i wi:kiy'apˀa:qtl'atni qwa: ˀah̲ko: qwa:ˀatlqin wi:kiy'apˀa:qtl ˀo:ˀoshowa haˀok ˀani tlolˀatlqin qwa:ˀatlqin ˀah̲ko ˀanitl'i:w'aqatlqa hiyi:l ˀayeˀi qoqwa:s ˀo:sa:h̲atl ˀanin ˀa:yoqatlqin haˀok," wawa:mah̲ tsi:qtsi:qa.

Cho: ˀah̲ˀa: hi:stm'intlah̲ ˀah̲ˀa:.

Cho:, ˀah̲ˀa:ˀatlma tsiqshiˀatl H̲in'aʔ̲om ʔ̲a:ʔ̲a:tiqshiˀatlma y'o:qwa:ʔatl Hin'aʔom hiy'iqwama ʔa:ʔa:tiqa ʔoʔowama ʔa:ʔa:tiqa ta:na yaqna:kshitlqin. Cho: hawi:ʔatlma ʔahʔa:.

Cho: tsiqshiʔatlma Ni:ti:naʔath Tl'iloxwaʔa wa:ʔatlma,

"Wa:wasameʔits wawa:tso:ʔa:niti:," wa:ʔatl'atin, **"Ha:chach'itleʔits wawa:tliti:s y'o:qwa siy'a:qitqo:s ts.shi:qtsi:qa hisi:k'a:hiti:s. ʔA:nachilʔa:qtl'atlah ʔatiqshiʔatl haʔomʔi,"** wa:ʔatlma, **"T'aqoqtleʔits wawe:ʔitqak ʔahn'i: ʔani ʔa:nimtqa qwa: hiʔi:s Ni:ti:naʔath Ho:ʔi:ʔath ʔokle:ʔi. Cho: qwatla: ʔahko: hiʔi:s y'o:qwa: Ho:ʔi:ʔath Ni:ti:naʔath nism'a:kʔi."**

ʔAhʔa:ʔatlma ʔa:ʔa:tiqshiʔatl haʔomʔi ʔanich ʔoshy'akshiʔatl tlolʔatl haʔok. Cho: hawi:ʔatlma ʔahʔa: ya:tsshiʔatlma.

ʔOʔaktlatin hini:ʔasʔatl. ʔOʔiʔatlin ʔani hilqa: toshqak'atl hi:lsʔatoʔi qo:ʔas ha:w'i:hatl Ni:ti:naʔath.

"Cho:, wikhin Ha:neʔi:chiʔatl ?" wa:ʔatl'atin.

"Cho:cho:, Ha:neʔi:chiʔatl'in," wa:ʔatlah.

"Ha:neʔi:chiʔatl'in," wa:ʔatlmaʔal hachatak'atl.

Qwam'a:qin chitakshiʔatlah ʔanin Ha:neʔi:chitl'asʔatl. ʔI:hʔatlah chitakshiʔatl ʔanis hawilchatlqas Ha:naʔaqsimchchatl.

Cho:, ya:tsshiʔatlin ʔotsachiʔatlin hilhʔa:qtli:ch'in. Wi:nappiʔatlin machinoʔatl. ʔAyi:chiʔatlma qo:ʔas ʔayi:chiʔatl, maksohtatlin tsaqi:tsqimlokwin ta:na: ʔish h̲ayoqwiml. ˀOˀokwinkshitlin W'a:yi:ˀath̲.[12] Hitachinkshiˀatlin ˀah̲ˀa:ˀatl wikin qi:chitl hiteˀitap'atlni sokwiˀatlin ta:ne:ˀi ˀo:tsi:chiˀatl. Tlakishiˀatlma ya:l yayaqwinkitqin ha:ˀinchiˀatlma Tlo:ˀowisˀath̲ˀi[13] ya:l.

"Hinat.shiˀatl'i qwam'e:ˀitqak Tlo:ˀowisˀath̲ h̲aˀoˀiˀa:ni," wa:ˀatlma.

Maksoh̲tatlma Tlo:ˀowisˀath̲ ˀowi:ˀatlma maksoh̲ta ˀayi:chiˀatlokma tlah̲ˀatl ˀayats'asˀath̲ ta:na:, maksoh̲tamin y'o:qwa: qwaˀi:y'ap'atlin qwam'a:ˀakˀitq. Hiy, hitachmkshiˀatlintla ˀi:h̲ˀatlin Ha:naˀatl ! ˀAˀayachink'atlin ˀaya:tlma qo:ˀas ya:ˀal. ˀAtlakwalin ˀa:ˀatlakwalaschimin. Chitak'atlah̲ qwa:ˀatlqin ˀo:no:tl wawa:mitqas kwi:kwi:la Ha:naˀaqsimchqas ˀoyi. Qi:chinkin hiteˀitap'atlintla: Tlo:ˀowisˀath̲ ˀo:yoqwa. Sokwiˀatlintla: ta:ne:ˀi ˀo:tsi:chiˀatl. Cho: tlakishiˀatlmatla: y'o:qwa Tlo:ˀowisˀath̲.

"Cho: kwa:tl'ichak," wa:ˀatlmatla: y'oqwa Cha:mat'akˀi P'a:chi:naˀath̲,[14] **"H̲aˀoˀi:ˀin y'o:qwa: yaqin P'a:chi:naˀath̲,"** wa:ˀatlmatla y'o:qwa:.

ˀAyi:chiˀatlokma hitapatlma qwam'a:ˀakitˀitq Tlo:ˀowisˀath̲ makwinksap'atlintla: ˀoˀomh̲i:chitlokwin qwam'e:ˀakˀitq. Hachatak'atlma na:ˀo:qsta Ni:ti:naˀath̲. Ha:ne:ˀi:chiˀatlintla:. ˀI:h̲ˀatlah̲ Ha:naˀatl tsoma:ˀatlah̲ Ha:naˀa ! Qwa:ˀatlah̲ t'apsshitltskwiqo:s hi:si:ˀato ch'aˀakˀi ˀo:no:tl ˀi:h̲ˀatl tl'opsimh̲i pipi:sath̲i ho:ya:l, wi:kˀaqtl hiteˀitl. Tlawa:ˀatlma n'a:sshitl ˀah̲ˀa:ˀatlin hiteˀitap'atl. Sokwiˀatlintla: ta:ne:ˀi ˀo:tsi:chiˀatl qachts'op'it'i:tapshiˀatlni.

"Hawi:ʔatlin," wa:ʔatlma Ni:ti:naʔath̲.

ʔAh̲ʔa:ʔatlin yatskwachiʔatl walkwachiʔatl. Cho: hi:stm'intlin ʔah̲ʔa: ʔah̲ʔa:ʔatlah̲ wa:ʔatl qwem'istaqin,

"Cho:, wik'atl'ichim hoʔa:s Ha:naʔa hite:ʔitlo:seʔitso: walshitlʔa:qtl'atlah̲," wa:ʔatlah̲, ʔah̲ʔa:ʔatlah̲ walshiʔatl ya:tsshiʔatlah̲ ʔotsachiʔatl Tsaxts'a:ʔa.[15]

ʔAh̲ʔa:ʔatlweʔinʔal Ha:naʔatl wik'i:t'atlqas ʔoyi hitaʔiʔatlʔal qachts'op'it'i:tlweʔinʔal. Cho: ʔah̲ʔa: hi:stm'intlma h̲achatakshiʔatlma. Qwa:ma: ʔah̲ʔa: Ha:naʔaqmis ʔo:shtsokma Ha:naʔaqtl'at, ʔoshtsokma hat'i:sʔat ʔo:simch'at ʔani hiteʔitapʔa:qtl'atqa ha:th̲a:naʔaqtlokʔi ma:tmas ʔanitli hayimh̲iy'ap'at k'omeʔi yayaqwink'atʔitq. Wikcho:qh̲ʔatl'atqo: ʔo:simchcho: Ha:naʔat hi:teʔiʔatl'at ʔah̲ʔa: wik'atl'at hiteʔitap ʔi:h̲ʔatlat w'aw'imsat we: h̲acho:qh̲ʔatlat ʔah̲ʔa: Ha:neʔaqsimchchat sa:ch'itso:ʔokw'ap'atl'at hi:teʔitap'at. T'aqomsma ʔo:simtmis.

115. How a Man Mishandled Beaver Power *(Sa:ya:ch'apis via Sapir)*[1]

ʔOʔoʔihweʔin miʔa:t ʔi:ch'im wik ʔa:naq̱ ʔi:ch'im qo:ʔas,
wik'atl saya: wik'i:t.shitl miʔa:t[2] tl'imshyaqmi:ʔatl
qo:ʔasʔi. Ho:ʔak hina:chitl ʔati̱: wiky'o:ʔi n'a:sshitl.
N'a:sshitl ʔachknaẖʔis n'a:s qatow'a:t ʔi:q̱he: ʔati̱:.
Hinasitl ʔO:qtl'as[3] ʔohak nism'aʔi ʔimti. Hi:lapas
ẖa:w'i:ẖatl ʔatltla kw'a:kw'a:lqe.

"Weẖhe:seʔi ha:ʔinʔateʔits ʔoẖat H̱aw'ilokqin," wa:ʔatl
ẖa:w'iẖatlʔi kw'a:kw'a:lqeʔi.

Wiẖhe:satl qo:ʔasʔi chi:san'a:p'atok ch'apats, hinni:ssoʔat
qo:ʔasʔi wik saya: maẖt'i:ʔi ʔi:ẖ. Hinni:ʔitl.

"Hilʔatlm'o::: !" wa:ʔatl.

"Hinnatsap'i," wa:ʔatl H̱aw'ilʔi.

ʔOʔi:ʔilʔap'at ya: qo:ʔasʔi hi:lts'aqilʔi. N'achoʔal hi:l
ʔayeʔi tl'a:q qwa:sasa qwe:ʔi:tq ʔi:ẖto:p tl'a:qʔi, ʔonna:k
tl'in'imch tla:qʔi mi:lẖi: ʔi:ẖto:p qwe:ʔi:tq.

"Cho ch'ichiʔicẖ ya:yil tl'a:qʔi," wa:ʔatl H̱aw'ilʔi,
"Tl'a:ʔi:sʔe:ʔit ya:yil qo:ʔasʔi."

Ch'ichitl ẖa:w'iẖatlʔi.

"ʔAya:p'ichim ch'ichitl," wa:ʔatl.

Tl'imshitlshiʔatl lo:tssa:maẖʔe siqachitlok. ʔAyaqtl'as
qo:ʔas ʔats'iksʔatẖ maʔasʔi takwa ʔo:kwi:l ch'a:ẖach'a:ẖa
hi:yishtop, ʔo:kwi:l ẖay'im ʔo:kwi:l ʔoxwa:p, takwa

kw'a:lqi: maˀasˀi.

"Cho ha:?̲inchiˀatl'i yaya:q chiqtl'asqin. Chokwa haˀok Kw'a:lap'almiˀe: !"[4] tlaˀo:ktla wa:, **"Kw'a:lap'almiˀe: !"**

Ch'o:chkil wawa: minkshitl ˀih̲ˀi mah̲t'i

"Kw'a:lap'almiˀe: !" n'opp'i:lok ?̲imti ch'o:chki:ts ?̲imti n'opp'i:lok.

Wa:qˀokshitl maˀasˀi, t'iqpitl hisi:k hi:lts'aqilˀi minikshitl mah̲t'i:ˀi.

"Wik'in ch'a:ni haˀok cha:niˀin no:ˀitl," wa:ˀatl maˀasˀi, **"Naˀa:tah̲ˀap'in ya:yil qo:ˀasˀi."**

No:ˀiˀatl no:k maˀasˀi.

> ***"Ha:ya::::***
> ***Niwa::::***
> ***Ha::ˀaya::shiwa::::   ˀaˀa:ya::::***
> ***Ho:::wi h̲owˀe"***[5]

wa:ˀatl maˀasˀi ya:tya:tatl.[6]

Hawi: nono:k maˀasˀi haˀokshiˀatl tl'a:qˀi. Qwa:sasa qwe:ˀi:tq ˀi:h̲to:p tl'a:qˀi tlaqmis ˀo:tsoˀokwˀah̲ qwe:ˀi:tq ˀi:h̲to:p.

"ˀAyi:sap'i qo:ˀasˀi !" wa:ˀatl H̲aw'ilˀi.

Haˀokshiˀatl qo:ˀasˀi haˀokshiˀatl Kw'a:lap'almiˀashtaqiml. Hawi: haˀok matlh̲sa:nop'atl'atok qo:ˀasˀi m'a:moti:lshiˀatl'ak.

"M'aw'inqsan'apchip'atl'ichak."

M'aw'inqsan'apchip'atl h̲a:w'ilatlˀi.

Hil to:pshiˀatl hini:ˀasˀatl mah̲t'i:ˀi qo:ˀasˀi hinna:chiˀatl qo:ˀasˀi, walshiˀatl mah̲t'i:ˀakˀi hitassaˀatl mah̲t'i:ˀakˀi ˀanaˀath̲ tsawa:ˀath̲ lo:tssma:kˀi ˀish h̲a:kwa:tlˀisokwˀi. Hinne:ˀitl mah̲t'i:ˀakˀi qo:ˀasˀi.

"Sokwitlchi hiy'ah̲sokwah̲ m'a:mot ch'apatsˀi."

Sokwitl t'an'eˀisˀi. Wi:katl tl'a:qi, wik'i:t tl'a:qqo:. Hoˀatsachitl ˀe:ˀe:ˀisha.

"Wik'i:tma," wa:ˀatl n'ow'i:qsakˀi.

"Hiy'ah̲sma ch'apats," wa:ˀatl t'an'eˀisokwˀi, **"Matlh̲sa:ma tl'a:q."**

Hoˀatsachiˀatl n'ashshiˀatltla t'an'eˀisˀi. Wi:katl ˀa:nasa hilyinˀi hiy'ah̲s matlh̲sa: ˀiniksy'i.

"Ha:ni, tl'a:qma hiy'ah̲s ch'apats'i ! Sow'a:ˀ̲atlchi sokwitl," wa:ˀatl lo:tssma:kˀi.

Hinni:ˀasˀatl lo:tssmeˀi. Wi:kaˀatltla tl'a:qˀi lo:tssmeˀi ˀa:nasa hiy'ah̲s matlh̲se:ˀi ˀinikssy'i, sokwiˀatl lo:tssmeˀi hinni:sˀatl hinne:ˀitl mah̲t'i:ˀakˀi. So:ˀatl ˀah̲ qwa: matlh̲se:ˀi ˀinikssy'i.

"Wik'i:tma tl'a:q ˀanama ˀah̲ko: qaqmaptˀi."

T'ichitl lo:tssmeˀi hilh hi:lpi:ˀilˀi. Katlhshitl qaqmapt ˀamashanlˀi ˀaˀamas qasi:ˀi ta:ch'eˀi tlitli:hsswi qaqmaptiˀi.[7] ˀAtwe:ˀinch'aʔashqwa: ʔat'o: maˀasˀi ya:qwilitˀitq hinne:ˀitl. ˀOhakweˀinch'aʔashqwa: ʔat'o: maˀasˀi ya:qwilitˀitq hinne:ˀitl. ˀOhakweˀinch'aʔashqwa: haˀom tl'a:qok qaqmaptˀi. Wik'ahs miʔa:tˀi qo:ˀasˀi.

"Tosha:kah we:ˀi ! Toshe:k ! Hilh maˀas ʔO:qtl'as ˀani wik'i:t maˀas wa:ˀakitlsok lim'aqsti wik'i:t maˀas ˀokwi !"

Ta:ta:tsswi qaqmapt yaʔisitˀitq haˀok ˀotsachitlkwachiˀatl[8] maht'i:ˀakˀi hitasaˀatlˀitq, n'achoˀalkwachiˀatl[9] m'a:motokwˀi tl'a:q tl'a:qokwˀi maˀasˀi hilhitˀitq haˀok. Tlihsswi:ˀatl qaqmapt hishsa:tsatˀi ˀannachak'atˀitq ˀositatˀi. ˀOhma: kamat.sap ˀani tl'a:qok haw'in ʔat'o: ˀoha:k qaqmaptˀi.

No:ˀiˀatl ˀah qo:ˀasˀi naˀa:tahˀap'atl lo:tssma:kˀi, no:ˀeˀatl mo:p'i:lˀi no:k ˀo:tsˀi no:k ʔat'o:. Qahshiˀatl qo:ˀasˀi hawi:ˀatlˀitq nonno:k. Takwi:chiˀatqa ʔasp'atatˀi qaqmapt ˀinikssy'i. Hina:chitl lo:tssmeˀi hini:ssoˀatl t'an'eˀisokwˀi. ˀOtsachiˀatl hilˀi:tq maˀas ˀayeˀi Ho:choqtlisˀath.

116. *Sa:ya:ch'apis Meets a Storm* (*Sa:ya:ch'apis via Thomas*)[1]

Ya:shmalin ʔaẖ n'a:s tlo:lapiʔisʔi ḥa:sitlni to:pshitl
ko:ne:ʔi, qachts'aqimy'aẖsin Si:xo:lmi:k.[2] Tlicha:ʔatlsi
ʔoḥʔatl ya:shmal Sixo:lmi:k. Wi:qsi:chiʔatl *tla:sʔi:*
wi:wi:ʔaloky'akʔi wiḥi:ʔotlmaʔi:qstotl *Ke:ptin*ʔakqin, *Santo*
ʔoḥʔatl w'asna wiḥi:ʔotl. ʔEʔimʔama qi:ts'okwitlt'ana ʔatḥi:
ḥayop'ilchapqach'a ʔatḥi: wi:qsi:chiʔatl hinin'atl hoy'a:k
ʔeʔi:ḥ. ʔOkla:ʔakni *Lo:ʔi: Ke:ptin ʔAlipe:k*[3] ʔokla:ʔakni
ko:na: yaqwi:q.

N'a:sshitl wi:qsi:ʔatl hi:y'aqtl'aẖssaqḥʔat naʔa:ʔat
ts'isto:pm'inḥʔi qwa: t'itska:qo: ʔo:no:tl ʔi:ḥ yoʔal.
T'ikwisachisht'atlqo: yaqwi:qqin, hiy winsyaqachisht'atlqo:!
Ya:l ʔI:ẖw'anim[5] ʔaẖʔa: ʔeʔinḥmaqak hoy'a:k. ʔOts'inama
ch'i:pmeʔi *Lo:ʔi:* ch'i:pts'inap ni:sa:kchimp ʔaẖʔa:ʔatl
tlaqa:lachiʔatl ts'iʔalachiʔatl Kwinʔo:yin ʔatlḥtachinoma
qwisʔap yaqwintlqin ʔa:ni ʔopy'ak. Qatkwachʔatl hoy'a:ki
ʔo:sa:ẖatl tlaqmisʔi yaqwa:lachisht'atlqin matla:lachisht
qwa:qwachimin ʔaẖʔa: n'a:sshitl. Tlaʔo:ʔasʔatlqo:
ḥa:w'i:ẖatl.

"Qaẖak'atlch'insh," wa:ʔatlqo:.

ʔAẖʔa:ʔatlaẖ wa:y'aqstoʔatl ʔi:naxi:chitlqo:s. Sokwitlaẖ
tl'opa:pi:ẖokqas tlitliḥʔaq m'och'ichotlaẖ, hitach'ichotlaẖ
ʔat'aqimlokqas chaqswi, hitach'ichotlsi *ko:tokqas*
ʔat'aqimlaqaq soch'aqimy'istskwaksi hist'atḥ Hiko:l *Mista
No:kom*.[6] Weʔich'atl Ts'isha:ʔatḥ. Qatw'a:t'atlitqach'ana
qaẖak ts'awa:k tsiqmanak yaqiti: Pishʔaktlim ʔokla:.
P'ishsoqstoʔatlaẖ hi:hi:qwi:ʔaschi:laqeʔi ʔani ʔaʔaniwaqa,
"Qaẖak'atlchinsh" wawa:lyoʔaqa.

"ʔO:qwatokma Hiyil ! Hani hawi:ʔatlʔich wawa: !" wa:maẖ

chichilshitl h̲a:w'i:h̲atlˀi. **"Ti:chikin. 'ˀA:nasaweˀin ti:ch wih̲i:ˀotl Ts'isha:ˀath̲,' wa:ˀatikin ma:tma:s,"** wa:mah̲. **"Wa:ˀatl'i ˀah̲n'i: H̲aw'e:l !"** wa:ˀatl'atah̲ ˀA:m'a:qchik,[7] **"Kwisto:psilatl'in ˀanik kwisto:p ˀo:cho: ˀokla: h̲aw'il. Ti:ch'ap'isim hini:tss se:ˀeˀisim,"** wa:ˀatah̲ ˀA:m'a:qchik.

Hini:ˀassi lilmi:y'amah̲ˀat matlshitl ˀah̲ t'oh̲ts'itatqas tsi:tsi:y'ih̲teˀi ˀatasish ˀeˀimqh̲ y'akwa:s t'i:t'iˀatoqoxschatl ˀo:no:tl ˀi:h̲ nashok po:x̲wa: yoˀi wi:qsi:.

"Ka:ˀatsskapo:h̲ matlto:p," wa:ˀatlah̲ yaya:qchisqas.

Matlshiˀatlah̲ ˀah̲ˀa: ma:ʔ̲i:tl'anop'atl ts'isto:ptskwiˀisˀi ˀoh̲tinˀap'atl qwa:qh̲ˀatlah̲ ˀah̲ˀa: hoˀi:ˀas hini:ˀas, tlawasˀatah̲ *Tik*[8] ʔ̲imt.shˀanit.

Hiy taka:tsyintlma ˀatleˀi hilyinˀi tlaqsim ˀotsachitlma, ˀanamah̲ ˀotsachitl tliche:ˀi tlaqsim. ˀOˀi:p'ichasah̲ hina:p'iqshitlah̲ ˀokatlah̲ ˀoch'akokwich Na:we:ˀi:kich'a wi:qsi: hina:p'aqy'ak ˀoch'akok wi:qy'a:noˀatlqo: ˀoˀo:tah̲qh̲ qwa:no:tlqh̲i:ch ˀo:ʔ̲aqstotl wi:qsi:, ˀah̲ˀa:ˀatlah̲ hi:talokshiˀatl hisi:kah̲ no:chyo: tsi:qtsi:qa ˀi:qh̲ok hisi:kah̲ hi:naˀisˀi Ts'o:maʔ̲as[9] ˀi:qh̲ok qwana:nakqas ˀah̲ˀa:.

"ˀO:sa:h̲ˀi tloyachitl tloyay'aʔ̲asah̲ so:til," wawa:mah̲, **"Ya:qsa:h̲iˀitqakˀa:la ˀoqomh̲iy'apchip si:chil ˀoyi hisi:k'atlqo:s ˀah̲ tsitsiqink so:til H̲aw'e:l !"** wawa:mah̲.

Kaˀopshitlah̲ yaqla:ˀakqas ʔ̲oyi ˀoksy'i ˀo:qomh̲iy'apy'ak ˀo:ts Na:we:ˀi:kich'a ˀo:qomh̲iy'apy'ak ˀah̲ˀa:ˀatlah̲ tlicha:noˀatl hawi:tlqas ˀoyi.

"Wik'im wi:ˀakshiˀa:h̲ wawe:ˀitq qo:ˀas," wa:ˀatl'atah̲

Lo:ˀi: ˀani wih̲i:ˀotl wawa:qa. **"Qwa:qwachatlin ti:ch ˀah̲ko: ˀanin hilts'a:toqin. Wik'i:t'atlma yo:l wih̲i:ˀeˀi,"** wawa:ˀatah̲. **"ˀOyo:sin qah̲shitl ˀoyi liˀa:ˀapqom ˀap'aqolˀi Ts'oma?̲as, ˀa:nasatlma yo:lna:k,"** wawa:ˀatah̲ *Ke:ptinˀ*akqin. **"Wa:w'it'asqasqo: wikmíh̲saqas wih̲i:ˀotlqon ˀoyi ˀanin qwa:qwachaqin ti:ch ˀanin wikqin wih̲i:ˀotl."**

"Ka:ˀak ˀah̲n'i: m'itlˀinˀi t'aqalˀap'i m'itlaxsimˀi ˀah̲n'i:," wa:ˀatlma *Lo:ˀi:* siqi:takˀi ˀo:kwil.

ˀOkchi:siˀatlah̲ *Lo:ˀi:* so:ˀatl tlich'yakˀi ˀaˀaptsaˀa:lokw'atl yaqwi:qqin, t'a:kaqtlsinh̲atlni ˀa:nah̲i. N'op'itts?iqimlokqatssa hawi:ˀatlqas hi:talokshitl. Toshe:k ! ˀOya:silatl ˀah̲ hina:yilˀi, kistaqswatl m'itle:ˀi ?oy'ih̲taqshiˀatl ˀani m'itla: t'aqsi:ˀilw'ayaˀak'atl ! Hiy Toshe:k ! Wa:kitswima k'ah̲pi:lts'intl ˀah̲ko: t'a:qtsqi:ˀakqin!

Hiy t'awatskshiˀatltla: qwa:ˀapˀitq ˀani hinasoqwa yaqwi:qqin *ko:ne:ˀ*i ! Toshe:k, tl'iqh̲sa:no:ˀatl ya?̲ih̲teˀitq ts'ityanim ˀo:sa:h̲atl wi:qsi:ˀi ! N'itlkwaqshiˀatl Hoshe:k *Si:nas*sa:ˀath̲, wiklm'a:ma hinosa *sipyanimˀ*akqin ˀono:tl ?̲ots'o: ts'ityanimˀakqin. Hina:tsyanoˀatl *Si:nas*sa:ˀath̲. Qi:kwa:l?̲atlqo: hinˀato Mamaln'im'inh̲ˀi ˀoyi t'awatskshiˀatlqo:, tlichshitlma Hoshe:ki cha:mo:lsapt'ana:ma. Hiy ˀa:nima wih̲chintl *Si:nas*sa:ˀath̲ ! Matlh̲sa:nop'atl ˀiqsilap ch'ityanimˀi *Si:nas*, ˀanitsin chama: ˀanitsˀitq ma:tlma:tla *Si:nasˀ*i. Hiy, n'achoˀalin hilqa: n'isx̲kwist'ah̲s hischits'oˀitq tlih̲ts'o: *sipyanimˀ*i hilyinˀi tlama ! Mo:minkkwists'otsh'a?̲ashqo: tlih̲kwists'o tlatsst'o:qsimˀi ˀaneˀi: ˀah̲ˀa: tlih̲kwisas hiniqsˀi mo:minkwisas Hoshe:k ! N'itlkwa?̲aqstotlma *Lo:ˀi:* qwisokˀitq *ko:na:*.

"ˀA:qinh̲in li:ˀa:h̲olˀatlh̲in qwiˀath̲qin," wa:ˀatlah̲ *Lo:ˀi:*.

Tl'op'inˀatlma tl'opswa:qtlatlma. Kachiˀatlma *Lo:ˀi:* nism'aqalˀi.

"Hilˀatlin ˀam'a:ˀach'insh ˀi:qhi: Hom'o:w'a,"[10] wa:ˀatlma.

"Cho: wihi:ˀoˀatl'in hatso:ˀat ˀanich'in ˀahn'i: ˀam'a:ˀa ˀi:qhi: Ho:m'o:ˀwa," wa:ˀatlah.

"Matlalaˀap'ap'i ma:tlˀitqinh kilano:s. Ha:ˀinchiˀi," wa:ˀatlˀatah.

Ha:ˀinchitlah ˀahˀa: qwam'istaqin.

"ˀOhˀap'ichim tl'atstl'a:tsqo: mo:qoml," wa:ˀap'atah.

Wik'atl *Santo* y'aksp'intl w'a:y'i:hatlma ˀani ˀoˀashtqa wik'ap wihi:ˀatl ˀani tsiˀinˀatlqa. Ha:chato:ˀatlˀat tsitsiˀinˀat qwam'istaqin ˀohˀat. Hiy li:tsapoˀatlin ˀahˀa: ts'axp'ichesma *tli:qi:htim*ˀi w'itskkwisas ˀani:sila hinihtolˀi hachat'aqtl tl'ach'aqtl ch'ityanimˀi ˀish ˀapw'inqsˀi li:tsapim, y'o:qwa:ma hachat'aqtl tl'ach'aqtl. Hiy tlichshiˀatlma *Lo:ˀi: ko:ne:*ˀi tak'o:p'atl, si:kshiˀatl toshe:kitˀi *ko:na:*mitˀi ! Sa:si:chp'inˀatlokwin yi:l matlahˀatl k'ilano:s, soch'i:lqach'a ˀe:ˀinchp'in matlshitl ˀatlqiml tl'atstl'a:tsˀi k'ilano:s, ˀatlqimltla: hilhiltsaqsˀi hilyinˀi. ˀOkwintl matlshitl. Mo:qomlalachitlin tl'atstl'a:tsˀi k'ilano:s ˀo:tsm'inh k'ilano:sˀi Tich'i:nim[11] wikitm'inhˀatl ˀa:nahi tl'ihaq.

Si:kshiˀatl *ko:ne:*ˀi yaqwi:qqin, qwama: ti:chachitlqo: kiki:shhichitl ˀo:no:tl ˀi:h si:ka:. Hi:kwalˀatlqon ts'ipt'axshitlik si:kasiˀatlqon ˀono:tl ˀeˀi:hmaqak ! Qathtachiˀatlqo: hoy'a:kˀi ˀo:sa:hi tlaqmisokˀi k'ilano:sˀi. Wikin qi:tl si:ka:, hiy nism'aqoˀalˀatlni hamopshitlni ˀani

Ch'ito:kwachist[12] ˀoh̲qa: ! Hiy n'achoˀalnitla: tlaˀo:ˀatla: nism'a, h̲amot.shitlnitla: ˀani ˀoh̲ˀatlqa Ts'isha: !

"Wa:sats'opitl'a:qtlh̲in ?" wa:ˀatl'atah̲ *Lo:ˀi: Ke:ptin*ˀakqin.

"Hisats'opiˀin Ts'isha:, m'oshink'atlqach'a: ya: ˀoh̲ Ho:m'o:w'a. Wik'i:t'atlokqach'a ˀoh̲ t'ashi:."

N'a:tssi:chitlni ts'aˀoleˀi ya:l *ko:na:* ˀatlqiml, n'a:tssi:chitlni n'opqimlma qachˀits'iqok tlaqsim hiy'aqtl'ih̲tama Ch'ito:kwachisht, n'opqimlch'aˀ̲ashqo: ˀatlts'iqok tlaqsim ˀihaqaqh n'opqiml *ship* qachˀits'iqpiqs, tsotsomch'aˀ̲ashqo: chita:l. Qah̲ak'atl h̲ima:ˀatl'a:h̲ˀatl li:tsapi:k ˀani ta:ˀoˀatlqa hi:kwalˀatl t'i:qsti:no:k ts'eˀi:ˀeˀi wih̲ˀe:ˀeˀi. Kih̲shiˀatl ya: hi:taˀotlˀi *ko:na: ship*ˀi:, n'a:tssi:chitlsa ˀani ya:lqa: ch'apatsasqa hi:taˀotlˀi ya:l *ko:na:*.

"Toshe:km'e:nh̲ hina:siˀichak ! Hilokqach'a ˀah̲ˀa: t'ashi: ! Ya:lma: ch'apatsas *ko:ne:*ˀi wi:h̲oˀotl. Hina:siˀichak tl'iqh̲sa:nop li:tsapimˀi," wa:ˀatl *Si:nas*okˀi *Ke:ptin*ˀi Qatqyo: !

ˀAteˀish ˀowi: li:tsapotl ˀatlts'iqpiqsˀi. Si:kshiˀatl qa:qatqyimtˀi *ship*m'inh̲ˀi hi:si:kwi:ch'atl k'ah̲e:ˀi ˀana:ts'atoqchikˀits'atl. Qwa:ma: ˀa:na:qinkˀits'atlqo: hilˀi: ˀa:minksteˀi Ts'isha: qwa: p'a:tsinkstatlqo: n'a:n'imsak'atl ˀoh̲ Ho:m'o:w'a. K'ah̲a: hosmatqts'os m'oshink'atl k'ah̲a: wik'i:t'atlok t'ashi: ˀo:no:tl ˀi:h̲, p'iyachitl wi:qsi:chitl. Hiy ! Qa:qatqyoˀi hisats'inoˀatl ˀa:ni y'o:qwa: hisats'intlqin *ship*m'inh̲ˀi ˀatlqiml yoˀa:ˀatl kwaˀat yaqwintlˀitq h̲isˀa:h̲ˀatl tl'ax̲kwist'aˀa:, sa:ch'itso:ˀokw'atl ta:tssist'aˀa si:kts'intl ˀotsah̲tachitl yi:. ʔAtoy'aqtlis[13] hi:na:p'alˀi Hi:kwis *shipm*'inhˀi.

T'ayo:kwiˀatlni ni:wa ˀoˀi:ts'osˀatl Tl'atl'inqowis[14] yaqqin *kona* hita:ˀatatl Ts'isha:ˀath kilʔa:ˀatlok ch'apats. ˀOˀaktlatlin ni:w'a hita:ʔato ˀanin ˀoˀapolasokqin ni:w'a ch'apats. Tlahti:p'atin tla:wa:noˀatlqin Ch'ili:t n'a:tssi:chiˀatlni ts'aˀolaˀi, ho:p'atoma Ch'ili:t kwaxn'a:qanoˀat ya:lˀat saya:ch'a ˀo:no:tl ˀi:h wi:qsi: ˀeˀi:hmaqak top'alˀi.

Shiqo:ˀahshˀatah n'achkomqtliqsiˀat Si:xo:lmi:k ˀo:no:tl ˀi:h to:hshitl qwe:ˀitq hisi:kw'aˀaqin ˀi:h ˀeˀi:hmaqak, qwahta:mah ˀahˀa: sakwʔatl yayaqqas.

"Wala:k'am ya:y'axsa Ch'i:naxt'a,"[15] wa:mah Ni:tinaqshitl Ni:tinaqt'i:ˀilshitlsi.

Wi:naqhithweˀin wa:nak Ni:ti:naˀath, ts'awa:kokweˀin himi:tss n'achalˀi ˀatimtweˀi:sh tahqh nat'o:tl tsiqshiˀatl k'a:hchi,

"Hi:mt," wa: qwa:ˀoˀatlqo: nism'eˀi.

"To:shyo: kwa:chiˀich, me:ˀiˀatin !" waˀatlweˀin.

Me:ˀitlqathˀatl'at ˀah ˀoyimtweˀin.

"Wala:k'i ya:y'ahsma Ch'i:naht'a," wa:nak'atl.

ˀOhqa:thˀap'atl Ch'i:naht'a ˀokla: ya:l himi:tssimˀakˀi ya:lwe:ˀin ˀoh ˀokla: Ch'i:naht'a hiy'athˀitq T'okw'a:ˀath hi:satsheˀitq wi:neˀi Ni:ti:naˀath, ˀahˀa: ˀo:t'iˀilshitltlah sakwʔatl Si:xo:lmi:k ˀo:kwil ˀo:ˀoktaqa ˀani ˀi:hqa: to:hokk'ok wi:qsi:ˀi. Hilts'a:tomin saya:ts'atoˀi Ho:m'o:w'a

yo:yo:y'itlata<u>h</u>   <u>h</u>o:hoqswis?atl   ch'ay'a:pok?i   wi:wi<u>h</u>isatl
ki:tlkwachi?atlok   ch'ay'a:pats   ts'e?i:yis?i   ?o:sa:<u>h</u>i.

"Wik'i: haya:qtl,"   wa:?atla<u>h</u>   Si:xo:lmi:k,   **"Siy'a:sa<u>h</u>
?a<u>h</u>ko: top'al?i   tloyay'apitla<u>h</u>,"**   wa:?atla<u>h</u>   ?i:<u>h</u>mayatl
qwa:?atl?itq   haya:qtl   n'a:tsa   ya: <u>h</u>o:<u>h</u>oqswis?atl?i.

K'a<u>h</u>a:?atlqo: hitaqo:?a   <u>h</u>assatl   Ho:m'o:w'a,   pi<u>h</u>a:?atla<u>h</u>
yaqchi?al?a:qtlqas   ya:qwila:qtlqas   hin?i:<u>h</u>.   Hiy
hi:talokshi?atlsi   ?okshi?atlsi   tin<u>h</u>sa:?asy'akokqas
hi:taloky'ak   Na:we:?i:k   ?o:ts   hi:taloky'ak.   Tli:<u>h</u>shi?atlni.
Qwa:sasama   ?a<u>h</u>   qwisqo: lo?ilim?i,   tin<u>h</u>satl   wi<u>h</u>i:sa?atlqin
hitinqis?i   Ho:m'o:w'a,   ?o:ts'issamin   t'aki:s   wik'attla:
tsitkshi?at   ?o:no:tl   tin<u>h</u>satl   !

?Ich'ay'ap'atokwin   ki:l?i?at   ?A:<u>h</u>o:s?at<u>h</u>,   ta:kowatin
yaqwi:qqin.   Kwa:<u>x</u>a:lts'isi:s   qwi:m'e:?itq   ts'ak'omts   lo<u>h</u>lo<u>h</u>sh
yaqwintlqin   ?o:?i:tstsi:?asokw'ap'at   ma<u>h</u>t'i:?akqin
ch'apatsokqin.   Tsaqi:tsts'iqas   ?A:<u>h</u>o:s?at<u>h</u>   hila:chisht
Tl'atl'inqowis.

Ts'a?olshi?atltla: qwiyiqin   wi<u>h</u>e:?i?atl
wi:k'i:t.shi?atloktla: sowi:y'ak.

"Kamat.shi?atl?itsk   ?anik   ?o:shcho: <u>H</u>aw'il,"   wa:?atl'ata<u>h</u>
?A:<u>h</u>o:s?at<u>h</u>,   **"N'opts'iqi?ashta?its   tin<u>h</u>sa:p   hi:s   top'al?i,"**
wa:?atl'ata<u>h</u>,   **"Cho: ?i:<u>qh</u>shi?atl?i,   wiky'o:ma   ?i:<u>qh</u>shitl   hil
hi:hiqsatl'i,   ?o<u>h</u>?atl'i   ?i:<u>q</u>hok,"**   wa:?atl'ata<u>h</u>.

"Top'alma   yaqi: hil   hilts'a:to?i,   wiky'o:ma<u>h</u>   qwayo?al,"
wa:?atla<u>h</u>,   **"M'itskwa:?a:qtla<u>h</u>   wikso:tlqo: ko:na:."**

Takokma   ?A:<u>h</u>o:s?at<u>h</u>,

"Hiy Qiltsmaˀ̲ath̲nit !"[17] wa:, **"Y'imqimy'o:tla Qiltsmaˀ̲ath̲ winix̲okwita** ***ko:na:*****,"** wa:.

ˀAtch'a:ˀ̲ashqo: ˀa:ni Qiltsmaˀ̲ath̲ qah̲shitl. ˀAh̲ ˀo:m'intlin.

ˀAh̲ˀa:ˀatl ˀam'i:chiˀatl ˀah̲ˀa:ˀatlah̲ h̲a:ˀ̲inˀap'atl Si:xo:lmi:k ˀ̲A:h̲o:sˀath̲ ˀo:kwil, ˀ̲asp'o:p'ap'atlisi ˀanin ch'i:san'ap'atokqin ch'apats, takwa:ˀak'amitah̲ˀa:la ˀo:shmis qwisˀatˀitq ˀo:shsilat ma:tma:s ˀoh̲ˀat, ˀo:sma: h̲aw'ilok Hashsa:th̲ ˀish N'an'achp'inyokwit. W'a:q'oqshiˀatl ˀ̲A:h̲o:sˀath̲ yatsa:qtas w'aqˀo: ˀatli:q ˀani ˀatli:qwasqa qo:ˀas *ko:ne:ˀ*i. Ni:sitl si:si:tsk'ok ˀo:kwilma ts'ichitl ni:sokqin kwaxw'ilta si:qachiˀatlˀitq ˀoyima ˀah̲ko: qwis wikh̲ma: ˀayo:lta si:si:tsk'okˀi.

"Sokwitlchi ***Tik,*****"** wa:mah̲ Si:xo:lmik ˀani Ha:naˀaqa hi:sh̲ hitinqisˀi.[18] ˀA:ni hini:ssa hine:ˀitl.

"Wa:ma:schi qo:ˀas. Kamitsokw'im h̲a:chat'im qwam'e:ˀitq qo:ˀas Ts'isha:ˀath̲ ! 'N'ashitlˀa:qtlweˀintso:,' wawe:ˀim," wa:mah̲.

Hiy wa:sqwi:mich h̲achati:ˀitl Ts'isha:ˀath̲ ! Hiy ts'i:qshitlsi ts'i:qy'a kokqas ! Hiy hixoqshiˀatl Ts'isha:ˀath̲ !

"Y'imh̲a:weˀin ˀanich h̲oqsn'i:ˀak H̲akomqh̲ ni:sna:k," wa:ˀap'atlah̲ tsiqna:k ya:l hahaqchimˀis kwaxkwists'oˀis.

No:ˀitlni ˀah̲ˀa: no:k. Ch'itinkkwitlah̲ ˀah̲ˀa: cha:mat'ak Hashsa:th̲ ˀah̲ˀa:ˀatlah̲ ts'a:tlts'a:wayi:chiˀatl, tsaqi:tschinopsi tl'isal ts'a:tlts'a:waya, ˀah̲ˀa:ˀatl tsaqi:tsqiml *ta:na:* ts'aqi:tschinop'atlsitla n'o:n'o:pqimlatltla:. Wik'i:th̲ qwis ya: h̲o:hoqswisatlʔi, wik'i:th̲ ʔ̲asp'o:p ʔani ʔoh̲ʔatqa sotlso:k' ʔ̲A:h̲o:sʔath̲ʔi. Qi:chiʔatah̲ ʔah̲ʔa: ʔo:qh̲lat ʔ̲A:h̲o:sʔath̲ ʔanitss wi:k'ith̲saqh̲ʔat mi:lh̲i:ʔat h̲aw'ilokʔi ma:tma:s ʔah̲ʔa: qwisitin h̲a:h̲a:h̲anoʔatltla.

117. Kanop the Shaman *(Sa:ya:ch'apis via Alex Thomas)*[1]

Nawa:yisitweˀin Kanop hi:s ˀapw'inqisˀi Hopitsˀath,[2] ˀApw'inˀasˀath[3] Kanop qo:ˀas ˀani:sˀis hi:laqsiˀis ts'aˀakˀisˀi ts'a:wahsoˀis, n'a:piˀi kotl'ohak milimlˀatl. Ne?i:chitlweˀin na:ˀa:ˀat tli:tli:hˀintl tla:tla:tw'eˀin. Ya:lwe:ˀin hitaqo:ˀa wi:na Ma:lts'a:s[4] tla:tla:tw'aya ! Hiy qwa: t'i:tskt'i:tskaqo: ˀo:no:tl ˀih ˀa:yo:tla:tla:tw'aya ˀi:h ˀayista wi:neˀi, ya:lwe:ˀin ˀi:haq wi:na ˀanahiqaq yi: p'inw'al.[5] Tlahqhwe:ˀin t'at'aqpanoˀat hi:sˀitq,

"Ch'ana:kshiˀin ch'a:lte:ˀin hi:s ts'aˀakˀi," wa:weˀin wi:neˀi.

Wi:napol tl'a:tl'ahachsatl hinolta Ha:wi:hatl ˀatla ch'ach'axwatsitss. Tsi:qtsi:qatl Waxni?ahsimch'a tsi:qtsi:qatl Qwayats'ahsimch'a, qwa:ˀatlqo:weˀin sitshitlqo: N'a:sˀi: ˀo:no:l ˀi:h ha:si?in ! Qwa:chil ˀahˀa: wik'i:tqh naˀa: Tlaˀo:kwiˀath wim'a:qtl'i wik'a:p'atqo: hi:lhilachisthˀi hasa:tok ˀaphti:sˀapwe:ˀin hi:nschis ch'a:lte:ˀi qa:hshiˀatl'at qa:t'yapt'a. Toshe:kitˀi Kanop t'it'imyisaˀat qa:t'yapt'a, hina:p'iqa Wiˀakw'ahsimcha hila:tsyimph yi: hilyinˀi, T'ama:. Tame:yi ya:y'ahs, Tla:chitot ya:y'ahs ˀO:shtaqyo?ahsimch'a, Ch'ich'ihink Ch'ich'ihinkˀi ya:y'ahs ˀo:mi:ko:sch'a, hiy'ahs Ya:tya:ta Ya:tya:teˀi tli:cha:tsow'atˀi hiy'ahsh Haw'iy'ahsimch'a.

Hisˀa:hˀatl tlawichik Kanop ˀani qahkwachyatl'atqa qa:ty'apt'a ˀani hopimyisˀatlqa. Ch'a:ts'inapshiˀatl ya: Ha:w'i:hatlˀi ˀatla ch'ay'a:xwatsokˀi. Hisˀa:hˀatl Kanop qwisˀi:k qwahtinamayi:ch ˀoyi ˀoyoˀalˀatl'atqo:ch, ˀoyi ?anich ˀo:ˀiˀatˀa:la qwamihsatˀitq ˀo:ˀiˀat. Wiˀakw'ahsimch'a ˀoyi wiˀakmihsatl'atqo:, ˀoˀiˀat ˀO:shtaqyo?ahsimch'a ˀoyi ˀo:shtaqyomihsatl'atqo:, we: ˀo:ˀiˀat Haw'iy'ahsimˀi ˀoyi haw'i:chitlmihsatl'atqo:ch.

Hitinqsaˀatl ˀahˀa: Ha:w'i:hatlˀi ch'ach'atsinoˀatlokˀitq ch'ay'a:xwatsokˀi. Tsi:qtsi:qatl Waxniˀahsimˀi tsi:qtsi:qatl Qwayats'ahsimˀi, hina:p'qatl Wiˀakw'ahsimˀi tsi:qtsi:qatl Qwayats'ahsimˀi, hina:p'qatl Wiˀakw'ahsimˀi hiy'ahs yi: hilyinˀi, Ch'ich'ihink'atl Chachimˀakw'ahsimˀi, T'ama:ˀatl T'amahsimˀi, Tla:chitolˀatl ˀO:shtaqyoˀahsimˀi, Ya:tya:tatl Haw'iy'ahsimˀi, Ha:tsho:lay'akˀi no:k ˀoˀoyaqhˀatl Ha:tsho:lay'akˀi no:k ˀaˀatlsahtakwiyahˀatl nono:k. Hitaqsitl Ha:w'i:hatlˀi ch'a:ltamitˀi ˀatla:. Wik'i:thˀatl hinˀalshitl Tlaˀo:kwiˀath wim'a:qtl'atlˀi wi:k'a:p'atqo: hi:hilachishˀi hasa:tok wi:na: tlihshiˀatl ˀahˀa: wi:neˀi. ˀO:sa:tok

"Ho ! Ho ! Ho !" wawa:qo: ˀo:no:tl ˀi:h ˀayo: ˀoxwa:pˀi tli:hak ˀoˀoma ch'ach'atits ˀam'ihtisˀi.

ˀEˀimˀapweˀin k'o:ts'a:tintl ti:chachiˀatl Kanop wiki:chiˀatl ˀani t'it'imyisˀa:nitqa qa:ty'apt'a. ˀOkwachiyoqatl koˀoqwa ˀani yi:lˀatlqa n'achi:tssˀatl ˀa:nahi wi:neˀi. Kamitqn'iqsatl ha:ha:yoxshitl Hosha:kitˀi Kanop ! Cho:ˀato hi:si:ˀato hila:chishtitˀitq wi:nimtˀi, qwacho:qh ˀahˀa: hinoschisˀatl machinoˀatl hiy'athˀitq. ˀO:hta:sa teˀilh n'a:sshitl Kanop.

ˀOna:kshitlweˀin p'atsmis Kanop cho:ˀatoˀitq ˀoyiˀoktok, qwa:we:ˀin qwe:ˀitq p'atsmis ˀa:nahi qattsk'in tli:htskwi: yaqwachisht'itlˀitq. N'a:tssi:chiˀatl Kanop ˀani hitaqsˀap'atqa ˀohˀat wi:neˀi yaqoˀalˀitq. Qa:hshitlshitl Kanop tapitl hishtspa:ˀat qo:ˀas so:ˀat. ˀO:n'ak'ohshiˀatl n'a:tssi:chitl ˀani ya:lqa: ˀiqachisht hila:chisht hitinqisˀi wi:neˀi. Wawi:chiˀat ˀoyi ts'axshiˀatqo: ta:tsswi:ˀap'at ˀani. ˀAni yawo:sqa tichachitl ˀoyi qwisqo: ˀoyi ˀeˀeˀishwat wawa:ˀat yaqoˀalˀitq.

"Wikʔa:qtleʔits ti:chachitl ʔoyi wik.wo:k ts'axswi:,"
wa:ʔatl'atqo:weʔin.

ʔAhʔa:ʔatl sokwitlnak'atl ʔo:ʔo:palokʔi. Hine:ʔitl
ʔo:tʔo:palʔi ya:qpa:lʔitq witwa:k - Ts'axsats'os, Tlan'iqol,
Hishnap, Kanoxwi:ʔitl, Ch'o:ha, Ts'eʔinwa - qwam'a: ʔahʔa:
witwa:k Tlaʔo:kwiʔath.

"Ts'axshitlʔa:qtlweʔintso: si:chil, ʔo:ʔatomah," wa:ʔatl,
"Ta:tsswi:ʔa:qtl'apweʔintso: si:chil ts'axy'ak," wa:ʔatl.

"Wa:yaqʔa:qtlhin ts'axshitl," wawa:lyo:chiʔatl ʔo:tʔo:palʔi.

"ʔOhʔap'i Tlan'iqol," wa:ʔatl'at Tlan'iqol.

ʔI:naxi:chitl Tlan'iqol sokwitl ts'axy'akʔi. Hiy
tlawi:chitl ts'ats'a:w'as Tlan'iqol wi:tsokwitl hoʔapshitl
ts'axshitlqo: ʔoyi. Haʔoqhshitl ʔahʔa: Hishnaq
ts'ats'a:w'astla: y'o:qwa:, hey wi:tsokwiʔatltla: y'o:qwa:
Hishnaq. Wi:tsokwitl wa: ʔa:ni ʔo:shtsok qa:qahakwa:piqo:
ʔotsokw'ap. Qa:hshitlshiʔatl Kanop qiqi:yaso:chiʔatl qahak,
ʔe:y wiksa:htakshitl qo:ʔasitʔi, na:tssa ʔani histopilʔatqa
yaʔatʔit wawa:ʔat ʔoyi ts'axswi:lqo: qahak'atlqo:
ʔoya:tlqo:weʔin, 'n'a:tsa hey qaqahtsimqh n'a:sshitl Kanop.
ʔI:naxi:chitl y'im'i:qsoʔi koʔal Ts'axsats'os ʔohʔatl
ʔi:naxi:chitl, ʔo:shatokqchikweʔin hinʔitl Hoshe:kʔi
mitxmi:qtln'okweʔin ts'axy'akokʔi.

"ʔOy ʔoy ʔoy," wawa:weʔin hinʔitl Ts'axsats'os.

Wa:tlhaweʔin ʔahʔa: tlawa:ʔatl'at hi:lʔi:tq Kanop.
T'iqwilʔatl teʔilʔi qwahta:ʔa:qtl'atʔitq ts'axsinqanop'at
ta:tsswi:lʔap'at ts'axy'ak Qatqyo:ʔi ʔataweʔish
ʔani:hsp'atoʔits'ap'atltla: ʔahko:ʔi ts'axy'akokʔi,

wi:tsokwiˀatltla: y'o:qwa: Ts'axsats'os. ˀO:htasa sokwil Kanop ts'axy'akˀi ts'axshitl, ˀo:tsahtaksa ta:ch'atˀi ch'apkw'atlasqo:, ˀa:ni ˀah hi:n'i:tl'asˀi ˀimin hista:ta ts'axshitl. Tl'oˀihta ts'axy'akˀi tsikimin qaqatsts'inkw'ihta tsikimin kwicho: ts'axy'akˀi. ˀO:tsahtaksa tlatqishkwispitl Hoshe:kitˀi Kanop tlakishitl hina:p'iqshiˀatl ts'iswa:s ts'i:yop'atˀi. Sokwil ˀaky'akokˀi ch'ichitl ˀom'a:shˀap ˀah tokwaqˀi ta:ch'a:tˀi, ch'ihtaˀap ts'iyop'atˀi laqshitl laqw'inqpitap ts'iyop'a:nitˀi, tl'ohmalsinqintl ˀah hista:teˀitq kohsa:p. Qwisˀatl wawa:ˀatˀitq, ˀa:na:tl ti:chachiˀatl Kanop. Kamitqwi:ˀasˀatl Hoshe:kitˀi ! T'aqiliny'ap'atl ya:yil moqwe:ˀi ts'iyop'a:nitˀi, t'aqswa:s hita:qtl'itl kohwanimˀakˀi. Hah'ah wiksto:pˀich Kanop.

Hitakwalqh ˀa:thshitl hitakwalqh n'a:sshitl hitakwalqhtla: tla:ˀokwilshitl. Mo:chi:y'aqtl'as mo:chi:lkwal. ˀO:shˀatl'atl naˀa:ˀat qwiyiˀitq mo:chi:lshiˀatl no:kna:k'atl hi:taht'as naˀa:ˀat, ˀiqsti:ˀitl hisi:ˀasitˀitq kohw'animˀakˀi, hine:ˀitl nonok.

Hashi:chiˀatl Tlaˀo:kwiˀath ˀani hitaht'asˀatlqa Kanop. Pokwiˀatl Tlaˀo:kwiˀath n'an'a:ch'as. T'iky'i:hi:chitl mahti:ˀi ˀi:h, nono:k ˀani nono:k Kanop ˀoˀoyaqh ˀahko:ˀi nono:k,

"Hiya ˀahiya ehe: ˀahiya
ˀana:ˀahiye: ˀangiye ˀahow hiye:
(ˀimt.shitl) ***Matwa:hsolokma Tlokwa:nakqana:***
ˀaho:w ˀahiye: ˀahiye: ˀahowˀahiye:
wawa:xniqshokma: ˀahiye: Tlokwa:nakqana
ˀaho:w ˀahiye:"

Sokwiˀatl ya:lsa:m'aqtli tl'ikmo:tokˀi[4] tsoma:ˀak

m'ots'isok tsak'o:p Hoshekˀi ˀinkokˀi. ˀInkw'achitl m'ots'isokˀi.

"Ka:ˀa lih̲alqo:," wa:ˀatl lo:tssma:kˀi, **"ˀOh̲ˀap'im tl'isalqo: lih̲at,"** wa:ˀatl lo:tssma:kˀi.

Litspitap ˀa:ˀapstilˀap ta:cho:ˀi toksti:lˀatl m'ots'isokˀi wik qi:kwa:l ya:yil m'ots'isok ˀi:qh̲i: tsak'o:tlitˀi, ˀo:sa:tok

"Hish:::," wa: lih̲alˀi.

"Ma: tots'inap'i," wa:ˀatl ˀo:kwil h̲a:w'ilatlˀi.

To:ts'inapshitl h̲a:w'ilatlˀi ˀiqsilak tsomintlok. Nono:k ˀani nono:kqa Kanop. Sokwitltla:m'ots'isokokˀi ˀiqsilaptla: tsak'o:p ˀinkˀi:, ˀi:qh̲i:tla: ˀanitskwal ˀanitskwalˀitqtla: toksta:ˀatla.

"Hish:::," wa:ˀatlqo:w'eˀin to:ˀalachitl lih̲alˀi.

To:ts'inaptla ˀiqsilaktla: tsomintl m'ots'isokˀi. P'ax̲ak'atl Tlaˀo:kwiˀath̲ ya:ˀal. Wawi:chiˀatl'attla: ˀoh̲ˀat Yaqtaqyo:chitlˀitq,

"Hita:ˀop'i h̲achat'op qwam'a:nako:sik tl'isal," wawi:chiˀatl'attla:.

ˀO:ktaqi:chiˀatl'attla: ˀah̲ˀa: qaqah̲atah̲sap'atl'attla: ˀah̲ˀa: ˀani w'asnaqa m'oya: tl'isalokˀi. M'oˀakwaˀap ˀah̲ˀa: kow'ila tl'isalokwilˀi, h̲achatkwaˀap kow'ila ˀani wawa:ˀatl'atqatla:,

"H̲achatkwaˀap'i m'oˀakwaˀap ˀani: !"

Wawa:ʔatl'atqatla: kow'ila hachatkwaʔap qwam'a:nakitʔitq tl'isal ʔani qaqahatahsap'atl'atqatla: ʔohʔat yaqtaqyo:chitlʔitq.

Tlo:kwatqtsaqa Tlaʔo:kwiʔath m'a:kway'i:hshiʔatl Tlaʔo:kwiʔath hi:sh ʔahʔa: ʔinxa n'o:psiyapi Ma:lts'a:s. ʔEʔimqhʔatl ʔahʔa: tlihkwisatl'asʔatlʔitq hiy qahshitl ʔahʔa: qo:ʔas qahna:k'atl, ʔoso:tl Haw'ilisimʔakitʔi maʔasʔi. Hiy n'itlkwaqshitl Tlaʔo:kwiʔath, ʔo:tsawinyokshiʔat pi:tsksy'iqi:lshiʔat ʔani hisili:y'apshiʔat'a:hqa hoʔosa ʔani sa:ch'iyi:ʔatoqa n'apxta: qahshitl. Hayimhat qwiy'i:hayi: qahshitlʔi ʔani ʔanasilaqa tlihatshitl qahshitl kwaxwahsol hismis ʔi:naxiqh ʔani M'a:kway'i:hw'it'asitqa. N'o:hshiʔat Haw'ilitʔi.

ʔAtaweʔish wik qi: ʔiqkwa:lʔap'at n'o:hshitlʔi hiy qahshiʔatltla: tlaʔo: qo:ʔas. ʔAtaweʔish wik'atltla: qi: to:pshiʔatlʔitq hiy qahshiʔatlweʔintla tlaʔo: qo:ʔas Tlaʔo:kwiʔath. Wiky'i:hatltla: ʔiqsilatltla: qwa:ʔapʔitq ʔani:silatltla: kwaxwahsol hismis qahshitl. N'itlkwaqshiʔatl ʔahʔa: maʔasitʔi Tlaʔo:kwiʔath ʔi:hʔatl n'itlkwaqshitl ʔani qachts'asawiʔatlqa ʔiqiya n'opchi:liya n'a:s, Haw'i:hʔi ʔo:sa:wi:l. Hiy tlaʔo:ʔatltla: qahshitl wiky'o:ʔitq qi:ts'okwitl ʔathi:.

ʔAhʔa:chiqhʔatl'atweʔin sokwiʔatl'at Kanop mo:sawiʔatlʔitq Tlaʔo:kwiʔath hiy sokwiʔatweʔin ʔahʔa: Kanop. Tla:chitshitl ʔo:tsahtaksa Kanop hito:hsolʔap, ti:chachitl qahshitlitʔi ʔa:hʔasa tlopkshitlqo: weʔichy'ihtaqshitl. Qwa:we:ʔin hi:n'aqo: ya:ʔitlʔitq yaqwahsolʔapʔitq Kanop. Hiy tlaʔo:tla qahshitl qo:ʔas. ʔIqstap'i:kap'attla: kamatshiʔat Kanop. Qahi:chiʔatl maʔasitʔi Tlaʔo:kwiʔath. Hi:to:hsawi:lchiʔap so:pa:ts'oʔal Kanop. Wiki:chiʔatl wala:kmi:chitl, ho:ʔo:saʔa:lshiʔatl qahshiʔatlqo:. Qwa:masa ya: qahshitl qachts'eʔi Haw'i:h yaqwi:ʔitq ya:qwilʔatʔitq wik'at sokwiʔat

Kanop. Ti:lticha ˀapshiˀatl Hoshe:kitˀi Kanop.

Qwisˀatl wa:qh̲ˀa:niti:ch h̲achat'op'i qwam'a:nako:sik tl'isal wa:ˀat ˀani ˀayanakshiˀatlqa tl'isal kamatokt'atlok. H̲aw'i:chiˀatl Hoshe:kˀi Kanop, h̲achatayatl'atqo:weˀin ya: qwam'a:nakˀitq ya:qwilˀitq hoˀosap ti:chaˀap. Wa:lˀichiˀatlni ˀah̲ˀa: ha:shichiˀatl ˀanich qwa:. ˀI:sokwiˀatl'at qo:ˀasitˀi ˀoh̲ˀatl ˀi:h̲ch'a: ˀi:sokwiˀat ˀoh̲ˀat yaqchiˀath̲ˀitq. ˀOya:tlweˀin hawi:ˀatl qwiyiˀitq m'o:ˀakwaˀapshilshiˀatl ya:qy'i:h̲ˀaˀa:lˀitq qwa:ˀapˀitq. Hawi:tl ˀah̲ˀa: qah̲a: Tlaˀokwiˀath̲. ˀO:shtaqyo:chiˀatl Kanop ˀiwachiˀatl ˀo:shtaqyo. ˀO:kwilitweˀinˀa:la ti:chaˀap ya: n'opchilˀatlˀi qah̲ak ts'awa:k ˀath̲i: ti:chaˀap'atlqo:weˀin ˀah̲ˀa:.

N'a:tssamah̲ yaqiti: Kanop ˀokla:. Nani:qsakitah̲ ˀo:ˀo:ˀop'atlsi now'i:qsakitqas n'ow'i:qsakitˀi[6] ˀoh̲qa ˀApw'in?̲asˀath̲. Cho: h̲a:h̲a:h̲anoˀatlah̲, ˀa:nama ˀah̲ˀa: ˀoyaqh̲mis.

118. Ch'it'oqwin'ak Becomes a Shaman
(Sa:ya:ch'apis via Alex Thomas)[1]

Hi:shmi:ʔatlqo:weʔin[2] Ch'it'oqwin'ak hilh̲ tl'ath̲sy'a:holʔi tl'ipo:s ʔoʔoʔi:h̲, Yo:loʔilʔath̲ Ha:yopiy'ataqiml Ch'it'oqwin'ak, t'apqiml qwi:ʔiqtl'apʔitq tli:h̲ʔaqstop tl'ipo:s weʔichqa tl'ipo:s ʔath̲i:ʔatlqo: qwe:ʔitlqa ʔah̲ʔa: sokwitl ts'itkh̲taʔapchip ts'ik'omts qah̲sa:p yaqo:si hi:shmi:ʔa. ʔOkla:ʔatlok ʔimtna:k "hi:shmi:ʔa" yaqo:si qwa:ʔap ʔah̲ʔa: tl'ipo:s ʔoʔoʔi:h̲. ʔAnasilaq soch'aqimlip ya: wiko:qh̲ʔi qwa:ʔap tlötlopkw'isatl ʔah̲ʔa: yi:lʔatl pop'ichitlh̲ʔat tl'ipo:s, wik'atl'at ʔoh̲ hinʔalshiʔat ya: hacho:qh̲ʔi ʔo:simchcho ʔatqo: hi:simy'aqsta·ʔatl wikh̲ʔatl'at tlopkshitl. Tl'atl'ath̲sy'aho:h̲ʔi hilqa: hoʔats'ol tl'ipo:s qwa:k'ok qwe:ʔitq ch'itma:k mah̲t'i: wi:ktaqyoqh̲ʔat n'a:tssa:t ʔatqo:ch qwa: ʔah̲ qwe:ʔitq chimʔil ʔoyi hacho:qh̲ʔatl'atl'atqo: hachaqshiʔatl'atqo:ch kwi:qa:ʔat qwisʔatl'at qwa:ʔatqo: ʔoyi hisimlasʔilqo: chimʔil, milʔa:ʔasaqakshitl tl'ath̲sa:m'its'olʔi hista:ta tlishtlinʔi kwi:qkwi:qa hi:shmi:ʔaqsimch'atlqo: ʔoyi.

Kits'asok ʔo:ʔom'ih̲toʔasok tl'ath̲akʔi tl'a:ska:n'olʔi tla:smapt, hisaqtatl ʔah̲ʔa: ts'isaqtatl tl'a:ska:n'olʔi ʔa:tlyaqan'olʔi matl'asʔatl ʔo:ʔokwasʔatl yi:l tl'aqaʔasʔi. Qwa:ʔatl'at qwa:ʔatʔitqʔa:la k'a:k'a:yopshiʔatl'atqo:, kwats'o:ʔatl'at ʔani no:t'ih̲taqa koh̲swi: hitih̲takʔi ʔa:tlyaqan'olʔi, mɑ̈lsa:p'atlqa ʔa:tlyaqan'olʔi ʔoyi tsoma:noʔatlokqo: ʔah̲ t'apw'animʔakʔi, k'o:k'o:qtl t'oh̲ts'itim'inh̲ʔatʔi ʔo:ʔokwim'inh̲ʔatl tl'ipo:sʔi.

"Chi:misanop'atl'is," wa:qh̲ʔatl.

Chi:chiʔatlqa qachts'eʔi chi:qh̲si: chi:misanop'atl maw'imsanop'atl cha:ni tl'ipo:sokʔi. Hiy ʔopqʔa:ʔatatla:

ˀahˀa: hinasitltla: hilˀi:tq ho:ˀich tl'ipo:s qa:hqa:hshitltla: ˀahˀa: ts'i:ts'inkwi:kshitl, wa:qin Qo:ˀasqin,

"Qatqyo: ! Qwi:qwichiwo:schk ya:lˀi wik t'iʔa:ˀato ˀoyi weˀich'atlqo: ˀoyi ?" wa:qin ˀah wi:ktaqyoqin.

ˀO:mi:k soch'i:q Ch'it'oqin'ak hi:shmi:ʔaʔaqtl so:ch'i:ʔahsi:l. Wik weˀichoˀat Ch'it'oqwin'ak hi:xwa:ʔaqtlch'a, tlopka:ʔiˀatlqo:weˀintla: Hoshe:kˀi ya:lˀatlqo:weˀintla: tsi:qtsi:. Hiy, yi:lˀatlqo:weˀintla: toxwa:chitl ! Hawi:tl ˀoˀo:taq ˀahko: kwala:ˀatli[3] ˀoyi hawi:ˀoˀo:taq hi:shmi:ˀa. Wa:ˀatl lo:tssma:kˀi ˀani n'amalshitlˀa:qtl'atlqa hi:nasimch'atl hi:xwa:ˀaqtlˀi Ch'it'oqwin'ak. Ha:t'inqshiˀatl ˀahˀa: ˀah ˀo:yi:ˀatl hi:lapi. ˀEˀimˀap'atlqo:weˀin hinalachitl ha:t'inqshitl, mo:chi:lshiˀatlqo:weˀin hat'i:s ˀeˀimˀatlqo: hinalachitl, ˀahˀa:ˀatl mi:limy'o:tlshitl ˀahˀa:ˀatlqo:weˀintla: ha:t'inqshiˀatltla: wik'atl hat'i:s ˀoyiya kwala:ˀatlqo: ˀoyi hopalˀi. Noma:kokwita yaqwi:mit ˀoyiya hat'i:s ˀoyi kwala:ˀatlqo: ˀoyi.

ˀOhokhweˀin Haw'il tl'ipo:s ˀahˀa: hi:xwa:ˀaqtlch'a. Wawa:ˀatl Ch'it'oqwin'ak ˀani weˀichopˀa:qtlqa hi:xwa:ˀaqtlch'a hat'i:s tl'op'i:chh ˀa:neˀitq ˀo:yi:ˀatop'atl ts'oˀichhshiˀi:kqo:. Shitlsti:sˀatl ʔi:chhshitlshiˀatlˀitq ˀoyi ch'ots'inoˀatlˀitq sats'op ts'a:maqakˀi Nam'int. Shi:tla:n'awiˀatl Yo:loˀilˀath ʔay'i:chhshiˀatl, ˀi:naxi:chiˀatl Ch'it'oqwin'ak.

"Wik'i:sim hi:ni:hah yatsm'o:pˀa:qtlah qi:kwa:lˀa:qtlah," wa:ˀatl Ch'it'oqwin'ak lo:tssma:kˀi, **"ˀOtsachitlˀa:qtlah M'itlow'e,"** wa:ˀatl.

?Okla:ma M'itlow'e yaqi: nochi: hil Nam'int. Ta:tlti:chitl Ch'it'oqwin'ak hi:nan'o:tlshitl ch'apats'isok?i, hinasitl toxol?i Nam'int ts'a?ak?i matl'i:tap ch'apatsok?i ?ah ?o:tsow'atok ?ah qwi:tsow'atqin ch'apats. Tlihw'in tsikimin?isok?i ts'oxy'ak?isok?i ya:tsshi?atl ?o?otsamatl hinap'i:?il?i, t'ashi:?is?i hisi:k'atl hinasitl ts'a:ht'e?e?is?i ts'aw'in ?o:kwil ?i:h?i: ts'a?ak, hitatssohta?a ts'a?ak?is?i ts'a:ht'a?a. Hisimlts'it?a?awe?in tl'isapi:h kwi:tch'ak ?o:x, qwa:we:?in hinqapi:hqo: ?a:ni. Kwaht'a:?atlqo:we?in ?ah win'okts'it?e?e?is?i ?o:x?i: kwi:tch'ak?i tl'isapi:h?i, we: ?ah?a:tlqo:we?intla: ho:?a:n'awi?atltla:. Hi:lapi?a Ch'it'oqwin'ak mamo:k lim'aqstat?i wa:ya?itltso:wo:si sokwitl, hiy ?omi:hsi:chitl ?o:x?i:. ?E?im?apwe?in kwaht'a:?am'inh?atl?itqtla: qwa:?ap?itq ?ani kwa:ht'a?o:lqa ?otl'otsach ?ana:chxwi?is?i, hiy sokwi?atl Hoshekit?i Ch'it'oqwin'ak ! Qwa: ?aptshitlqo: tl'isapi:hit?i kwi:tch'akit?i, hayimhichi?at qwitsachitlo:si, qwa:we?in hi:st'aqstotlsapo: m'oksy'i?i.

Ya:tsshitl wala:k hinap'i:?il?i qwi:tso?ok?itq. So ?ani so:qa: so:wi:qtlinl hishtsoqwa ?o:x?i:, ?ona:kshi?atl Hoshe:kit?i hininqiml M'itlow'a. Hilh ?ah?a: ?a:thshitl. Hiy Toshe:k ! Ne?i:chitl ?ani nono:kokqa ya?aqtln'ok?itq Ch'it'oqwin'ak ! Qwa:?atlqo:we?in ?aya:tokqo: na?a:?at nono:k qwa: tla:chitolqo:. Ne?i:chitl ?oyi we?icho?atlqo: ?oyi. Hi?i:s?atl wi:nap'as ?o:n'ak'ohshi?atl ?o:?o:shtaqyo Hoshe:kit?i ! ?O:n'akoh?atlqo:we?in ?ani machi:lqa maht'i:?i ?i:h ?ayi:l ?o:?o:shtaqyo ?o:?o:shtaqyoqalshm'inh. Mo:chi:y'as hilna:qi yaqi: M'itlow'a ?okla:.

?Ah?a:?atl ya:tsshi?atl mo:chi:lshi?atl?itq hita:?atatl tlo:ch'intl wiky'o:qh ?ost?i:tl. Hiy totopw'isatl hi:kwal?atl?itq ?ost?i:tl. N'a:tssi:chitlsatlwe?intla: ya:lwe:?in qwa: ?inkqo t'it'i:tsswaqtlasqo: qwi:tso?ok?itq. Ho?atschi?atlwe?intla: qwa: ?inkqo: hopkiml ?otsachi?atltla:

tl'aqaʔ̲asˀi ˀataweˀish hilh̲ˀatltla: t'ipˀa:ˀa ˀapqi:ˀi tl'aqaʔ̲asˀi saya:ch'eˀi. H̲isˀa:h̲ˀatl ˀani ˀo:y'aqtln'okqa. Mo:p'itoˀalweˀin ˀinkˀi: ˀah̲ˀa:ˀatl wik'i:chiˀatl, ˀatwe:ˀinch'aʔ̲ashqo: t'itsst'alˀatl tl'aqaʔ̲as ˀo:ˀo:shtaqyoqwalshˀatl. ˀOˀo:tawiˀatltla: ˀah̲ˀa: ˀani,

"Wikchka:ʔ̲ash ˀa:naqh̲ ˀo:shtaqyomih̲sa ˀanik wikh̲so:k sokwitl ˀinkitˀi hopkiml."

Hi:ˀissotl weˀich, ʔ̲o:y'ichi:lshiˀatl yaqwi:pˀitq ˀoy'oksap'atl p'oˀop ˀish yaqwˀichˀitq, histˀatap'atl ts'isqˀatap chimtsi:lok yaqwˀichˀitq matla:sitap'atl yaqwi:pˀitq Ch'it'oqwin'ak. Ha:ya:poˀatl ya:qsimchitˀitq ˀo:shtaqyosimchshiˀatl, n'o:ˀi:chiˀatl ya:qwin'ak'oh̲shitlˀitq ha:ya:poˀatl ˀani h̲i:xwa:ʔ̲aqtlch'a tl'ipo:s ˀo:simchitqa ˀo:shtaqyims ˀani ˀo:kwi:qstintlqa ˀo:shtaqyims. ˀAtlakwalchilkwalweˀin Ch'it'oqwin'ak hitah̲t'aˀatl ˀah̲ˀa: ˀatlakwalchilkwalshiˀatlˀitq. N'an'ach'inˀatlqo:weˀin[4] ˀath̲i: Ch'it'oqwin'ak, wik'atlqo:weˀin weˀichotl N'a:chna:cha qwaya:tok qwaya:tokˀitqˀa:la ˀo:ˀo:shtaqyo ˀoyi Tlotlokwatʔ̲inˀatlqo: ˀoyi.

Hiy'ath̲ maˀas T'iqo:ˀis[5] ˀokle:ˀi mamaˀo: hi:la:n'ol ts'aˀakˀi Nam'int h̲a:yopiy'shtaqiml ˀo:ts mamaˀo:. Tana:k maˀasˀi T'iqo:ˀisˀath̲ teˀil hil ya: hini:y'oˀasˀi hiy'ath̲ˀitq Ch'it'oqwin'ak, wiksto:pshiˀatlok ya: tana:kˀi. ˀAchy'a:p'atl Ch'it'oqwin'ak taka:tis ts'aˀakˀi Nam'int, ˀom'eˀi:ˀatl mo:lshiˀatlˀitq hi:na:n'osaˀatl si:n'olˀatl ˀinksy'i Ch'it'oqwin'ak. ˀOʔ̲iˀatl ˀani tl'a:yo:ˀalqa yaqchiˀath̲ˀitq ya: tana:kitˀi, wachi:soˀatl ˀinksy'i hine:ˀiˀatl.

"ˀAqaqh̲a tl'a:lyo:ˀi naˀa:ˀat," wa:ˀatl lo:tssma:kˀi.

"ˀAqaqha ˀani qahna:k'atlqa ˀahn'i: tana:kitˀi. Cha:niqachka ti:chaˀapchip qwishtaqyoqho:sikˀa:la Tlotlokwat'in tla:ˀokwilshiˀatlqo: tlopka:ˀap hapoxtso:meˀitsˀa:la," wa:ˀaˀatl'at lo:tssma:kˀi hana:qtlˀatlˀat.

"Wiky'o:ha n'o:hshitl ?" wa:ˀatltla: Ch'it'oqwin'ak lo:tssmeˀi.

"Wiky'o:qach'a ˀiqilokqach'a," wa:ˀatl lo:tssmeˀi.

Ya:tsshitl Ch'it'oqwin'ak hine:ˀitl ˀoˀitl ˀani ya:lqa: matlqimyilˀatl ma:qyoˀi.

"Cha:ch ch'a:ch ch'a:ch, li:ˀa:qtl'ichas," wawa:qchik'atl hi:neˀitl Ch'it'oqwin'ak.

ˀO:hta:sa kwawiqspitl ma:qyoˀi kwa:sitl ne:ˀi:chitlsa qwa:wosiˀa:la tlahˀatlqo: qahshitl qo:ˀas, hilwe:ˀin naˀa:ˀat ti:ch wik qiya:s kwa:s hoˀakwisasˀatl tlakishitl.

"Tl'iqhsa:nop'ich tliqhsa:nop'ich ˀe:ˀe:ˀisha !" wa:ˀatl.

Wik'atok tl'iqhsa:nop'at.

"Tl'iqhsa:nop'ich," wa:ˀatltla: hoˀas.

Ts'awa:khˀatl lo:tssma,

"Tl'iqhsa:nop'ich hi:lˀi:h," wa:ˀatl.

Hahaqchimˀat tl'iqhsa:nop'at pi:tsksy'iˀi ˀi:ta:kp'ichhˀat tl'iqhsa:nop'at pi:tsksy'iˀi ˀi:ta:kp'ichhˀat qiˀi:p'at lowiqsimˀi. Hiy tl'olsta:qs Hoshe:kˀi Ch'it'oqwin'ak tl'olsimqintl qah̲akʔi !

"Hi:," wawe:ʔin n'op'itʔ̲atl ʔeʔimʔitq tl'olasitl.

Hiy Qatqyo: sokwiʔatlweʔin chiwah̲solʔap Ch'it'oqwin'ak ! Mi:lshitlsaweʔin t'iʔ̲ah̲sitl qah̲akitʔi, tsotsqalaweʔin t'it'i:h̲malsol sach'a:s t'iʔ̲ah̲sitl. Ya:lwe:ʔin Qatqyo:ʔi qwa:ʔak qwe:ʔi:tq ya:qwilʔatokʔitqʔa:la Tsiqtskwi: wa:ʔat wa:ʔ̲it ! N'an'a:chmalinkweʔin ʔa:nah̲i qwam'i:lʔitq ʔ̲ih̲wi:ʔasit ʔo:no:tl ʔi:h̲ ʔo:shp'alat, qwa:we:ʔin ham'i wa:qo: tl'a:lyo:mitʔi. Hinolta ʔoʔi:ʔil yi: qah̲shitlitʔi. T'apqiml ʔi:qh̲i: Ch'it'oqwin'ak ʔani tlah̲satlqa ʔiʔ̲ah̲sisokʔi:qh̲i: ʔinksy'i. Hiy kamatʔatap'at Hoshe:kitʔi h̲achatayat qwaqwats'aqalitʔitq ya: qah̲shitlitʔi qo:ʔasi. Kamatshiʔatl ʔani ʔo:shtayo:chitlqa Ch'it'oqwin'aki.

Matchiʔatl ʔoyaqh̲mis hishtsa:kwachiʔatl qwam'e:ʔitq ma:tma:s ʔo:ts'inaqak Ch'it'oqwin'ak. W'asna:tkqo:weʔin ʔoya:tl'atqo: kamatshiʔat ʔoyi ti:ch'atlqo: teʔilʔi, ʔaniyalqo:weʔin ya: n'opchi:ltskwatlʔi qah̲ak ʔo:ʔatop'atl'atqo: hiy tlah̲ʔatlqo:weʔin hixwalolʔatl tlawi:chitl ! Kamat'ani:chiʔatl ʔah̲ qwam'a:qin ma:tma:s Ch'it'oqwin'ak. ʔAʔa:to:ʔatlqo:weʔin kamat'asʔatl'atqo:,

"Qah̲ak'atlh̲a ya:qwa:ʔatopi:so:," wa:ʔatlqo:weʔin.

H̲aw'i:chiʔatl Ch'it'oqwin'ak hinʔitshiʔatl'at h̲aw'ilmis. Ts'ayiʔ̲asʔatl Ts'isha:ʔath̲ ʔotsachitl Hinap'i:ʔis,[6] ʔowaqsak n'ow'i:qsakich nani:qsakitqas ʔah̲ʔa: ʔanits'atlma. Ts'ayiqi:ʔiʔatl Yo:loʔilʔath̲, hiy Toshe:k katlh̲shitlweʔin Ch'it'oqwin'ak ʔowi:h̲tilweʔin hinʔitlʔi Yo:loʔilʔath̲ Tsayiqi:ʔitl.

"Qwa:ʔa:po:kwi:s m'inoqy'a:k kow'ila:p'ich ʔowiʔi:tl

ˀo:ˀo:shtaqyoˀi:," wawa:ˀakweˀin no:k hin'itl Ch'it'oqwin'ak.

Mamatltsaqts'o:ˀakweˀin yaqiti: ch'ochmaqtskwi ˀokla: n'opy'alok ˀa:na la:ha:n'olweˀin hinˀitl. Tl'ahqhˀatlweˀin nats'o:piˀatlˀitq matlshiˀatl ˀah ˀa:ˀam'a:sˀatˀi, ˀahˀa:ˀatl tl'ik'aqtlasiˀatl kwikwimksatˀi ˀashsa:p'atl wim'a:qtlˀi ˀashshitl ˀani ˀayop'inqsap matlsa:p. ˀAna:ˀaqtl'ihtaweˀin yi: ˀashtskwi:ˀi hi:mapatl'at tohto:hn'ok, qi:ˀatweˀin hi:mapat Ts'isha:ˀath totsxtskwi:ˀi, hishimy'o:p'atl ˀashtskwi:ˀakˀi ˀahˀa:ˀatl po:tqshiˀatl Qatqyo:ˀi qwahta:ˀatl ˀahˀa: ! Ya:lˀatlweˀintla: n'opy'alˀatloktla: ˀi:qhi:ˀatloktla: qwa:ˀakitˀitq. Ya:lwe:ˀin ˀi:qhi:ˀatloktla: n'opy'alˀatloktla: ˀa:na, ˀanasilatlqo:weˀintla: totsxhtaˀap ya:lˀatlqo:weˀintla: ˀahˀa: ˀi:qhi:ˀatloktla: ˀa:na n'opy'al. ˀA:na:tlweˀin ˀo:shp'altso:ˀatl ˀi:hˀatlweˀin ˀa:ni ˀo:shp'ala Ts'isha:ˀath Ts'ayiˀasˀi.

119. The Youth Who Followed a Shag *(Sa:ya:ch'apis via Sapir)*[1]

Tl'i:tstl'i:yimtweʔin ha:w'ilatlʔi, tl'iy'aqstop tl'ipo:sʔi, tl'i:y'aqtl'i:hshitl ha:w'ilatlʔi ʔotsachitl Ho:choqtlisʔath ts'aʔakʔi. Hi:na:n'otl ts'aʔakʔi tl'ipo:sʔi tl'iy'aqtl ts'ihatiʔi, hitats'intl ʔaʔokʔi tl'ipo:sʔi. Hinasitl kwistsʔi:ʔi, tl'i:tstl'i:ya ha:w'ilatlʔi wik tl'iy'aqstotl. Hi:na:n'otltla kwistsʔi:ʔi. Hinkway'i:h ha:w'ilatlʔi, ʔi:kwista qala:tikʔisokʔi hi:na:n'otl kwistsʔi:ʔi. Hinasitl tl'athakʔi toxow'ischaʔatl tl'ipo:sʔi histaqtl'itl tl'ipo:sʔi lo:lxʔasʔi ʔitsmakt. Tlawas ha:w'ilatlʔi toxow'ilta, kwits.shitl ʔitsmaktʔi n'achoʔal ye:::: nism'a tlol ! Hine:ʔitl ha:w'ilatlʔi. Wahshiʔatl'atok ts'i:hatiʔi. N'achoʔal hil so:ha ʔaya ʔeʔinhʔis[2] ts'a:ts'a:kʔi, ʔaʔanisʔap tl'aqaptʔi ts'ixwatin[3] ʔo:no:tl ʔaya, ʔaya:tl ʔa:tosh ʔaya:tl chims ʔaya:tl tl'itl'ihiy'o:h ʔaya:tl ch'a:stimts ʔaya:tl wa:xni ʔaya:tl tl'apisim ʔaya:tl tl'o:nim.

Walshitl ha:w'ilatlʔi ʔotsachiʔatl mahtʼi:ʔakʔi,

"Wik'im ʔi:qhok ha: n'o:w'is ʔo:m'is."

ʔOna:k lo:chimo:p ha:w'ilatlʔi.

"ʔOyoʔalah tlol nism'a ʔotsachi:kin," wa:ʔatl.

Hini:soʔatl lo:chm'o:pokʔi ha:w'ilatlʔi ʔathi: weʔichatlʔitq ch'o:chkʔatl maʔas, hayimhi:chiʔatl n'ow'i:qsoʔi qwitsachitlo:si. Wik'i:t n'achoʔal pawalshitl hachischihʔi:. ʔAtli:chiʔatlok t'an'a takwa:ʔak meʔitlqats. Qi:kwa:lʔatl mo:ʔatlok ts'oʔichh hitakwal.

"Cho: n'ashiʔikeʔitso: yaqokwi:so nani:qso. ʔAya:tlok

so:h̲asht tl'oshyo: ʔoh̲okma ʔ̲i:mti:," wa:ʔatl h̲a:w'ilatlʔi, **"ʔOn'a:h̲in nani:qsakchin ʔo:ts'atlin t'an'a pawalshitlich'a ho:ʔak ʔoyi."**

Hitah̲t'aʔatl ma:tlʔitqinh̲ʔi hisi:k'atl tli:h̲ak ʔ̲aʔokʔi[4] hinasiʔatl maʔasʔi ʔeʔim ʔa:th̲shitl. Hinoschisʔatl t'a:tn'eʔisʔi n'an'a:chimeʔiʔatl ma:tma:sʔi, hi:lsʔato t'ashi:ʔi t'a:tn'eʔisʔi hilʔatl h̲a:w'ilatl, sokwitl h̲a:w'ilatlʔi.

"ʔAchiqh̲aso: ?" wa:ʔatl.

"ʔOh̲ʔatlin ʔo:ts'atlin t'an'a pawalshitlich'a ho:ʔak ʔoyi, ʔon'a:h̲ʔap'atl'atin n'o:w'is nani:qsakch'in."

"Chokwa:chak," wa:ʔatl h̲a:w'ilatlʔi qo:ʔasʔi, **"ʔOtsachiʔe:ʔits yi:lokma maʔas,"** wa:ʔatl.

Hini:soʔatl t'a:tn'eʔis.

"ʔOn'a:h̲ʔateʔits hiyil t'a:tn'eʔisʔi, ʔoh̲ʔatlokweʔin n'ow'i:qso pawalshitlit ho:ʔak ʔoyi."

N'itlkwaqshitl ʔeʔi:ch'im.

"Chokwa: chokwa: chokwa: !" wa:ʔatl ʔeʔich'im.

Sokwitl ts'api:sotl t'an'eʔisʔi ka:ʔotsokʔi lo:tssmeʔi.

"ʔAyi:ty'amin so:h̲ashtʔi chokwa:chak p'a:tʔ̲itl."

"ʔAyaweʔin so:h̲asht !" wa:ʔatl ʔeʔi:ch'imʔi.

P'atqshitlshiʔatl hine:ʔiʔatl so:h̲asht ʔaya,

chocho:kwaʔinmeʔiʔatl chʔo::::chk ma:tma:s qwam'e:ʔitq.
Waqʔo:ʔatl Ho:choqtlisʔat<u>h</u> ch'o:chk'atl waqʔo, haʔokshiʔatl
maʔasʔi nasha:k'atl maʔasʔi. ʔA:t<u>h</u>shitl tla:ʔo:k ʔa:t<u>h</u>shitl.
Weʔichoʔatl maʔas ch'o:chk, hina:chiʔatl t'a:tn'eʔisʔi
wikʔalsap'atltla: nani:qsakʔi, wik'i:t<u>h</u>ʔatl n'a:sshitl
t'a:tn'eʔisʔi.

Hilʔatltla: qe:::: wik'i:t. ʔAtlqich<u>h</u>kwalʔatl.

Hita<u>h</u>t'aʔatltla: ʔoh ʔatl pawalshitlitʔi ho:ʔak ʔoyi.
Hishink'atl lo:chm'o:pokʔi. ʔOqsʔatl chims ts'isqmisokʔi
ʔish ʔaya motsmo<u>h</u>aq matliqs⁵ ts'isto:pʔi ch'apatsʔi.
Hitasatl maʔasʔi ʔayaʔat<u>h</u>ʔi. Hinoschis ha:w'ilatlʔi
ʔo:wi:<u>h</u>tis chakopʔi ʔoʔaktlis lo:tssmeʔi. Tsiqshiʔatl
ts'awa:k lo:tssmeʔi hil<u>h</u>ʔatl ʔayeʔi maʔas,

"**Chachashxhtaʔe::::,**" wa:ʔatl, "**<u>H</u>achitsnakito::::
ya:sikwisʔe::::.**"

No:ʔitl lo:tssmeʔi ya:qwilʔatʔitq wa:ʔat,

"**Hoʔoq<u>h</u>ta:::: maʔa:<u>h</u> chachashxhta::::nge:
he::::yo::::ngo:q motsmo<u>h</u>a:nga: ya
yaya:q<u>h</u>ta::::ye:ʔi:s chachash<u>x</u>hta::::.**"⁶

Tl'i:ʔilʔatltla: ʔi:ch'imʔi, y'im<u>h</u>shiʔatl <u>h</u>a:kwa:tlʔi.
ʔA:t<u>h</u>shitltla: weʔichotl maʔas ch'o:chk hina:chiʔatltla
<u>h</u>a:w'ilatlʔi ch'an'iʔinʔatltla: hina:chitl ʔat<u>h</u>i:,
sa:ch'ink'atl walshitl <u>h</u>a:kwa:tlʔi <u>h</u>a:w'ilatl hishink,
sa:ch'inkatl pawalshitl wik'atl hoʔatsachitl.

120. A Runaway Slave Comes to the Chief of Wanin

(Sa:ya:ch'apis via Sapir)[1]

Shi:lats'itlweʔin[2] histaqshitl kwistsʔi:ʔi qatsch'achinik Haw'i:h ʔaʔi:k ts'awa:kok n'ow'i:qso ʔomʔi:qso, ʔa:naʔathsatl n'optaqmil hishtsaqts'o ʔa:nahi.[3] Hitaht'aʔatl shi:tlats'itl ʔotsachitl hilʔi:tq ʔaya qo:ʔas hini:sʔatl shitlatsʔi. Hini:ʔatl qatsts'istatl tli:hshiʔatl ʔotsachiʔatl ʔaʔokwʔi, hisi:k'atl tli:hak. Hitaqo:ʔa apqo:ʔeʔi, ya:y'aʔa ko:kohw'isa hita:ʔeʔi. N'a:tssa:tl qoqwa:sʔi qachts'eʔi tli:hak'atl. Ya:l toxsohtaʔa k'ayo:min ! N'ikshitlchip t'ohts'itatʔi ko:kohw'iseʔi. Ts'awa:k'atl n'a:tssa ʔani wikqa k'ayo:min.

ʔAtla:tl, **"K'ayo:minma,"** wawe:ʔi.

Ts'aw'a:k, **"Wikma k'ayo:min,"** wawe:ʔi. **"Hishtsaqts'o:ma t'ohts'iti !"** wawe:ʔi ts'awa:k.

ʔAtla:tl **"K'ayo:minma"** wawa: ts'awa:k'atl **"Wikma"** wawe:ʔi.

Hitaqsip'atl ko:kohw'iseʔi, hilʔatlhisa: t'ohts'itatʔi ko:kohw'iseʔi ʔanahʔis ko:kohw'iseʔi. Tli:hshiʔatl hitasatl to:pshitl maht'i:ʔakʔi. ʔI:qhshiʔatltla ʔani n'ikshitlqa k'ayo:min.

"Wikma k'ayo:min," wa:ʔatltla ts'awa:kʔi.

ʔOʔokwink'atl ʔi:qhok lo:tssamihokwʔi.

"Ha:ni ʔet'aqtleʔits !" wa:tsst'alʔatl.

Siqachiʔatl ko:kohwiseʔi. Kamat.sap'atl qo:lʔi wawe:ʔitq ya ts'awa:kʔi, **'Histsaqts'o:ma t'ohts'iti,'** ʔani wawa:qa.

ˀO:kwilˀatl qo:lˀi kamat.sap ˀani hilˀatqa n'ikw'i: t'ohts'itatˀi, ˀanich ˀana qwa:ˀap T'ot'ohtsaqts'o:ch'a, wa:ˀatl t'apat.shitl qo:lˀi ˀani ˀohqa T'ot'ohtsiqts'o:ch'a. ˀO:kwilˀatl t'a:qa:k ya ts'awa:kˀi wawe:ˀitq.

"Chokwa chokwe: hina:chiˀa:ni," wa:ˀatl meˀitlqatsokwˀi.

Hinachiˀatl to:pshitl mimityaqshˀatl,[4] shi:tlts'imsy'akw'iˀatl shi:tlokwˀa:qtl'atl ˀam'i:chiˀi:kqo:. Walshiˀatl ˀapw'inˀitlˀitq ˀathi: hine:ˀitl maht'i:ˀakˀi. ˀOhok ˀimti: qo:lˀi T'i:t'iqwinˀa,[5] ˀokla:ˀak t'an'a Tlo:swi.[6]

"Tlopkshiˀi," wa:ˀatl lo:tssma:kˀi T'i:.

Hil qahak lotssmeˀi ! Tlawi:chiˀatl tlaˀo:ˀi qo:ˀas chaqshitl hil qahaktla y'o:qwa:. Tlawi:chitl Haw'ilokwitˀi, chaqshitltla: hiltla qahak y'o:qwa:. Cho:chk qahak qwom'a:qtl'asˀitq lo:tssa:mih t'a:tn'eˀis, ˀo:sa:hatl ko:kohw'iseˀi ˀani haˀokqa[7] T'ot'ohtsaqts'oqhˀatˀi n'ikshiˀat. ˀAlqshitlchip p'atqokwitˀi Haw'ilˀi, wahshitl miˀa:tokwitˀi haˀo:qsip'atl p'atqokokwitˀi Haw'ilˀi. Tli:hshiˀatl hitaht'aˀatl ts'aˀakˀi, hinasitl N'ima[8] ˀokle:ˀi nism'a. N'a:sshiˀatl to:m'itanop ch'apatsokwi, hita:qtl'itl hopt.shitl hiˀi:s ˀahˀa: n'a:s wi:nap'as.[9] Tli:hshiˀatl to:pshitl ˀotsachiˀatl ˀO:qwa:tis ˀokle:ˀi nism'a hinasitl ˀathi: nism'eˀi, hisasatl Tl'asimyis[10] ˀokle:ˀi nism'a ˀane:ˀis ˀo:kwil ˀO:qwa:tis. Hoptsa:p'atl ch'apatsokwˀi hiˀi:s ˀahˀa: n'a:sshitl.

Nawa:yisaˀatl Ho:hinkwop.[11] Koˀalhˀatl nawa:yis, hi:sˀatl Wanin ˀokle:ˀi nism'a. Tl'itl'imˀasˀatl meˀitlqats ˀohok ˀimti: Tl'isˀa:chim,[12] qwa: ˀohok ˀimti: ma:ˀak tl'isokwatˀi ta:ch'i:tˀi, ˀo:no:tl ˀani ˀoˀoˀihokqwa n'ow'i:qso maːˀak. Tl'itl'imˀasˀatl meˀitlqatsˀi ˀoˀoˀih̲ˀatl ch'okn'a haxwinmots, ˀotsachiˀatl Tl'asimyis ˀokle:ˀi. Hinasitl Tl'asimkiyis meˀitlqatsˀi. Wa:ˀatl'at ts'imiskshiˀatl'at[13] meˀitlqatsˀi, n'ashitl meˀitlqatsˀi.

"Chokwa," wa:ˀatl'at.

Ya:l hiy'ah̲s t'iˀah̲s ch'apatsokwˀi.[14]

"Hiti:lh̲a n'ow'i ?" wa:ˀatl'at meˀitlqatsˀi. **"ˀI:yaqh̲ˀaschi ˀo:ts:ˀokwah̲. 'ˀO:tsoˀokw'atweˀintsok hiˀi:sma ya qo:ˀas,' we:ˀim,"** wa:ˀatlat t'an'eˀisˀi.

Hoˀatsachitl t'an'eˀisˀi, tl'ichitl ts'i:h̲atakˀi, sokwitltla ts'i:h̲atakˀi tl'ichitltla ˀo:tso:ˀokw'atl hi:sokwˀitq n'ow'iqso.[15] Hinasitl hi:sokwˀitq n'ow'iqso.

"Hawi N'o:w'i hiˀi:sma ya: qo:ˀas ˀatla," wa:ˀatl n'ow'i:qsakˀi, **"Sokwitlˀa:qtlweˀintsok ˀo:tsoˀokw'atweˀintsok."**

Hinoschis Ho:h̲inkwop mah̲t'i:ˀakˀi.

"Chokwa:chak hilwe:ˀin ya qo:ˀas," wa:ˀatl qaqla:tikokwˀi.

Ya:tsshitl ch'o:chk'atl qa:qla:tikokwˀi, hinasitl hiˀi:sˀitq ˀatleˀi qoqwa:s. Sokwil Ho:h̲inkwop ˀotsa:sokw ˀah̲ n'ow'i:qsoˀi ˀotsa:sokwˀah̲ t'an'eˀi, kwoti:sotl ˀotsachitl mah̲t'i:ˀakˀi hine:ˀitap. Sokwiˀatl qa:qla:tikˀi ch'apatsˀi hini:soˀatl ˀotsi:ˀap'atl mah̲t'i:ˀakˀi Ho:h̲inkwop Waninˀath̲ˀe[16] H̲aw'il. Wik'i:th̲ˀatok sokwiˀat ˀO:qwa:tisˀath̲ H̲aw'i:h̲ˀi ˀono:tl ˀani ˀo:tsqa: nism'a Wanin, ˀono:ˀatl ˀah̲ˀa: ˀoh̲ˀatlok ˀ̲imti: Tl'asimyisˀath̲. Wika:h̲ ˀo:h̲sasak Waninˀath̲ ˀ̲imti: Ma:ktlˀ̲i:ˀath̲qa Waninˀath̲. Ha:ˀ̲inma

Ho:h̲inkwop ˀo:ˀitl H̲aw'ilok ˀO:qwa:tisˀath waqˀo: H̲aw'ilˀi. ˀOtsachitl ˀokle:ˀi nism'a ˀ̲Asimil,[17] waqˀo: H̲aw'il ˀO:qwa:tisˀath. No:ˀeˀatl ts'i:qshiˀatl Ho:h̲inkwop.[18]

"Wa:ˀanga:::: ya:ye:ˀi kwa:sˀish yongo::::
ˀOh̲tinˀatokseˀim wah̲ch'ak ˀeˀi:h̲ˀe ch'iti:ˀasim
ˀOh̲tinˀatokseˀim wah̲ch'ak h̲ayo:ˀatlokqo:s h̲aw'ilmis,"

wawa:ˀatl Ho:h̲inkwop ts'i:qa:, p'achitl ˀO:qwa:tisˀath̲ h̲an'ilok Ho:h̲inkwop. ˀOyi:ˀatl ch'iti:ˀasim. Walshitl ˀO:qwa:tisˀath̲, tloyachiˀat lim'aqsti H̲aw'ilˀi ˀO:qwa:tisˀath̲. Ha:ˀ̲inˀatl h̲aˀokwitl. P'achiˀatl h̲aˀokwitl H̲aw'ilˀi ˀO:qwa:tisˀath̲, p'achiˀatl'at Ho:h̲inkwop. ˀOyi:ˀatl'at ts'aˀak ˀonitˀi tsow'it ˀayint ts'aˀakˀi ˀoh̲okwˀi ˀ̲imti: Wanin. Qwish̲ˀatl ˀotlˀotsachiˀatl Ho:h̲inkwop, ˀah̲ko: ˀokwinoˀatlok maˀas Wanin. ˀOh̲ichiˀatlok ˀ̲imti: Waninˀath̲.

121. Wealth From a Shag (Sa:ya:ch'apis via A. Thomas)[1]

Wikmaqakweˀin ha:wilatlˀi Haw'il ʔOts'o:sˀath.[2] ˀO:mi:kokweˀin n'ow'i:qso ˀi:hto:p ma:ˀak, ˀoksy'aqstak Haw'il n'ow'i:qso ʔOts'o:sˀath. Wiki:lok lo:tssma ha:w'ilatlˀi yaqwintlˀitq ˀi:hˀat p'ishso:qtl'at ˀohˀat n'ow'i:qsakˀi. Wahshiˀatl n'ow'i:qsoˀi qwa:ˀamiti: yaqwi:mit ˀani wahshitlitqaˀa:la wikmaqak'atlokqo: ˀoyi t'an'a. ˀOhˀat so:ˀat neˀi:qsakˀi qala:tikok n'ow'i:qsoˀi wikal ˀo:h wahshitl wi:ˀo:ˀakˀi ha:ˀomsaqh ˀa:nahi wi:ˀo:ˀakˀi wikqh so:. YaʔatlˀItq ha:ho:pa qwisiki: ˀoyi ˀoˀo:sho:ˀalqo:, ch'o:chkil ka:ka:ˀopa qwisˀati:chˀa:la ˀoyi ˀo:ˀo:shoˀalˀatl'atqo: ˀoyi hisi:kˀa:qtlˀitq hat'i:s histiya:qtlˀitq hat'i:s wawa: ˀi:qhok ha:ho:pa neˀi:qsoˀi wi:ˀo:ˀakˀi.

Qwa:ˀatl kow'ila k'o:k'ots'itl'i:k[3] wawa:ˀatˀitq ha:ho:pat neˀi:qsakˀi. K'o:k'ots'itl'i:k ˀokla:ˀap'atl'at n'ow'i:qsakˀi ˀohˀat ˀo:ˀoktaqat ˀani ˀaˀa:nataqqa k'ots'im ˀoˀoˀi:h, ˀana:kqa haˀom ha:w'ilatlˀi. ˀAtlchi:lm'op'atlqo:weˀinkwaˀat k'o:ts'itl'asˀatlqo: ˀoyi ˀop'it'atlqo:weˀin qi:kwa:l n'opochilkwal, hilh ˀahˀa: hat'i:s ha:pat'inqy'iha hitssnopˀi. Qwam'o:p'atlqo:weˀin ˀahˀa: qi:m'o:p ˀani hat'inqm'opqa. Qa:tsi:ˀatl'atqo:weˀinqo: tl'a:q ˀoyi ˀoy'ip'atlokqo: ˀoyi n'ow'i:qso wahshitlchip'atlqo:weˀin wikchi:p haˀok ˀon'a:h y'o:qwa: qwishˀa:hi: ˀoˀo:kwaqh qoˀi:chitl wa: ˀani ha:ho:patqa ˀohˀat neˀi:qsakˀi yaqwintlˀitq ˀi:h wi:ʔaqtl n'ow'i:qsakˀi.

ˀAtaweˀish wa:lshitlh Toshe:kˀi ya:lweˀin ˀahˀa: hi:tinqsatl tl'ipo:s ˀi:h ! ˀO:hta:sa kamat.sap wa:ˀatˀitqˀa:la neˀi:qsakˀi, ˀo:hta:sa toxw'ilta kamitqshitl hi:tinqsatlqa ya:l tl'ipo:sˀi ya:tsok, qwa:qa: qwaˀalˀitq ˀani ya:lqa: ʔaʔaskyiml wik'i:t'at laphsp'at'o ˀona:kqh lapẖsp'at'o ˀa:naẖatl ˀ̲a̲ˀ̲a:skan'o:ẖˀatl'at. ˀO:ẖta:sa sokwitl.

"Ka:ˀa qwi:qtli:k," wa:. **"Ka:ˀa qwi:qtli:k,"** wa: tla:ˀo:k. **"Hini:ˀism qwi:qtli:k la·:kshitl,"** wawa:.

Mo:p'itˀ̲atl'ap'atweˀin ka:ˀa wa: ya:lwe:ˀin ˀaẖˀa: tliẖwa:ktli ẖi:xwa: !

"Cho: ka:ˀa tlaˀo: hitssnop'ap'i," wa:.

Hiy hitawaktlitla: tlaˀo: hitssnopshiˀatlok ! ˀAẖˀa:ˀatl lachiˀatl.

"Cho: wala:ˀatlchi," wa:ˀatl.

Hina:chiˀatl tl'ipo:sˀi cho:ˀatatl. Hiy ˀo:shna:kshitl Hoshe:kitˀi K'o:k'ots'itl'i:k ! Cha:na:tltla ẖam'okwiˀatl ts'e:ˀiy'iˀatl yaqoˀalˀitq, ˀaẖˀa:ˀatl walshiˀatl hiy'atẖˀisˀitq, ni:schisˀatlqo:weˀin k'ots'im yaˀ̲aẖsˀitq yaqnaqˀitq yaqla:ˀap'atl'atˀitq ˀ̲imtna:k'ap'at maschimˀakˀi. T'apatsap'atl hitaqsip'atl hopinkokˀi ya:qwakwinˀilokˀitq chimˀilokˀi, hitaqsẖˀatlok ˀa:tẖshitl yaqna:kshitlˀitq. N'a:sshitl ˀalqshiˀatl, hilwe:ˀin ˀapẖtaˀats'nˀil ẖi:xwa: ẖoqwinkˀi, hilsp'i:qsmaqshitlweˀin hi:lsp'i:qssa cho:tlsho:yeˀi ẖi:xwa: hitssnop x̲achshiˀatl ˀaẖˀa: takok qa:chts'asiyapap qa:chts'asiyapiqa ẖi:xwa:. ˀA:tẖchitltla: tlaˀo:k hiltla: ˀi:qẖi:ˀak n'a:sshiˀatlˀitq, hilwe:ˀin ˀapẖtaˀats'oˀilˀatltla: ẖoqwinkˀi ẖi:xwa:. Wasqwi:ˀak ˀa:yichitlshitl ˀoẖok mamoms x̲a:chẖtaˀapshiˀatlqo: ˀeˀi:ẖtskwiˀi wasqwi:ˀis ˀa:yichitlshitlok Hoshe:kitˀi ! Liẖtqi:lchikok takok qwi:ˀiˀilokˀitq ch'ich'itaqsopitap'atl. Wikˀay'inˀatl ˀani qwaqwa:qa ˀo:no:tl ˀani wi:y'a:tqa hine:ˀiˀat K'o:k'ots'itl'i:k ˀo:shẖˀat. Hiy ˀayanakshitl h̲i:xwa: Hoshe:kitˀi !

Tl'op'i:chh̲shitl qwaqwa: x̲a:chapitap ˀeˀi:h̲tskwiˀi ˀa:ph̲n'a:kˀi ˀeˀinh̲tskwiˀisˀi, wikˀay'in ˀani wikˀay'inqa ˀani h̲i:xwa: ˀa:yatsaqaqa. Tl'op'i:chh̲shiˀatl ˀah̲ˀa: makn'a:h̲misˀatlweˀin ˀah̲ˀa: Tl'a:ˀasˀath̲[4] tso:tsom p'atqok h̲i:xwa:qh̲im,[5] hi:katl kakimˀisokqa h̲i:xwa: maˀassy'aqstiˀi lakh̲li:ˀ̲aqi:chiˀatl Tl'a:ˀasˀath̲ˀi,

"Hi:y wi:kimsaqtlch'anaˀ̲ash kakimˀisokqa hil maˀasˀi h̲i:xwa:."

"ˀOtsachitltsso: ya:yis n'opqimyisˀi maˀas, ˀanama ˀaya:k h̲i:xwa: tsoma:ma," wa:nak'atltla: hana:qtl'atl maˀasˀi ˀo:kwilˀatl'at K'o:k'ots'itl'i:k.

"Qwa:h̲a: ˀah̲ˀa: ˀa:ni ?" wa:ˀatl ˀah̲ˀa: qach'its'iqˀi.

H̲a:m'i:tlnak'atl n'opts'iˀ̲atl tlih̲shitl hitapˀis n'ashitl, wi:napatl ˀoh̲ qachˀitsˀiqˀi ˀani hashi:chitlqa ˀani no:no:ts'isaqh̲ˀatqa ˀani wikmaqakqa K'o:k'ots'itl'i:k.

"Chiti:nokwinoh̲win," wa:ˀatl tsiqshitl Tl'a:ˀasˀath̲ˀi.

Wa:mitaˀa:la Tl'a:ˀasˀath̲ ˀo:kwil h̲i:xwa: "chitinok".[6]

"ˀAya:kweˀintsik h̲i:xwa: wa:wateˀits ya: kwi:sow'atisˀath̲ˀi," wa:ˀatl Tl'a:ˀasˀath̲ˀi, **"ˀAnitsso: tsoma:ˀak ˀah̲ hiy'ath̲ˀitqso:, wa:lˀaltsh̲amin,"** wa:ˀatl.

"ˀO: n'ashiˀich ˀah̲n'i:lma hi:lsˀatoˀi qwan'ah̲o:sik," wa:ˀatl K'o:k'ots'itl'i:k.

Kwitsshitl Tl'a:ˀasˀath̲ˀi, qwa:we:ˀin tlih̲swi:qotlqo: hil

Kwitsshitl Tl'a:ʔasʔathʔi, qwa:we:ʔin tlihswi:qotlqo: hil ʔayeʔi hi:xwa: toʔil ch'itaqsoʔilʔi.

"Ya:lma:tla: kwisitolʔi kwitsshiʔitla:," wa:ʔatltla: K'o:k'ots'itl'i:k. **"Ya:lma:la: hi:lts'aqilʔi, kwitsshiʔitla: qwan'a:ho:sik,"** wa:ʔatltla: K'o:k'ots'itl'i:k, **"Mila:mihsakah ʔahn'i: ʔeʔinhtskwiʔisʔi ʔish ya: ʔa:phn'a:kʔi mila:mihsatokwah makshiʔat,"** wa:ʔatl K'o:k'ots'itl'i:k.

Makshitlshiʔatl ch'a:pokwitʔi Tl'a:ʔasʔath, ʔa:phi: K'ok'ots'itli:k wik qwaqtl'ap qwaqtl'i:tq hi:xwa: ʔaʔa:tqsy'op. Makto:p'ato:chitl wasqwi: Tl'a:ʔasʔathitʔi, hitapʔis tlawi:chitl yaʔa:yaqts'iqʔitq ʔi:qhshitl yaʔa:ya:qts'iqʔitq,

"ʔA:nina: tsoma: hi:xwa: ya:yis maht'i:ʔi, makto:p'ati:chitlin," wawa: ʔi:qhok. **"Wikma: qwaqtlok qwaqtlokʔitqʔa:la maʔasʔi, ʔa:phi:ma,"** wawa: ʔi:qhok Tl'a:ʔasʔathʔi.

Hitapʔis qachʔits'iqʔi ch'ay'a:pok makshitlshiʔatl ch'ay'a:pokʔi Tl'a:ʔasʔathm'inh, makto:p'ati:chitlaqatltla: y'o:qwa: wasqwi:. ʔAhʔa:ʔatl walshiʔatl mo:ts'iqʔi ch'o:chk'atl walshitl mo:ts'iq, hitasatl nism'a:kʔi Ni:ya:.[7] T'apatinkshiʔatl mo:ts'iqʔi ʔani wik'i:tokwitlqa ʔiyaqhmis. ʔAtlchi:yil hitasatl qwiʔathʔitq, tlihshiʔatl ʔahʔa: wala:k'atl Kwinyo:tʔath[8] ch'o:chkts'iʔatltla: mo:ts'iq hinasw'it'as yi: Kwi:na:yilʔathch'a[9] ʔI:ts'oqʔathch'a ʔanich hi:sta:ʔatomitʔa:la ʔahʔa: makn'ah Tl'a:ʔasʔath. ʔAnich hilit ʔahʔa: ʔi:hw'aqtl'ap hi:xwa: tl'a:ʔayisʔi. Walshitl ʔahʔa: t'at'awak haw'ilmis mo:ts'iqʔi Tl'a:ʔasʔath hitasatl qwiʔathʔitq.

Yoxti:chiʔatltla: ʔi:qtsoʔokshiʔatltla: ʔOts'o:sʔath

mo:ts'iqʔi, ch'o:shokwiʔatl'at ʔah̲ʔa: ʔani tli:h̲n'ah̲i:chiʔatlqatla: mo:ts'iqpanachʔi. Ts'awa:k'atl ʔi:qh̲na:k'atl ya: mo:ts'iqpanachʔi ʔo:kwilʔatl ʔi:qh̲ok ʔow'a:t'inʔakʔi. Wa:ʔatl ʔani ʔattso:qa ʔatqo: hi:shsa:th̲owat tlih̲awat yaqi: ʔaya h̲i:xwa: wiktla: ʔ̲ax̲shitltsk'in'is ʔani ch'ich'itaqsoʔilqa qa:chts'isiyapi. ʔO:yaqh̲ts'inaqshiʔatl Tl'a:ʔasʔath̲ wi:napilitʔi, yox̲ti:chiʔatl y'o:qwa: tlatlo:ʔi Tl'a:ʔasʔath̲ wi:napilm'inh̲itʔi.

Ts'i:ya:y'aknakshiʔatl K'o:k'ots'itl'i:k, ʔoh̲okwita kach'ak n'o:ph̲ta:yok yaqwi:mit n'opy'al ʔa:na t'a:ktlcho: h̲ayop'il n'on'opy'al "No:ph̲ta:yok" ʔokla:noʔatlok, ya:qtisʔatlʔitq K'o:k'ots'itl'i:k t'a:kstop'atl h̲i:xwa:ʔakʔi, ʔo:ktisʔatl ʔah̲ʔa: ʔ̲opʔ̲ah̲sip'atl ya: yaqʔa:qtlokʔitq ts'i:ya:y'ak ʔah̲ʔa: qwa:qh̲ʔaqtl'atok wiktsok ʔoyi ma:kwʔati:kqo: ʔani ts'i:ya:y'aknak'atlqa.

Tlih̲shiʔatl Tl'a:ʔasʔath̲ h̲ayots'iq tlih̲aʔo:ʔi, ʔo:malapatl ya mo:ts'iqʔi mo:ts'iqpanachʔi h̲ayots'iʔatl ʔish mo: Tl'a:ʔasʔath̲ makw'asʔatl h̲i:xwa: ʔo:tsiy'okw'atl'at K'o:k'ots'itl'i:k, hinah̲awiʔatl Hoshe:kitʔi wi:na K'o:k'ots'itl'i:k h̲ayots'iq ʔish mo:ts'iq ! KeʔisʔatI'at hiy'ath̲ʔitq Hoshe:kitʔi wi:neʔi ʔoh̲ʔat ! Makshitlshiʔatl'at qo:ʔasitʔi, h̲a:yoh̲tayokw'is qo:lʔi: qolʔato ʔo:sh qwamih̲seʔi Tl'a:ʔasʔath̲ʔi h̲a:wi:h̲ so:ch'ahtayokw'is ma:tl'itqinh̲ʔisʔi qo:l ʔeʔinh̲ʔatlʔi ʔeʔinh̲ʔatlʔitq No:tx̲asʔaktli ʔish Ma:ma:tli:ts.[10] Ya:ʔalʔatl ʔoh̲ ʔa:nah̲i ya:l kwi:sow'atisʔi matsy'oqmeʔi. Soch'anakshitl qaqo:l K'o:k'ots'itl'i:k ʔatla h̲a:tha:kwatl qachts'a ch'a:kopi:h̲. Hiyitop ʔo:ʔap'atl ch'ochmaqal qwiqqwi:qokwiti:ch h̲aw'ilmis yaqwi:mit. Wik'i:t cha:ni tl'isal, lokoka:polok ʔo:sh Tl'a:ʔasʔath̲, ʔoh̲a:tla: kwan'is tikwatqyoʔi ʔoh̲okwitaʔa:la makto:p Tl'a:ʔasʔath̲, tsaqi:tsh̲tah̲a kwan'isʔi tikwatqyo soch'i:q tl'a:qa:sht ʔoh̲a:tla chikmo:t n'opqimy'ap tlaqmis ʔo:ʔatop kwan'isokʔi.

Y'imha:ˀatl ya: hana:qtl'atlitˀi, **'ˀAnama ya: tsoma: hi:xwa: kwi:sow'atisˀathˀi.'**

No:saqa ˀaxpitapt'ama ˀaphtapitap ˀayeˀi hi:xwa:, makto:p'ati:chiˀatltla: ˀoh Tl'a:ˀasˀath walshiˀatl. Tsoma:noˀatl haw'ilmis K'o:k'ots'itl'i:kitˀi. Tl'i:ˀaˀatl kwi:sow'atsatl K'o:k'ots'itl'i:k, tl'i:ˀilˀatl kwa:n'iy'inlˀatl hi:lhchip'atl maht'i:ˀakˀi n'ow'i:qsakˀi, tl'i:ˀil tl'a:qa:sht ˀoˀi:sˀap ˀatlp'itsap haˀok hi:lh maht'i:ˀakˀi n'ow'i:qsoˀi.

Hashi:chiˀatl y'o:qwa: Ni:ti:naˀath[11] ˀoˀo:tstoˀatl ya: wa:lˀaqeˀi Tla:ˀasˀath tsotsom hi:xwa. Wa: ˀani ˀattso:ma ˀatqo: hi:shsathowat makshiˀat yaqi: ˀaya hi:xwa: wiktla: ˀaxshitl.

"Wiksakwimim ˀaxsa:ptsk'inˀis qwa:yi: ˀi:h ˀaya."

ˀO:hta:satl y'oqwa: Ni:ti:naˀath tl'i:qsitl tsaqi:tsts'iˀatl ˀoh Ni:ti:naˀath. Hitaqo:ˀatltla: y'o:qwa: Ni:ti:naˀath Qatqyo: tlahˀatl ˀaya:tl tsaqi:tsts'iˀatl ! Y'o:qwa:ˀatltla: Ni:ti:naˀath hiyiqtop ˀoqsˀatl makto:p ch'ochmaqal, makshitlshiˀatltla: y'o:qwa: Ni:ti:naˀath. Qo:lˀatloktla: y'oqwa: makto:p Ni:ti:naˀath hi:xwa: ˀohim, soch'aˀap'atltla: qo:l K'o:k'ots'itl'i:k. Ma:kok ch'ochmaqal ˀatla:toˀi ˀo:sh haw'i:hˀi Ni:ti:naˀath. Tlahˀatl ˀa:ni wikpitap'atl, latsla:ksolˀatl ˀa:nahi ya:yis kwi:sow'atisˀi matssy'oqmeˀi, ˀa:nahatl ya:ˀal ya:tis ma:ktsa:qeˀi. Tl'it'oqyatlok cha:ni sho:tlsho:yakˀi hi:xwa: wik'atlok cha:ni qwis qwa:ˀakˀitqˀa:la.

Mana:ksap'atl qaqo:li:chitlokˀi wik hishinkw'aqtlas, sayi:sˀap hishtsaqts'o:ˀap maˀas qaqo:lokˀi. Loyi:ˀatl'at maschimˀakˀi ˀohˀat ˀaˀa:tlayatl'at homaqtlhˀat, t'aqi:y'apchip'atl taka: ya?at?itq hi:xwa: ?o?o:yi:?atl qwam'a:qh?at?itq lo?ok ?oyi:?at. Hiy hash?ato ha?ato hi:xwa:?akit?i cha:ni ! Kamat'aphwe?in ya: sho:tlsho:ye?i hi:xwa: ?oyi wikw'it'as?ap'atl'atqo: ?oyi shoma:p hi:xwa: wik'atl ?ah?a: shoma:p qwa:?ap?itq, ?okwiqs?ap'atl tl'ochtskwi:?is?i matlinksap ?oyi hawi:?ap'atlqo: cha:ni sho:tlsho:ya. Kamat'ap'atl ?oyi wacha:ksa?as?ap'atl'atqo: ?oyi, ?o?i:qs?ap'atl'atqo: ?oyi ?i:h?i: ya: tl'ahiqs ?e:?e:?ishatl ?ah?a: wacha:kshi?atl !

?Ah?a:?atltla: k'o:ts'i?atltla: K'o:k'ots'itl'i:k qwa:?ap?itq hishistatltla: k'ok'ots'i:hshitltla: ?ah?a:qwa:?ap?itq?a:la ?ani ?ama:kqa ha?om k'ots'im. ?A:?a:thw'isatl ?aha?a: wa:lshitl, ?o:pxaqwiqtlinyiswe?in chap?is, hil?atl ?ink ya: chap?e:?e?is?i. Hiy ?i:hshi?atlwe?in nay'aqak?is?i na?a:?at !

"?A:ho:," wa:?atl na?a:?at ?om?i:qso Na:ni:qe?i.

"Na:ni:qa" wa:ma: ?oh Hili:n?ato?ath ?ana:tlin "Ya?i:" wa:?atl ?oh ?o:kwil ?ah?a:ch'a. ?O:sh?atl'atl ya:?a:ktlinl?api:ch ya:qsa:hati:ch?a:la to:hshi?at, kwatsi:qshitl tli:hak K'o:k'ots'itl'i:k. Qwa:we:?in ?ohqo: sa:xtishitl nism'e?i loqtlshi?atl?itq qwa:?ap?itq ya:?a:ktlinl?api:ch, qwa:sa:hi ?ah?a: qaqah?aqstotl K'o:k'o:ts'itl'i:k. Chachimhi qwaya:tok?itq?a:la lo:tssa:mi:h ?oyi "?Aho: ?aho:" wawa:?atlqo: tl'atl'a:hsy'op ?oyi ?ihak'atlokqo: nay'aqak. Ts'axsatl K'o:k'ots'itl'i:k ?opxaqis?is?i.

"Cho: Qahshe:tl toxw'iltatl'i !" wa:?atl lo:tssmak.

Malsa:p'atlqo:we?in yaqwi:q?itq?al, **'Cho: Toshe:k toxw'iltatl'i !'** wa:.

Moqwi:y'o:tl K'o:k'ots'itl'i:k qahkwachiˀat qa:ty'apt'a hopimy'o:tl hisili:chiˀa:h ya:tsshitl.

"Toshe:kˀish ha:y'ahs chimw'a:psileˀish !" wa:ˀatl lo:tssmeˀi.

Toxw'ilta lo:tssma ˀo:htasa tlawi:chitl ya:y'eˀeˀi so:ˀi: nay'aqak Na:ni:qeˀi. Hiy hina:hin sokwitlchip nay'aqak K'o:k'ots'itl'i:k ˀotshi !

"Ka:ˀas nay'aqak," wa:ˀatl, **"ˀOhokma maqinqanim Hiˀitl'i:k ˀoˀitlchip'i,"** wa:ˀatl, **"ˀOhokma Hihi:qtoy'i:k maqiqamin ˀo:ˀitlchip'i,"** wa:ˀatl, **"ˀOhokma ˀaˀachtsito:ma Kw'akw'atl chimtsitolˀatˀi,"** wa:ˀatl, **"ˀOhokma Ko:kohw'isa ˀaˀachtsito:ma qaqatsitolˀatˀi,"** wa:ˀatl.

Qwoqwam'achilˀap ˀahˀa: t'ichiˀatl t'ikoqtlinop'atl, so:patl Na:ni:qeˀi wik'atlok t'iˀi:tl, wik'i:t.shiˀatl ˀinkitˀi qwa: t'aplshitlqo: ˀani hini:ˀatlqa qweˀi:mitˀitq ts'amaqkaˀi.

ˀOtsachiˀatl Ma:n'oˀisˀathtspa[12] ˀo:y'ichi:lshiˀatl ˀahˀa:, wik ho:paˀak'ap qa:tw'a:t'ipshi:l. Noma:kweˀin homaqtl'ap'at ˀoy'i hashahshitl, sitsa:p'at ˀah ˀo:ˀiˀatok chimtso:t'atˀi wahshiˀatl'atok qatso:t'atˀi. ˀOkwi:sip'atl tlatmapt, ˀohwe:ˀin hohtak ˀoˀoy'iˀa:lok tlatmapt ˀish homismapt ˀanikitˀisˀi qo:ˀichitlˀisˀi ˀi:qhi: homismapt. ˀOhˀap tlatmaqchintl Hiˀitl'i:kˀi Hihi:qtoy'i:kˀi homischinoˀatl ˀoh Kw'akw'atlˀi Ko:kohw'iseˀi ˀokwichink'atl. Hilˀatl ˀahˀa: ts'e:ˀiy'asˀatl mo:chi:lkwalˀatl wi:napatl. Hilhˀatlweˀintla: ˀahˀa: Qwayats'i:k ˀoyoˀalˀatltla: hayoqoml. ˀOhˀatlweˀinch'aˀashqo: kwi:kwi:sahakch'a Qwayats'i:k. ˀOyi:ˀatltlattla: kw'a:lok qwacho:qhm'inhˀitq kwi:sahi, ˀahˀa:ˀatltla: ˀo:nasˀi:ˀatltla: ts'e:ˀiyiˀatltla:.

ʔAh̲ʔa:ʔatl walshiʔatl ʔatlakwalchi:lkwalshiʔatlʔitq ʔoyi. Wa:lshitlshiʔatl ʔath̲i:, hinasitl ya: tlolʔe:ʔeʔi w'ichx̲ʔe:ʔeʔi tsaqa:t'aʔa. Histʔ̲atl hix̲oqshit naʔa:ʔat ko:koh̲w'isa, qwa:ʔatl k'ah̲sa:pqo: nism'eʔi ! ʔO:h̲ta:sa wih̲i:ʔotl K'o:k'ots'itl'i:k tlawi:chitl histʔ̲atlʔitq hix̲oqshitlʔi ʔateweʔish tlawa:ts'atap'atl'attla: hiy hix̲oqshiʔatlʔatltla: naʔa:ʔat ! Hinolta K'o:k'ots'itl'i:k hinimqaʔotl, ʔo:h̲ta:sa n'achista:ʔa ʔo:h̲ta:sa n'a:tssichitl qwa: t'at'o:sqo: ʔo:no:tl ʔa:yo:ʔat n'achmisat ko:koh̲w'isa. Hitinʔ̲otl wiwikata, wa: ʔani ʔo:shnakshitlqa wiktla: sosoh̲tatsk'in. Hitasatl ʔath̲i: mah̲t'i:ʔisokʔi.

"ʔ̲Ah̲miy'ah̲sqach'ama K'o:k'ots'itl'i:k qwiy'okw'alo:siʔa:la ʔats'iyokw'al," hashi:chʔatltla:, ʔani wawa:ʔatqa K'o:k'ots'itl'i:k.

Qi:ʔilt'a:na n'opochiyitltla: ʔah̲ʔa: ʔiqtsachiʔatltla: histo:kw'alʔatltla: ʔah̲ʔa: h̲am'o:kw'al. Hinoltaʔatl histoʔalʔitq ʔa:qtlilol. ʔOʔitl yaqh̲n'olʔitq ʔi:h̲ ko:koh̲w'isa wik ʔo:ʔitl ʔe:ʔih̲seʔi, hini:sn'iʔ̲otl hitaqsip yaqwi:qʔitq. Ch'ichitlchip hilh̲okw'ap ʔapsta:qsʔatʔi ʔ̲e:ʔi:qath̲okw'ap hitasaʔatl hisasatl ya: matssy'oqmeʔi kwi:sow'atisʔath̲ʔi.

"Hiy ! Kw'ichinkshitlin ʔa:ʔa:sila ho:n'iqi:min Ko:koh̲w'isama hiy'ah̲s. N'ashiʔichak yaqiti:so: lacha:tl," wa:ʔatl K'o:k'ots'itl'i:k.

Hitinqsatl kwi:kwi:sah̲i h̲amopshitl'as.

"Siy'a:qit.s ʔah̲ hista:tachip chiwiʔakitsish," wa:ʔatl ts'awa:qh̲ kwi:sah̲i.

"Cho: cho:cho: sokwiʔi," wa:ʔatl K'o:k'ots'itl'i:k.

Hiy sokwitl ʔa<u>h</u>ʔa: kwisa<u>h</u>iʔi hinoltap hini:tssw'ischis ! Hiy ch'ichaqshitl tli:ʔil hini:pqat<u>h</u>ʔatokʔi ! Wawa:lyatl <u>h</u>i:ʔiyilʔi nasha:kq<u>h</u>ʔatl ʔani ʔo:shy'akqa K'o:k'ots'itl'i:k ʔani pisa:qa.

"Wik'i:kitqin ʔa<u>h</u>ko:ʔi hini:p ʔoyi wikitqo: ya: pis<u>x</u>wa: K'o:k'ots'itl'i:k," wawa:lyatl.

Qi:ʔilʔatltla: K'o:k'ots'itl'i:k hina:chiʔatltla: ʔa<u>h</u>ʔa:. Hitakwe:l ʔatlchi:lkwalʔatl ʔatla:tlok ʔat<u>h</u>i: hino:kw'al ʔa<u>h</u>ʔa:ʔatl walshiʔatl. ʔO:ʔiʔatl ʔi:<u>h</u>ʔi: ko:ko<u>h</u>w'isa ʔi<u>h</u>aqaqʔi ʔo:ʔiʔatl hitinqsan'ap hitaqsip yaqwi:qʔitq, ʔi:q<u>h</u>i:ʔap'atltla: <u>ʔ</u>acho:ʔap ts'i:ts'iswa:sʔap'atl.

"Hiy ʔaminkshiʔatlnishtla yaqin his<u>x</u>wa: qaqa:qi:ʔak !" wa:ʔatltla: K'o:k'ots'itl'i:k, **"Hitinqsaʔichaktla: kwi:kwi:sahe: <u>h</u>amopshiʔichaktla: yaqiti:so: qwa<u>h</u>ta: ʔa<u>h</u> ts'a<u>x</u>shitl, hiy'a<u>h</u>sʔatlʔishtla: ko:ko<u>h</u>w'isa,"** wa:ʔatltla: K'o:k'ots'itl'i:k.

Ts'awa:kq<u>h</u>ʔatltla: <u>h</u>amopshitl ʔani ʔo<u>h</u>itqa qwa<u>h</u>ta: ʔi:<u>h</u>ata. Hiy hini:tssw'ischisʔatltla: ʔa<u>h</u>ʔa: ! Hiy tl'i:ʔilʔatltla: ! Chi:tak'atl ʔani tl'i:ya:m'in<u>h</u>ʔatlqa, <u>ʔ</u>a:<u>ʔ</u>a:tiqatl'at K'o:k'ots'itl'i:k ʔani ʔo<u>h</u>qa: hi:nipshi:l ya: lachaʔa:lʔatʔi ko:ko<u>h</u>w'isa.

Qi:ʔilʔatl ch'a:ni K'o:k'ots'itl'i:k wik hina:chitl ʔatlakwalchiyilʔatl ʔa<u>h</u>ʔa:ʔatl hina:chiʔatltla:. Hitakwa:l ʔatlchi:lokwalʔatltla: ʔa<u>h</u>ʔa:ʔatl walshiʔatl ʔa:tlqimy'iʔatl ʔa:qtlisalolokʔi n'opqimlʔap ʔi:<u>h</u> ʔa<u>h</u>ʔa:ʔatl ʔap<u>h</u>nolʔi ʔana<u>h</u>. Hitaqsip'atltla: yaqwi:qʔitq ʔatlqimy'a<u>h</u>siʔatl, ʔiqsilap'atltla: <u>ʔ</u>a:<u>ʔ</u>achinop'atltla: ts'i:ts'iswasm'in<u>h</u>ʔap ts'iyop, ʔoʔomatltla: matsy'oqmeʔi tli:<u>h</u>ak.

"Ts'axwa:ʔatlch'aso:sh ʔa:ni ko:kohw'isa, tlahʔatlin chimchitlchip'atl !" wa:ʔatltla:.

Kachitl sayatssk'ap nism'a histi:pm'inhʔitq. Hiy hi:tinqsatltla: kwi:kwi:sahi hinalts'atltla: !

"Siy'a:sah ʔahn'i: ʔi:hʔi: siy'a:qtah ʔi:hchinop ts'axshitl," wa:ʔatl ts'awa:k.

Hiy hitatssmaʔaqi:chitl ʔatleʔi ʔohqathm'inh ʔi:hchinop ts'axshitl ! ʔO:ʔokchintl ya: tlicha:ʔakitʔi ʔohi:chitlok t'a:qoch'ak ʔani ʔohitqa ʔi:hchinop ts'axshitl, wawa: tlicha:tskwiʔi ʔani hi:kwalshitlqa hoqsa:p'atik ʔo:no:tl ʔi:hchiyoqwa ʔi:h nashok litka: ! Hi:ʔinchiʔatl ʔatleʔi, wawa:lst'alshiʔatl ʔani y'o:qwa:qa hohtak ʔi:hi:p. Hiy wi:ʔakshitl ts'awa:k ʔohi:chitlok ʔanaht'ane:ʔisʔi. Tl'i:w'inʔap'atl K'o:k'ots'itl'i:k haʔokwiʔatlqa sokwink'atl ʔani tl'itl'i:xts'ap'atqa:. Walyaqpitl K'o:k'ots'itl'i:k hiy'athʔitq. Tl'i:ya:ʔatl ya: ʔatleʔi ko:hw'isaʔinlayatl wi:ksto:panakshi:lqa K'o:k'ots'itl'i:kʔi, yaqwintlʔitq t'a:qa:k'at ʔani ʔa:na:nakshilsaqa ʔoxwa:pokʔi.

Ha:ʔinʔatl neʔi:qsakʔi yaʔatʔitq la:kshiʔat, tsiqsa:p'atl qwa:tso:yi: w'asna ʔon'a:hmisqo: milsy'i m'achy'ak.

"ʔApa:kqasqo: ʔon'a:hʔapqo:k," wa:ʔatl neʔi:qsoʔi.

Tlihshitl wala:k yi: Hishkwi:ʔath[13] ʔon'a:hshitl m'achy'ak t'a:qa:n'olha ch'apxto:p ʔani wa:ʔatqa wi:ʔo:ʔakʔi ʔoyi t'a:qa:nolhaqo: ʔoyi. Wikʔay'inʔatl milsha:y'asitʔi ʔani ʔathiyasatlqa wi:ʔo:ʔakʔi hiy'athʔitq.

"ʔI:qshiʔim[14] ch'apatsokʔitqak," wa:ʔatl neʔi:qsakʔi ʔo:kwil.

ˀI:qapak mo:y'al ch'apatsokˀi neˀi:qsoˀi. Ts'isan'ap tl'oshi:y'ap ch'apatsok neˀi:qsoˀi, ʔ̲i:qshitl to:pshitl ʔ̲i:qyaqish̲ok n'a:sshitl, chi:y'a:p'atl to:pshitl ho:p'atatlˀitq kwi:sow'atsaˀatl hiy'ath̲okˀitq wi:ˀo:. Hiy hitinqsatl Hoshe:k K'o:k'ots'itl'i:k ya:lweˀin milsi:tss hi:tinqsatl ! Wik ˀayaqh̲ ch'oshʔ̲atl ˀatlaqh̲ ˀah̲ˀa:,

"ˀO:no:tlch'aʔ̲ash ho:n'i:qipshi:lqath̲ hawits'aqyoch'aʔ̲ash ˀa:ni yi:lˀatlqa chachimˀak'atl," wa: ch'oshʔ̲atl.

"ˀI:h̲si:ˀatlma chachimˀak K'o:k'ots'itl'i:k ˀatikchk tsomintl," wa:ˀatl'attla: mots'isshiˀatl K'o:k'ots'itl'i:k.

ˀOtspintlweˀin tli:h̲shitl tl'a:ˀay'eˀeˀi sima:tsyinweˀin Hoshe:kˀi milsy'i. ˀAnasilaweˀin ˀotspintl ˀah̲ tl'a:ˀay'eˀeˀi ˀah̲ˀa:ˀatlweˀin wi:napachishtoˀatl. Tlah̲ti:p'atl tom'aqstoˀatlˀitq ˀah̲ˀa:ˀatl hoˀats'inoˀatl tli:h̲shiˀatl ˀath̲i: ˀo:kway'i:h̲shiˀatl hilokˀitq ˀa:qtlilol. Hinasitl hilokˀitq ˀimts'ak ˀi:qh̲i: wiky'o: ˀapw'intl ˀath̲i. Hinoltaˀa ma:matlach'ap ch'apatsakˀi qa:h̲qa:h̲shiˀatl ko:koh̲w'iseˀi na:yisˀatl ˀoh̲ neˀi:qsoˀi hi:tinʔ̲op. Qa:h̲qa:h̲a h̲ayoqomlsawop ˀish soch'aqiml ˀeˀi:h̲ˀi la:shla:sha. Hiy hitaqsip'atl n'an'a:n'ichshshitl qwisˀa:qtlokwi: yaqwi:q ya:lwe:ˀin ˀah̲ˀa: ˀe:ˀih̲ach ch'apatsˀi ˀiqsim, hinoschaˀa hoˀaschaˀa so:ch'aqimy'iˀatl. Hiy hitinʔ̲optla hiy hitaqsiptla: hiy ˀa:na:tl tlah̲ˀatl ni:qstoˀatl tsaqi:tsqimy'ah̲sitlh̲ˀatl.

Tli:h̲shiˀatl ˀath̲i:, ˀotspa:noˀatltla: qwitsachitlitˀitq tl'a:ˀay'eˀeˀi ˀotsachiˀatltla: wi:napachishtoˀatltla:, hilh̲ ˀah̲ˀa: n'a:sshitl. Wik'ap'atl'at qiyachisht n'a:sshiˀatl ˀah̲ˀa: h̲asilap n'eˀitlsap ˀah̲ˀa:ˀatl tli:h̲shiˀatl, yaqwintli:ch ˀeˀimˀits'ap hopkwist'aˀa, hiy hitaqo:ˀatlweˀin Hoshe:kˀi K'o:k'ots'itl'i:k ! N'itlkwaqshiˀatl maˀasitˀi po:ya:s.

"Toksp'alma ko:koh̲w'isa K'o:k'ots'itl'i:k ˀani !" wa:ˀatqa.

Ts'i:san'olokweˀin m'achy'akokˀi ya:lwe:ˀin wiky'akw'ah̲sok, ˀoˀ̲ashtqath̲ˀatlok. Pon'i:qsaˀatl qo:ˀas tl'a:tl'ah̲achsaˀatl K'o:k'ots'itl'i:k, pon'i:qsaˀatl qo:ˀas ho:maqn'iqsatl maˀasˀi hinalts'a. Hitinqseˀiktla: kwi:kwi:sah̲e: sokwitlchip'iktla:.

"Hilma: koh̲w'isaˀ̲ah̲sˀatltla: yaqwi:tsawayi:k sotlso:kchip," wawa:lyoweˀin ˀo:sh qo:ˀas, **"ˀA:na:nich'akshˀa:la ˀo:ts'ah̲sˀat. Hitinqsaˀatl'ik sokwitlchip'atl'iktla: ˀanik qwa:ˀap,"** wawa:lyoweˀin ˀo:sh.

Machintl yaya:qchimitˀitqˀa:la sotlso:k machintl y'imh̲a:. Hinltisshitlok ˀ̲a:ˀ̲achak takwa:ˀak ˀ̲acho: ˀoˀ̲ashtqath̲ˀatlok milsy'a:kˀi. Ch'o:chkokw'ap tlicha:ˀokt neˀi:qsakˀi qwam'a:qsˀitq tsaqi:tsqimlˀi ko:koh̲w'isa. Hitapˀisˀatl ˀah̲ˀa: hini:ˀ̲atl ch'apatsˀi ˀotsachiˀatl hiy'ath̲ˀitq wik'ah̲sh̲ˀatl ko:koh̲w'isa. Ki:lˀiˀatl qaqo:lˀi ts'i:pisan'ap'atl ch'apatsˀi ˀoh̲ˀatl ya: h̲i:xwa:ˀ̲ischkwim'inh̲ˀi qaqo:l.

Ha:yochilh̲n'ak'atltla: ˀats.shiˀatltla: ˀiˀiqh̲ˀ̲atltla: neˀi:qsakˀi. ˀIqtsachiˀatltla: ˀah̲ˀa: tl'e:ˀilˀi ˀani ˀotlˀotsachqth̲qa. Tlah̲ti:p'atltla: ˀah̲ˀa: tl'e:ˀilˀi ˀani ˀotlˀotsachqth̲qa. Tlah̲ti:p'atltla: ˀah̲ˀa: tom'aqstoˀatlˀitq hoˀatsachiˀatl ˀotsachiˀatl qwitlqwitsachˀitq ˀa:qtlililokˀi. Hinasitltla: hilokˀitq ˀa:qtlilol ˀath̲i: qa:h̲qa:h̲shitltla: ko:koh̲w'isa. Wik'ap'atl mi:lh̲i: ˀeˀi:h̲ ˀoh̲ˀapiˀ̲atl ˀoˀoˀomh̲iˀi ˀa:ph̲n'a:kˀi ˀeˀi:h̲. Hi:tinˀ̲opshitltla: ˀah̲ˀa: ˀath̲i:, chamalts'aqa ˀani qwa: ˀah̲ˀa: tsaqa:t'aˀa yaqwintlˀitq chamol wiktsok ts'a:wo:tsok hi:tinˀop'at. Tsaqi:tsqimy'ah̲siˀatl ˀoh̲ˀish soch'aqiml ko:koh̲wisa ˀah̲ˀa:, kwa:ʔatatl ch'apatsʔi ʔe:ʔinh̲achotlʔits'atl. Tli:h̲shiʔatltla: ʔath̲i: ʔiqsilatltla: hitapatltla: hisa:chitlʔitq ʔiqtsachiʔatltla: ʔotsachitl tl'a:ʔayapiʔi. Wik'ap'atl'attla: qi:yachisht n'a:sshiʔatltla: koʔalqo:ʔatltla: hitaqo:ʔis. Hiy koh̲w'ih̲saʔ̲ah̲sk'okw'atltla: K'o:k'ots'itl'i:k hi:taqo:ʔa sima:tsyinʔatltla: m'achy'akokʔi ! Hiy hinalts'attla: pon'i:qsaʔatltla: maʔasitʔi ! Hiy ʔayasatlk'okw'atlweʔin tlah̲ʔatl ko:koh̲w'isa tsaqi:tsqiml ʔish soch'aqiml ! Ch'ichaqshiʔatltla: ʔah̲ʔa: neʔi:qsoʔi ʔani ch'o:chkokw'ap'atl'atqatla: tlicha:ʔokt tsaqi:tsqimlʔi ʔish soch'aqiml ko:koh̲w'isa. Tl'opaqshiʔatltla: ʔah̲ʔa: t'i:siʔatl ʔaya m'oksy'i ʔa:yaqsaʔaʔ̲atlʔi hita:ʔa ʔinksy'i ʔinkʔi:, w'aqʔoqpiʔatl ʔ̲Ots'o:sʔath̲. ʔOya:tl haw'a:qatlʔitq hine:ʔiʔatl K'o:k'ots'itl'i:k, ʔ̲imtna:k'ap'atl'at ʔoh̲ʔat n'ow'i:qsakʔi ʔoya:t ʔ̲imtna:ksap'at tlaʔo:kʔitqtla: ʔayaqs ko:koh̲w'isa ko:h̲w'isaʔ̲inlʔitqtla: neʔi:qsoʔi.

"Wikts'aqsimah̲ tlatlaʔokwilshitlqo:so:. ʔO:ʔokwilseʔisim K'o:k'ots'itl'i:k," wa:ʔatl tsiqshitl K'o:k'ots'itl'i:k, **"Wikmh̲saqas y'imh̲a:ʔapqo:s so:til ʔanik ʔoh ʔokla:ʔap ʔoyi wah̲shitlchipqo:s."**

ʔAh̲ʔa: wa:ltaqshitl hini:ʔasʔatl walshiʔatl hiy'ath̲ʔitq. ʔAh̲ʔa:ʔatl tla:ʔo:kw'atltla: wik'atl ʔayaqs h̲ayoqomy'ah̲sʔatl ʔoma:k'atl ch'o:shokwiʔatqo: ʔoyi n'an'a:ch'i:h̲shiʔatqo:. Hinasitl ts'oʔichh̲ ʔatsyo:ʔatl sa:ch'ink. Hi:stm'a:ʔatlok hayoqoml ʔoqs wik'atl ʔo:ʔo:potlsa ʔayaqs. ʔInx̲i:chiʔatl ts'oʔichh̲shiʔatlʔitq ʔo:ʔotah̲n'ah̲i:chiʔatl. Ma:kokw'atl hi:na:n'oh̲sim ma:kok ʔ̲a:tlyaqan'ol, ʔokwi:lshiʔatl ʔa:nachil tokwaqiml ʔokwachi:l, h̲a:nah̲i:chitl. ʔI:shqawop'atl ya: h̲i:xwa:ʔ̲istskwakʔi tl'a:ʔasʔath̲i:tstskwak chapx̲to:pʔi. Ma:kshiʔatl p'inw'al ʔoʔo:tah̲sats. H̲a:n'ah̲iqh tl'op'ichh̲shiʔatlʔitq, h̲ana:kqh̲ ch'okwiʔatl ma:ʔak.

Hinachishtoˀatlok ˀoˀoˀotah ma:tma:s ˀOts'o:sˀath y'o:qwa:ˀatlok hinachishtotlok ˀoˀoˀotahokˀi. ˀOya:tl ha:chiˀatlˀitq hina:chitl ˀoˀoˀotah hina:chiˀatl y'o:qwa: K'o:k'ots'itl'i:k. ˀA:nasatloktla: tlicha: kwaqi: neˀi:qsakˀi takwistatl qaqo:lokˀi mo:ˀap kwaqi: qaqo:lokˀi n'opostaqa yaqo:si ˀo:ˀo:tah, ˀoksma wik'ahs ˀapw'inqsˀi ˀani hiy'ahsqa ˀa:tlyaqan'olˀi cha:maqsaˀahs tokwaqapi:hˀi, yaqwa:notlˀitq n'an'amatsaqts'o: qaqachts'atsaqts'o: qo:ˀas. Tli:hshitl ˀotsachitl tl'a:ˀay'eˀeˀi hiyilhˀitq hi:natahqa ˀoˀoˀotahˀi matlachishtotl hosmin ˀo:ˀokwichishtotl. Hik'ap'at qi:yachisht hiy n'itlxshiˀatl hil hilyinˀakˀi hila:chishtˀitq?al ! Hihshitl hilwi:ˀishˀat ˀah chimtsitwi:ˀisokˀiˀal ma:ˀak. ˀA:tlqimy'itl tli:hshitl tli:tlicheˀi ˀo:no:tl ˀi:h ˀane:ˀis ma:ˀak. Hiy tsaxshiˀatl Hoshe:kˀi K'o:k'ots'itl'i:k hopqas matl'ihchinˀi[15] hi:na:n'ohsimˀi ˀo:no:tl ts'opqa: ! N'apxta: ˀanasila kiki:shhichitl ma:ˀakˀi. ˀAnasilat tlawi:chiˀat ma:tlshiˀatok K'o:k'ots'itl'i:k ˀoˀoˀotahˀi ˀohˀat. Matlahosan'ap hiy'athokˀitq n'ow'i:qso. Ch'iya:ˀap ho:maqtlo:ˀap yaqchiˀathˀitq takwa: tl'a:ˀi:h tl'a:qkway'i:hˀap ch'iˀas qwam'e:ˀitq qo:ˀas. Hisoschisˀatlok chakwa:si hiy'athokˀitq n'ow'i:qso, cho:pipiˀatlok hi:lts'aqilˀi ˀo:ˀi:yapilok.

ˀAm'i:chitltla: ˀoˀo:tahtla: hina:chitl K'o:k'ots'itl'i:k ma:tlshiˀatoktla:. ˀAni:silat n'apxta:ˀaktla: ˀo:sa:hatlok qwa:ˀap Yaˀi:ˀi yaqoˀalitˀitq. Matlahawoptla: n'ow'i:qsakˀi hiy'athˀitq ma:ˀakˀi, ˀiqsilatla: ˀo:ˀo:kwa:ˀatop'ap ch'iya: qwa:me:ˀitq qo:ˀas. ˀA:nasa hiche:ˀi tli:cha: ˀoktnakshi:l neˀi:qsoˀi, mo:p'italok ˀani:ts'ot tl'a:q ˀapw'inˀat tlokw'animˀatˀi ma:ˀak, ˀachkhtachitl ˀani:sila ˀanikitˀitq. Hisoschisoktla: hinoschis chakwa:si hiy'athokˀitq n'ow'i:qsakˀi, ˀa:tlqimlapipiˀatlok chakwa:si mahti:ˀakˀi n'ow'i:qsoˀi. Mo:chi:lshitl hi:nachi:l mo:y'ipshitl ˀahˀa:ˀatl wi:nappiˀatl cha:ni. ˀAˀayanakshiˀatl tl'a:q maˀasi:tˀi mo:p'i:lmotshiˀatlqa ma:ˀak. ˀAhˀa:ˀatl siqaˀap'atl chakwa:si mo:qomltsaqa chakwa:si K'o:k'ots'itl'i:k, w'a:qˀoqshiˀatl maˀasˀi siqachiˀatlˀitq chakwa:siˀi mo:qoml. ˀAna:tl lo:tssa:mi:h̲ hinal w'aqˀo: ya:l wi:y'a:tlˀi noma:k, wi:kay'iˀatl'at ˀoh̲ ya: ˀi:qh̲i:ˀi no:maˀ̲i:k. ˀOyi cha:kwa:siˀ̲inlˀatlqo: ˀo:shh̲, wi:napilˀatlok ya:qwapotlˀitq wik'i:t'atlok m'a:mot, hi:sa:tsh̲aˀa:lˀatl ˀah̲ˀa: ha:w'asshi:lˀatl siqyaqilˀi chakwa:si. Tsiqshiˀatl ˀah̲ˀa: K'o:k'ots'itl'i:k homaqtlilˀatlˀitq ˀoyi chakwa:siˀ̲is,

"Na:ˀo:chiˀatleˀits ˀah̲ yaqchiˀath̲qe:s ˀah̲ yaˀ̲i:sqas," wa:ˀatl. **"K'ots'imˀatlma ˀah̲ko: ˀoh̲ˀatlma yaˀ̲i:sqas. K'ots'i:sˀatleˀits,"** wa:ˀatl.

Y'imh̲a:ˀatl ya:ˀakh̲itˀiˀa:la ˀo:ts'os tl'i:w'inˀap ˀani k'ots'im ˀonaqqa. ˀAh̲ˀa:atl ˀatsyo:chitltla: mo:chi:lshiˀtltla: ts'a:wi:y'ipshi:l ma:ˀak ˀi:qm'a:pipitltla: mo:qomlapipitl chakwa:si.

"ˀOkwi:tsah̲ ˀo:y'ip ˀah̲ko: yaˀ̲i:sˀatlitqak," wa:ˀatltla: yaqchiˀath̲ˀitq. **"Wika:h̲ ˀo:tsh̲w'al ya:yil n'ow'i:qsakqas ˀani ˀo:mi:kqa,"** wa:ˀatltla:, **"Wikalchipqas qwa:ˀako:si tsitsiqi."**

Mats'intlmaˀi:qtl'ap'atl n'ow'i:qsoˀi mah̲t'i:ˀakˀi. Wik K'o:k'ots'itl'i:k ˀi:qma:ˀak'ap'atl'at mo:p'i:lˀi ma:ˀak, ˀotsh̲inˀatl'at ch'iya:ˀatok K'o:k'ots'itl'i:k, ˀah̲ˀa:ˀatl hi:nawi:qshchiˀatl ma:tma:s ma:kwawi:qshchiˀatl tl'a:qokˀi. Makw'asˀatl Tlaˀo:kwiˀath̲ makw'asˀatl tl'a:q Qiltsmaˀ̲ath̲ ˀ̲A:ho:sˀath̲ Hishkwi:ˀath̲ Mowach'ath̲. H̲aw'i:chiˀatl Hoshe:kitˀi K'o:k'ots'itl'i:k tsoma:noˀatlok mah̲t'i: h̲aw'ilmis. ˀAh̲ˀa:ˀatl ˀa:tsshiˀatltla: ˀoˀo:tah̲ˀatltla: K'o:k'ots'itl'i:k. ˀAnasilatl ˀa:tlp'i:w'itl[16] h̲aya:y'ipshiˀatl ˀah̲ˀa:ˀatl lachiˀatl cha:ni ˀah̲ˀa: qwisitweˀin. ˀO:ma:ma ˀah̲ˀa: ˀoyah̲mis K'o:k'ots'itl'i:k.

122. Tla:tla:qokw'ap Sees the Thunderbird and Gets Power From a Sea Egg *(William via Sapir)*[1]

Hina:chitlweˀin hisa:chitl Ts'isha: ˀoˀo:tah hitahtachitl saya:ts'achintl, hinaˀatak ˀeˀinhˀisˀi chaˀak. Hinoˀal ˀi:hto:p ts'axshiˀatl, hinyoqwi:chiˀatl. Hoptshitl ˀi:hto:p ˀayimtˀi wik'i:tshitl. ˀO:qomhi:ˀi hitato:yoqwi:chiˀatl. Histaqshitl hilts'a:toˀi hopkiml liw'ahmis. Wiki:chitlok hinosa yaqchi:yoqweˀitq ˀe:ˀe:ishatlqo:weˀin hinosa. Ya:l hinatshitl tom'aqtl m'itla: t'a:qshqi:noˀat. Hi:!. Tl'ihshiˀatl. ˀO:tsahtaksa wi:napotl ˀi:hto:pˀi ˀatowe:ˀinchaˀashqwa to:hshitl ho:ˀakweˀinch'aˀashqwa n'a:tssa:.

T'itskˀatl'atl. Wi:napotl hishinkshitl yaqts'iqˀitq qa:qla:tikokwˀi. Cho:chisht'atl i:hto:pˀi hawi:tl hinaˀato. Qa:tsshiˀatl ˀeˀi:h katso:minˀi ˀo:ˀo:soqtaˀa:lˀap, sokwitl li:tsyanimˀak tl'ahts'a:sqnitl, ch'o:chk qwam'i:ˀitq qwam'isteˀitq. Sokwiˀatl'atok n'i:kw'iˀatl'atok, ts'awa:k'atl n'a:tssa qwe:ˀi:tq ya:l qo:ˀas chamihta kamatsap ya:l hinki:ts. Chachimhi ˀich'ay'ap'atok ˀana:t ˀich'achiˀat t'ohts'itatˀilachiˀatl t'i:chishto'atltla. Ch'an'i:chitltla ˀah qa:ts.shiˀatltla. ˀIqsilatl qwa:ˀapˀitq sokwiˀatoktla n'i:kw'iˀatoktla ˀa:nasatl'atqo:weˀin ˀich'achiˀat t'ohts'itatˀi lachiˀatoktla. ˀIch'achiˀattla mo:p'it.shiˀatokweˀin n'i:kw'iˀat lachiˀatl'atokweˀin. ˀOtsachiˀatl ch'an'i:chiˀatl nism'eˀi.[2] Nism'aqchinoˀatl hi:la:chisht.saqhˀap'atl qahsa:p'atl.

Tsiqshiˀatl Tlatla:qokw'op, **"Waˀatl'atlichim n'a:tssimitah kamat.samah qwa:yi: ma:ma:ti hashahˀa:qtlokwah,"** wa:ˀatl.

Ma:tlshiˀatl matl'aktlinoˀatl hitasatl Ts'isha: matl'aktlatl. N'achoˀalˀatl ya:l qwa:ˀat ˀahaˀa: chakwa:si ts'awa:k'at ˀanahˀis ts'awa:k'at ˀi:h, wiky'o: qwayoˀal. Wi:nappiˀatl wik'atl hina:chitl wa:ˀatlok lim'aqsti ˀani topa:taqtlokqa hashahshiˀatlok qwayoˀalˀitq.

Hina:chiˀatltla ˀohˀatl qala:tik ts'axshitl. Hitachi:yoqwi:chiˀatltla wik qi:chi:yoqwa qahshiˀatlokw ˀahaˀa: matli:tssoˀatl n'achoˀalˀatl ya:lweˀin qwa:ˀat ˀahaˀa: nach'a ts'awa:k'at, ˀatowe:ˀinch'aˀaqwa ˀoh Ts'ats'awaktlich'a. Matli:tssoˀatl wehi:ˀop'atl. Ya:lweˀin weˀichoˀatl qo:ˀasˀi, nanatlaˀop weˀi:chitl ya:l nono:k yaqwi:pˀitq. Ya:lweˀin nono:k po:w'its.shiˀatl.

Hina:chiˀatltla hitahtachitl wikoˀal n'opchi:l hilts'a:to wik hinoˀal ˀi:hto:p. ˀAha ˀahaˀa: wa:lshitlshiˀatl wi:hiˀotlshiˀatl. ˀAna:ts'atoqhˀits'atl ˀoyoˀalˀatl ma:ˀak ts'axshitl ˀotsahtaksa, ˀatowe:ˀinch'aˀaqwa ˀohˀatl Kw'akw'a:ˀaktli, qwa:ˀat nach'a kw'ayo:ˀatqo:.

Walshiˀatl wihi:ˀoˀatl wi:nappiˀatl ˀo:tsa:qshiˀatl chakwa:si qatsts'a: qatsts'op'iltskwi. Tl'i:ˀilˀatl homaqstotl ˀa:t w'aqˀo: t'a:tn'eˀisˀi. Qitsshiˀatl qwisˀap'atl qwayoˀalˀitq ˀokwiˀalˀap'atl tl'oqwˀi: loˀok, ˀoˀalˀap'atl t'i:tsk'in ˀani ˀoyoˀal ˀani n'ikwhenmaˀi:qtl'a:nit ˀi:qhokw'atl ˀoˀokwink'atl yaqchiˀathˀitq. Topa:tichiˀatlok qi:ˀa:qtl'atlok ha:tlha:oqsach ˀona:k, ˀahaˀa: qwaˀo:ktokwah ˀona:k ˀahaˀa:ˀatlah[3] ˀoˀoˀi:hshiˀatl kw'akw'atl.

ˀOˀo:tahshiˀatltla hinasiˀatltla saye:ˀi saya:ts'atoˀi, hilhˀatl hina:yoqwi:chiˀatl ˀatlachi:yoqwi:chitl ts'ats'awi:pshitl.

"Qwaqwa:m'achi:qasatl'in," wa:ˀatl.

ʔAʔa:tlachi:qatl wih̲i:ʔol. Qatsts'achilʔatl wi:napil ʔah̲ʔa: hina:chiʔatltla. Ts'axshiʔatltla ʔoh̲ʔatl ts'axshitl Nanatla:ʔ̲op qa:la:tiksa, oh̲maʔ̲i:qtl'ap'at hini:yoqwa ʔoh̲mih̲sa hopi: ta:ta:yiʔi. Wiklm'a: qah̲shitl, ʔatlchi:lshiʔatl ʔatla:tlok ʔath̲i: hawi:ʔatl qa:h̲sap p'osshiʔatl, cha:na:tl ho:xsʔatatl ʔah̲ʔa: qa:h̲sapshiʔatltla. To:pshiʔatl wik'atlok qah̲shitl ! WeʔichoʔatI yaqʔi:tq hinyoqwa.

Tsiqshiʔat, ***"Wikʔa:qtlah̲ qah̲shitl,"*** wa:ʔatl'at. ***"Hawi:ʔatl'is qa:h̲sapʔa:qtl,"*** wa:ʔatl'at po:w'itsshiʔatl. ***"Nono:kw'is ʔani:yawo:sah̲ wih̲i:ʔotl."***

"Tlimkshiʔich," wa:ʔatl ta:ta:yakʔi.

ʔI:naxichiʔatl ʔi:naxmakʔi, nonokshiʔatl hinʔatatl ʔi:h̲to:pʔi. Kami kamitqshiʔatl ʔi:h̲to:mitʔi, sos.shiʔatl ! Hawi:ʔatl qah̲sa:pmaʔiqtl sosa:ʔatl cho:chiʔatqchik sach'i:yachishtqchik, matlalʔatl ʔa:nah̲i, hinasitl Ch'otsi:t ʔeʔimʔap hawi:tl ʔapw'in. Ka:mitqoksaqh̲ qah̲shiʔatl hinasiʔatlʔitq Ch'otsi:t. ʔAni:silatl Ts'isha: hitasatl ch'ichiʔatl ʔatowe:inch'aʔ̲ashqwa ʔoh̲ Tlitlo:qtlch'a[4] qwa:qtl qwe:ʔitq tli:yop ʔatl'aqtl, ʔatowe:ʔinch'aʔ̲ashqwa ʔo:no:tl wiklm'a: qah̲shitl. ʔO:qtl tl'ims. ʔAnah̲ʔits'at chakwa:siʔis.

Hitah̲tachiʔatltla hinoʔalʔatl ʔoyoʔal ya:l chaʔak ya:l wih̲ʔa:ʔa[5] wik saya:ts'atoqh̲, tlawi:toʔatl ya:lweʔin ch'ih̲a: wi:napachitoʔatl ya:lweʔin p'o:ʔi ʔi:h̲, ʔatowe:ʔinch'aʔ̲shaqwa ʔoyoʔal ch'oya:ch'a.[6]

"ʔAqistso:h̲en," wa:ʔatl qa:qla:tikok.

"Ts'axshiʔin," wa:ʔatl ʔoh̲ʔatl ʔo:ʔats'oʔi ts'axmaʔ̲i:qtl.

"Wik'in," wa:ʔatl ta:yi:ʔi. **"Wim'a:qtlin, pawalshitlo:sin**

p'atqok," wa:ʔatl.

"Take:ʔin," wa:ʔatl, "Qaḥsa:p'in."

"Cho:," wa:ʔatl.

Wiḥchi:chiʔat qwa qwe:ʔitq chaʔak wik ḥachintl
tsaxshiʔatl hinʔatyatl p'o:ʔiʔi kamitqshiʔatl ʔoyoʔal ʔani
wik'ahsʔatlokqa tokwaqiml ʔo:no:tl kamitqokok.⁷ Qi:kwa:l
t'anak⁸ po:sa:ʔatlok, ʔatoweʔinch'aʔashqwa hitawatlǫk,
ʔatowe:ʔinch'aʔashqwa ch'itiʔisya p'o:ʔiʔi. Chi:ya:sʔatl
xwishimlʔi, lachiʔatl qwi:sasa haya:ʔakshitl
qwitsachitlitlo:si. N'a:chokshiʔatl ʔi:ḥto:p ʔon'a:ḥshitl.
Ts'axshiʔatl ta:yi:ʔi, qaḥshitlok k'a:chchi:yoqweʔis
n'apxta:ʔak.

"ʔAʔa:yachi:qatl'in," wa:ʔatl.

Ts'axshiʔatl ʔo:ʔats'oʔi qaḥshiʔatloktla. Tlawi:chiʔatl
qwisʔatltla hishinkshiʔatl matlinksap'atl. Ts'axshiʔatl
tlaʔo:tla qaḥsa:pchip'atl qala:tikokwʔi, ts'axshiʔatl
qa:la:tikseʔi, mo:chinkitweʔin mo:mo:chi:qa hi:tatsaʔa.
ʔAtla:k ʔatḥi: wihe:ʔoʔatl, wi:nappiʔatl cha:ni ho:xsʔatol
cha:na:tl.

Hina:chiʔatltla n'ochi:lʔatl hilts'a:to walshiʔatl wiki:s
wiki:p wi:y'aʔi wik'aktli.⁹ Ya:ʔak'at lim'aqsti ʔani wi:y'a
wiki:p. To:pshitl ya:tsshiʔatl, ʔotsachiʔatl tl'a:ʔay'aʔeʔi
Ts'isha:. Topshitl ḥan'aḥtoʔatl sosshitl ʔatḥi: ch'it'e:ʔi
tom'aqtl. ʔOtsachiʔatl sosshitl Ts'otsi:t, saya:ts'atoma¹⁰
Ts'otsi:t. N'achoʔalʔatl ʔoyoʔal ʔi:ḥ qwa hopy'akqo,
cho:ʔato sokwitlmaʔiqtl qwiqo:si qwe:ʔi: qwe:ʔi:tq hopy'ak.
Sokwiʔatl tlitli:hswatweʔin¹¹ ʔaḥa kwikwiniksatʔi
ʔatowe:ʔinch'aʔashqwa ch'itisya ʔoḥʔatl t'ots'opch'a.¹² So:

hinosa sosshiˀatl ˀotsachitl Ts'otsi:t yats'o:tl hiy'a:ˀaqh n'a:sshitl. Ya:tsshitl ˀotsachitl ˀapqi:ˀi hilhˀatl ˀoˀoy'ichi:lshiˀatl, hilwe:ˀin ˀo:qtl tl'imis. Hi:lasatlok hopta:ˀatlok ˀapqe:ˀi, hi:y'a:ˀasaqh topshitl.

Tlahti:p'atl tom'aqatoˀatl ya:tsshiˀatl qa:la:tikseˀi n'a:chokshiˀatl ta:yi:ˀakˀi. Wik kamat'ap ˀotsachitlokqo: nawa:y'oˀatl qala:tikˀi n'a:choˀalsa ya:l qo:ˀas hinoschaˀa ˀatowe:ˀinch'aˀashqwa ch'itisya ˀohˀatlok ta:yi:. Kamitqshiˀatl tlawi:chitl !

"Sow'a:ˀatlhak," wa:ˀatl.

Kashiˀop'awiˀatl ch'itasshiˀatlok ˀani qi:ˀatl sosa: wihi:ˀotl histaqshitl Ts'otsi:t, yats'o:p'atl ta:yi:ˀak.

"ˀO:y'imah ch'iha:," wa:ˀatl ˀi:qhokw'atl qala:tikokwˀi. **"Walshiˀatlchi,"** wa:ˀatl, **"Mo:chi:lˀa:qtlah wik walshitl,"** wa:ˀatl.

Walshiˀatl qala:tikˀi hitaht'asshitl. Hinasitl mo:chi:l, mo:chi:l wik weˀichotl, mo:chi:l wik haˀok. Hitaht'asˀatl wik haˀok hinasipmqaˀi:qtl hayochil wik haˀok, wiˀi:ˀak hayochil hinasip n'opo haˀokshitl, wi:nappiˀatl ts'e:ˀiyipiˀatl.[13]

Mo:chi:lshitl hina:chiˀatl ˀoˀo:tahˀatl. ˀAnasilatl tl'a:ˀay'otl Ts'isha: ˀoyoˀalˀatl ˀi:hto:p ts'axshiˀatl k'achchi:yoqweˀis. Hitahtachiˀatl n'opts'iˀatl qa:la:tikseˀi ˀohˀatl matl'aktlatl wihi:ˀop'atl ˀotsachitl Ts'isha:. ˀAhˀa:ˀatl hina:chiˀatl wa:ˀatlok lim'aqsti ˀani n'a:chokshitlˀa:qtlqa ta:ta:yak. N'a:chokshiˀatl hinoˀalˀatl ˀapstachink'atl ˀoˀaˀiˀatl ˀani ma:tlma:tlatlqa wi:hiˀoˀatl. Walshiˀatl hitasaˀatl hisasaˀatltla Ts'isha:. Qatsts'i:pweˀin

n'opʼitḥ hina:chitl, ʔo:sa:ḥatl ʔani ʔona:kshitl tʼotsʼop
tlʼimyʼaqtl[14] ʔoktayo:chiʔatl.

Qwa:ʔapshiʔatl ʔatla ʔo:yʼipʼatlqo:weʔin nʼopʼitḥ
hina:chitl, ʔoʔoʔi:ḥshiʔatl tlʼatsʔi:, ʔo:poʔatl yaqchiqḥʔitq
ʔoʔoʔotaḥ ʔo:sa:ḥatl ʔani chʼiḥna:kshitlqa. ʔO:no:tl ʔanich
qwa:ʔamit ya: ʔona:kshitlʔi chʼiḥa: takwa qwa:ʔap. Wikatl
qwa: wikʔi ʔo:yʼip chʼiḥa: wikʔi nashokwʼat limʼaqsti
ʔa:nasa ʔo:yʼip chʼiḥa: nashokshiʔatl limʼaqsti, wikʼatl
qwis wi:ʔakʼatʔi limʼaqsti.

123. How the Nitinats Get the Thunderbird and Lightning Snake

(Captain Bill via Sapir)[1]

Mo:lshitlitoweˀin qwiyi:ch mo:lshitl top'al, lo:h̲shiˀatl top'al wik'i:tshitl n̦issm'a ˀah̲ko:. N'opqiml wih̲chi nochi:ˀi ˀokla: Ka:ka:piya[2] ˀoˀi:ˀaˀatl Xitlxitl'iˀi Xitlxi:tl'alatl. ˀOna:k h̲a:kwa:tl ˀokla:ˀak Chi:ˀilim.[3] Qi: mo:lok mo:chi:l mo:lok ˀoyi:ʔ̲atl ch'apats ˀi:h̲ˀi: ch'apats. H̲a:y'awiˀatl hawi:ˀatl mo:lok. Qi:ˀatl ˀoḳwi cha:ni Ka:ka:piya. Litsit.shiˀatl h̲a:kwa:tlˀi Chi:ˀilim wik'i:th̲ok chakop. Hi:lsaqh̲ˀatl nochi:ˀi ˀo:h̲sasatl kamat'ap yoqotsoyˀitq t'an'a ˀoyoˀalˀatl kamatsap ˀani ˀo:tsok Yaʔ̲i:ch'a. Nay'aqnakshiˀatl meˀitlqatsok, ˀi:wachitlok, wik'atl ˀe:ˀe:ˀisha walshitl. Meˀitlqats t'an'eˀi ʔ̲imtnakshiˀatl t'an'eˀi ˀokla:noˀatl H̲a:wilxim, ˀohˀatl ʔ̲imtayi n'ow'i:qso Yaʔ̲i:ˀi. Walshiˀatl[4] ˀi:wachitl ha:w'ilatlˀi yosha:ts'otl ˀo:no:tl ˀani kwisto:pqa. Walshiˀatl ˀotschiˀatl maˀasokˀi hita:ˀatatl histaqshiˀatl nochi:ˀi Ka:ka:piya.

H̲a:w'ilatlshiˀatl H̲a:wilxim ˀoˀoˀih̲shiˀatl ma:?ak ˀoˀo:tah̲shiˀatl ˀoˀoˀih̲shiˀatl toyi:s ma:ˀak.[5] Wi:na:po:l ma:?ak ˀo:tsiy'ok toshowisok'i hiyist'i:h̲ˀitq ˀo:y'ipshi:l soch'a ts'awa:k n'a:s, qi: qwa: ˀo:mi:k. ˀAne:ˀis maˀas hilh̲ˀi:tq n'a:chsa ˀoyi wi:napoˀatlqo: ma:ˀakˀi hina:chiˀatl. T'an'anakshiˀatl Xitlxitl'iˀi:[6] h̲a:kwa:tl'atlok ˀokla:ˀatlok Chi:ˀilimtla. Tla:ˀo:tl t'an'anakshitl h̲a:w'ilatl'tlok, ˀatli:chiˀatlok t'an'a ts'awa:k h̲a:kwa:tl ts'awa:k h̲a:w'ilatl. Qoˀi:chiˀatl h̲a:w'ilatlˀi Tla:tla:qoksapshi:l[7] ˀokla:ˀatl. ˀI:qh̲okw'atl n'ow'i:qsoˀi ˀani ˀona:k nochi:ˀi qwiyiˀitq mo:lshiyl, ˀani ˀoh̲ˀatlok nochi:ˀi Ka:ka:piya. Kamatsap'atl h̲a:w'ilatlˀi wa:ˀatˀitq ˀoh̲ˀat n'ow'i:qsakˀi. Wik'atl ˀi:qh̲ok n'ow'i:qsakˀi ˀani ˀotsachitlˀa:qtl nochi:ˀi ˀoh̲ˀa:tl Tla:tla:qoksapshi:l, ya:tsshiˀatl Tla:tla:qoksapshi:l ˀotsachitl nochi:ˀi ts'awa:k n'a:s ˀoya:tl to:pshitl hinasiʔatl. Hi:ya:ʔatl mo:chi:latl hilp'iqa nochi:ʔi. M'itlshiʔatl ʔathi: weʔichoʔatl ha:w'ilatlʔi. N'a:sshiʔatl ʔoyoʔalʔatl ʔani ya:ʔyaʔa ma:ma:ti ʔi:h ʔohʔatl T'i:tsk'inch'a mat'a:ʔatl ʔoyitskwi mat'o:tl ʔathi. Mitle:ʔitq. Tlawi:chiʔatl ha:m'i:chiʔatl qwe:ʔi:tq qwa:ʔatʔitq t'ohts'iti, ʔah qwe:ʔe:ʔiny'apsatl walshiʔatl ʔoma:k'atl qahshitlqo: mat.shiʔi:kqo: ʔani ʔi:hqa: ! Walshiʔatl hitaht'asʔatl ha:w'ilatlʔi, ʔotsachiʔatl maʔasokʔi.

ʔIts'a:t.shiʔatl lo:chim'o:pokʔi Tla:tla:qokshi:l ʔoʔi:ʔilʔatl hi:lts'aqil maht'i:ʔakʔi ch'itaqsoʔilim.[8] Qits.shiʔatl ʔokwiʔalʔap ʔitsaqsoʔilim yaqoʔalʔitq ma:ma:tiʔi T'i:tsk'inʔi ʔatlakwalchiyil hi:l ts'awi:l ha:kwa:tlʔi.[9] ʔAh ʔoyoʔalʔatl ha:kwa:tlʔi ʔani ya:yilqa ʔohʔatl Hiʔitl'i:kch'a ts'ahw'i:l. Ch'ihshiʔatl'at ʔits'a:tʔi ʔoyoʔalʔatl Hiʔitl'i:k hi:lʔi:tq ha:kwa:tlʔi ts'ahw'i:l.

ʔO:y'ichi:lshiʔatl ʔohʔatl n'ow'i:qsoʔi Xitlxitl'iʔi:. ʔO:y'ip'atl ʔimti: Wa:lt'i:lamaʔoq,[10] ʔokwi:lshiʔatl Hiʔitl'i:k ʔokwi:lshiʔatl qitsyo: qwe:ʔi:tq ʔokwiʔalʔap loʔak, ʔokwi:lshiʔatltla: qwa:ʔatʔitq t'ohts'iti ʔokwi:lshiʔatl hinkits'im qwa:ʔakqas hinki:tsim ʔah ʔo:t'i:ʔilatlma.[11] Qitsshiʔatl Xitlxitl'iʔi: ʔohʔatl Tla:tla:qoksapshi:l t'an'eʔi ʔokwi:lshiʔatl ʔahko: n'ow'i:qsakʔi ʔamasholʔatʔi ʔokwi:lʔatl T'i:tsk'in. ʔOkwi:lshiʔatl y'o:qwa: maht'i:, ʔokwi:lshiʔatl hi:ltsi:ʔasʔi qitsyo:ʔi qwayoʔalʔitq ha:kwa:tlʔi ʔits'a:tʔi machi:l histoʔal topa:ti:lshiʔatl. Tlo:kwa:ni:chiʔatl Xitlxitl'iʔi, ʔohʔapʔatl Tla:tla:qoksapshi:l ʔo:n'ak'atl Hiʔitl'i:k ʔi:qhokw'atl qwayoʔalqa ha:kwa:tlʔi, ʔohʔatl n'ow'i:qsoʔi ʔi:qhok. ʔAni wats.sti:yilʔatqa ʔo:mitaqatl ʔi:qhok n'ow'i:qsoʔi, ʔimtna:kshiʔatl ʔokla:noʔatl Wa:lti:lamaʔoq.

124. A H̲iko:lʔath̲ Sees the Thunderbird and the Northern Lights Women (William via Sapir)¹

T'apashiʔat lim'aqsti wa:ʔak lim'aqsti ya:tspanachatlqo:cha:na:tl.

"Ne:!" wa:ʔatl lo:tssma:kʔi, "ʔOkwi:lchip'is ko:k ya:tspanachʔa:qtlah̲," wa:ʔatl lo:tssma:kʔi, "ʔOya:qtlah̲ ya:tsshitl koʔalʔi:kqo: wiky'o:ʔi:kqo: tlimkshit̲l qo:ʔas."

Matlhsa:nop'atl lo:tssmaʔi ko:k, ʔo:qsti:ʔak'ap mo:tl'a:qa:sht. Ya:tsshiʔatl. Ha:t'inqshiʔatl, hat'is ʔa:neʔitq n'a:s ti:tlti:ya. Mo:p'it'atlqo:weʔin hitats'oqshitl ʔoma:k ʔoyi ko:kwʔa:ti:chitlqo: qi:kwa:lw'it'asqa, hishsa:tsa:qtlqa ya:tsok hat'i:s ʔath̲i:ʔi ti:tlti:ya. ʔAh̲ʔa:ʔatlqo:weʔin ʔinkw'achiʔenk koʔi:chiʔatlqo:, ʔah̲ʔa:ʔatlqo:weʔin haʔokshiʔatltla. Mo:p'it.ts'oqshiʔatlqo:weʔin qwa:qtlh̲ʔatlqo:weʔin hat'i:s. Hat'i:s n'a:s ti:tlti:ya ha:ti:saqh̲ʔatlqo:weʔin topshitl, ʔinkw'achiʔatlqo:weʔin koʔi:chiʔatlqo:. Ta:yachitlmaʔi:qstoʔatlqo:weʔin ʔah̲ʔa:ʔatlqoweʔin, n'apxshiʔatl tlimkshitl ʔe:ʔe:ʔisha! Hil wik'i:t yaʔato:si. T'iʔo:ʔatl, mamo:kshiʔatl lim'aqstatʔi, kamatsap ʔani n'achinkshiʔatlqa.³ Ha:t'inqshiʔatltla. Hawi:tl hat'i:s ʔoya:tl hawi:tl ʔapw'anoʔatl n'a:s. Ya:tsshiʔatl ya:tspanachiʔatl. Neʔi:chitl hista:tok k'i:tqa:, haya:ʔak hista:toko:si. N'a:chok wi:napotl t'iʔa:ʔa, n'achoʔalmaʔi:qtl wik n'achoʔal. N'achimsanoʔatl ʔoyoʔal ye:::: histoʔal n'a:sʔi n'achoʔal hilʔatl mitxwa: hi:taʔato, tlawi:chiʔat hi:lapiʔeʔitq. N'a:tssa:tl hinatshitl tlawi:chiʔatl qo:ʔasʔi, ya:l ʔIya:l sokwiʔatl hi:st'itl ʔane:ʔisʔi. Qah̲shiʔatl qo:ʔasʔi sokwitlkwachitl ʔIya:lʔi.

Tsiqshitl, "ʔO:shoʔalʔa:tleʔits," wa:ʔatl'at ʔoh̲ʔatl'at ya ʔIya:lʔi.

Po:w'itsshiˀatl. Wa:ˀatl'at ˀahko: ˀani ˀoshoˀalˀa:qtlqa. Tlimkshiˀatl ti:chachiˀatl. So: ˀIya:lˀi wik'atl lachitl wik hopt.sa:p. N'opchi:lˀap'at t'itsk'atl'atl ˀatweˀinch'aˀash t'itsk'atqi:ts ˀIya:lˀi yaqwi:pˀitq. T'iˀo:ˀatl naˀa:tahshiˀatl t'itske:ˀi. Saya:ˀi hista:tok, wi:ˀok hinitshitl. Ha:m'i:chitl t'itsk'atl'atl qa:tsshiˀsatl nashokshitl qatsa: ˀoˀi:p'ich'aˀa tl'aqaˀasˀi qatsa:ˀatl to:hshitl n'achoˀal qo:ˀasˀi. ˀOyoˀal ya:y'aˀa ˀink, hiy'a:ˀa hilˀi:tq m'oksy'iˀi ˀatweˀinch'aˀash ˀohˀatl Hiˀitl'i:kch'a ˀatweˀinch'aˀash wawo:satl T'i:tsk'inˀi. Nashokshiˀatl t'itska:, n'achoˀal qo:ˀasˀi ˀoyo?atl ya:y'a ˀaqa mat'a:ˀa ma:ma:ti. Qahshitl qo:ˀasˀi qahkwachiˀat qa:ty'apta, ti:chqh hisli:chiˀa:h tlawi:chik ! ˀA:nahwink'atl qasi:ˀatˀi na:tssa:tl kamat.sap chamihta qwe:ˀitq ma:ma:tiˀi, n'a:tssi:chiˀatl qwe:ˀi:tq Hiˀitl'i:kˀi qwe:ˀi:tq ˀi:naxi, ha:n'ak'ohshitl qwa:qwa:tsy'akˀitq. Ch'an'i:chiˀatl ˀich'achitl ma:ma:tiˀi. Ti:chachitl qo:ˀasˀi ti:chachiˀat qay'apt'a. Wi:nap'oˀatl hi:y'a:ˀasa mo:chi:y'a:ˀa hilhˀi:tq ch'ihshiˀat.

Ya:tsshiˀatl wiktsachiˀatl, wik ch'a:ni: walshitl ˀo:ˀoty'ak ˀani ch'ihshiˀatqa n'achoˀal ˀoyoˀal qo:ˀas hayo ˀatweˀinch'aˀash wi:napoˀatl qo:ˀasˀi hilhˀi:tq ˀo:shoˀal qoˀatsoˀal. Hi:y'a:ˀasaqh topshitl. N'achoˀalˀatl to:pshiˀatlˀitq ya:lweˀin ˀink hayoqoml ya:l ˀeˀi:wachitl ˀinkˀi n'eˀitlshitl qwa n'a:sshitlqo: ˀinkw'achiˀatl, ˀatweˀinch'aˀash ˀohˀatl N'a:n'a:st'o:ch'a.[4] Wi:nap'aˀa qo:ˀasˀi n'a:tssa: ha:wits'aqhiˀi n'a:sa:p qwa: n'a:tssi:chiˀatl qo:ˀasˀi ˀoyoˀal ya:l ha:thakwatl ˀatweˀinch'aˀash ha:tha:kwatl ya hayoˀi yaqoˀalˀitq qoˀatsoˀal. Ya:lwe:ˀin ts'i:tlts'i:y ts'i:ˀo:p'a:l ˀo:kwil ˀinkokˀi, ˀohˀatlweˀin Ts'i:tlts'i:yaˀotltaqiml.[5] Tloyachitl n'a:sshitl. Hawi:ˀatl ho:hin qwisa:p'atl'at.[6] ˀAtltaqoˀalˀatl ch'ihshiˀat. Ya:tsshiˀatl wa:lshitlshiˀatl, walshiˀatl hini:ˀiˀatl.

"Chokwa," wa:ʔatl ʔo:kwilʔatl qala:tikokʔi.

ʔO:shts'inaqshiʔatl ʔi:qh̲shiʔatl qala:tikokʔi ʔo:motaqshiʔatl qwayoʔalʔitq ʔani ʔoyoʔal ʔi:h̲ ma:ma:ti. Kamatap qwiqʔi:tq ʔi:qh̲ok ʔani ʔoyoʔal N'a:n'a:st'o:ch'a ʔatlsa:h̲takoʔal.

"Topa:takitlin," wa:ʔatl.

ʔO:no:ʔatl wa: ʔani wa:ʔatqa ʔoyiʔat ʔ̲imti: ʔaya kamat'ap'atl qwam'a:yatʔitq ʔ̲imtayat. ʔAh̲ʔa:ʔatl ʔokwi:lshiʔatl qitsshiʔatl ʔokwiʔalay'ap'atl laʔok, tl'oqʔi laʔok ʔatlah̲timʔap'atl. ʔOʔalay'ap'atl ma:ma:tiʔi qwa:ʔap'atl qwayoʔalʔitq ʔoʔalay'ap'atl H̲iʔitl'i:k qwayoʔalʔitqtla, qwayoʔalʔitq ʔ̲Iya:l ʔashiʔah̲soʔalʔitq qwa:ʔap'atl qwe:ʔi:tq qitsyo: tl'ih̲okokweʔin ʔapqi: ʔ̲Iya:lʔi topkokh̲ʔatlok ʔapm'iyaqtli, qwa:ʔatlok qitsshitl. ʔOʔi:ʔilʔatlok ya: hi:lts'aqilokʔi ch'itpiʔatlok. Topa:ti:chiʔatlok, ʔi:yaqh̲mi:chiʔatlok, ʔo:yi:ʔatlshiʔatlok ʔits'a:t.shitlokʔi:kqo: h̲a:kwa:tl ʔi:tst'o:latl.

ʔI:qh̲okw'atl ʔoʔokwink'atl yaqchiʔath̲ʔitq ʔo:motaqatl qwish̲ʔi:tq ʔona:kshitl T'i:tsk'in, hawi:ʔatl ʔi:qh̲ok. To:pshiʔatl ʔo:ksn'a:ʔ̲alshiʔatl qwayoʔalitʔitq tlaʔo:yoʔaltla N'a:n'a:st'o: ʔo:ksn'a:ʔ̲alshiʔatl to:pshiʔatl'itq ʔoyi, hilh̲ʔatlok mah̲t'i:ʔakʔi qwa:ʔap'atlok ya:ʔalʔatl yaqchiʔath̲ʔitq. Haya:ʔak'atok qwa:qwa:tsy'akoko:si ʔani wiky'o: qwayoʔal. Mo:chi:lshitl qwa:ʔap h̲achi:lshitl mo: ʔono:tl qwam'a:chilshitl ʔani wa:ʔat mo:chi:lokqaʔa:la ʔo:ksn'a:ʔ̲al. Hawi:ʔatl ʔi:qh̲shiʔatl qwaʔo:ktokʔitq ʔona:kshitl h̲a:chatmotaqa. ʔOkla:noʔatlok h̲a:kwa:tl Ts'i:tlts'i:yaʔotl, Ts'e:tlʔis. N'a:n'a:swiʔis,[7] N'a:n'a:sat'aqs,[8] N'a:n'a:y'alok,[9] ʔo:ts'atlok ʔ̲imti: chimmis.[10] ʔOh̲i:chiʔatlok H̲ah̲i:qtoʔa[11] ʔ̲imti:, ʔoh̲i:chiʔatlok

ʔimti: Yaya:tspiya,[12] ʔoh̲i:chiʔatlok ʔimti: H̲ah̲awitoʔa,[13] ʔoh̲i:chiʔatlok ʔimti: H̲ah̲awah̲soʔa,[14] ʔoh̲i:chiʔatlok ʔimti: Mi:xtachi:k,[15] qwam'a:yat ʔimtayat. Qwa:qwa:tsta:ʔakah̲ qwaʔo:ktokwah̲ ʔona:k T'i:tsk'in.

125. A M'o:ho:lʔath Youth Visits the Thunderbird

(Tyee Bob via Sapir)[1]

Wikmaqakitweʔin qo:ʔas, wik'at chamih̲ta h̲a:h̲o:pat. T'apat'aqstoʔatl h̲a:w'ilatlʔi ʔani ʔon'a:h̲shitlʔa:qtl hilh̲ʔa:qtli: hat'i:s. Ya:tsshiʔatl hiy'ath̲ toxol Tl'a:sʔaʔa:l[2] tl'op'i:chh̲. Hat'i:schiʔatl ti:tlti:chiʔatl, h̲ayosah̲takokweʔin tichim ti:tlti:chiʔatl. ʔEʔim mo:chi:lkwal ti:tlti:yatl, ʔa:nasatlok mamoms ti:tlti:ya, ti:tlti:ya koʔal ti:tlti:ya to:pshitl hishtsaqts'oʔak. Weʔichotltla: n'a:sshitltla: ti:tlti:chitltla: koʔal to:pshitltla: ti:tlti:chitltla:, p'iyachiʔatl'at tokwaʔatʔi qachts'achilshiʔatlʔitq ti:tlti:ya, ʔo:h̲w'inkshiʔatl tlolʔisʔi kw'a:lok n'opcho:lshiʔatl ʔo:h̲wink. ʔAh̲a:ʔatlweʔin mo:chi:lshiʔatl washiʔatl mo:ch'i:yilʔatltla: wi:napil tloyay'ap'atl tokwaʔ̲atʔi.

ʔAh̲ʔa:ʔatltla: ya:tsshiʔatltla: ʔiqsilatltla: ti:tlti:chiʔatltla: ʔiqh̲ʔatloktla: kw'a:lok qwiqwi:tspakʔitq. Titlti:chiʔatltla: to:pshitl. Weʔichotltla: hi:y'a:qtl'assatlqo:weʔin hita:qtlasʔi weʔich. ʔAtlchi:lshiʔatl ti:tlti:yatla: koʔal ti:tlti:yatla: to:pshitl ti:tlti:yatla: koʔal ʔish to:pshitl. Ti:tlti:yatla: koʔal qwistla: to:pshitl mo:chi:lshitltla: ti:tlti:ya.[3] ʔAh̲ʔa:ʔatl walshiʔatl mo:chi:yilʔatltla: wi:napil.

Ya:tsshiʔatltla: ti:tlti:chiʔatltla:, mo:p'itshitlweʔin mo:mo:chilkwala. ʔAh̲ʔa:ʔatlweʔin weʔichoʔatl po:w'itsshiʔatl.

"ʔOtsachiʔa:ni:," wa:ʔatl'at ʔi:ch'im qo:ʔas ʔoh̲ʔat. **"ʔOtschiʔatl'im hiy'ath̲i:ts T'i:tsk'in."**

Tlopkshiʔatl hashah̲shiʔatlok ʔani po:w'itsaqa. Wala:k'atl

wa:ˀatl[4] ˀoˀokwink'atl ˀomˀi:qsakˀi, ˀi:qh̲okw'atl ˀani ya:tspanachˀa:qtl.

"Wik'i:sim qa:h̲awilshiˀa:h̲ h̲ayochilkwalqo:s," wa:ˀatl ˀomˀi:qsakˀi, **"'Qah̲shitlch'aˀash' we:ˀisim h̲ayochilkwalqo:s ˀish mo: qa:h̲awilshiˀatlsok ˀah̲ˀa:."**

Wala:k'atl h̲a:w'ilatlˀi ˀotsachiˀatl hihist'itolˀitq po:w'itsa. Ti:tlti:chiˀatl ˀo:tsiy'okh̲ˀatl[5] mah̲t'i:ˀakˀi T'i:tsk'in. Mo:chilo:ˀokweˀin hi:ninqintl nochi:ˀi ˀokla: To:ta:.[6] Ti:tlti:yatlqo:weˀin hi:niqintl ˀoyoˀalˀatlqo: ch'aˀak ya:tsshiˀatlqo:weˀintla hawi:ˀatlqo: hat'i:s. Qatachiˀatl'at tokwaʔ̲atˀi mo:chi:lshiˀatl ya:tsok ˀah̲ˀa:ˀatl hinasiˀatl. Wik'it t'ashi: tl'ath̲ak ye:::: n'o:piˀak h̲isili:chiˀa:hˀatl hininqintl, walshiˀatl hita:ʔ̲atatl n'o:pchilo:ˀokw'atl hi:taʔ̲ach. Walyaqshiˀatl ˀatlakwalchilkwal, ˀi:qh̲shiˀatl ˀomi:qsakˀi.

"ˀOtsachitlitah̲," wa:ˀatl, **"Mah̲t'i:ˀakˀi T'i:tsk'in."**

Kamat'ap'at hilqa: maˀas T'i:tsk'in To:ta: ˀokle:ˀi nochi:. H̲a:h̲o:pshiˀatl ˀomˀi:qsoˀi.

"Qi:chiˀim ti:tlti:ya wik'im lochna:kshitl," wa:ˀatl ˀomˀi:qsoˀi t'an'a:k ˀokwil.

Qi:chitl h̲a:ho:pa ˀomˀiqsoˀi wik ˀi:qh̲ok chakopokˀi qwa:ˀakˀitqˀal t'an'a ˀo:no:tl ˀani wikqa: chamih̲ta h̲a:h̲o:pa t'an'a:k n'ow'i:qsoˀi. ˀAh̲ˀa:ˀatlweˀin hawi:ˀatl h̲a:h̲o:pa. ˀAh̲ˀa:ˀatltla: hita:qtl'iˀatltla: wa:ltaqshiˀatl ˀomˀi:qsakˀi ˀani h̲ayochilkwalˀa:qtl. Ti:tlti:chiˀatltla:, tlahˀatl ˀi:h̲ˀatl[7] qwaqwa: mo:shtaqalachiˀatlok kw'a:lok. Weˀichoˀatltla: koˀi:chitltla:. Ti:tlti:chiˀatltla: koˀal, h̲ayoshtaqak'atlok tl'aqapt qwam'e:ˀitq ˀish mo:.

To:pshitltla:. Qi:chiʔatl ti:tlti:ya wawi:chiʔatl ʔoyi t'ashna:ksap'atqo: qwitsachitlʔa:qtlʔitq wawi:chiʔatl ʔaʔaniwi:chiʔatl ti:tlti:yatlqo: ʔo:kshiʔatl t'ashi:. Wawa:ʔatl sa:ch'ink koʔalʔatlqo:, to:pshiʔatlqo: qwam'e:ʔitq n'a:sshitl wawa: t'ashi: ʔoyi:ʔatqo:.

Hayochilshiʔatl walshiʔatl hinassiʔatlok hayochil qwisʔatl wawa:ʔa:nitʔitq ʔomʔi:qsakʔi ha:ho:pat. Hinawiʔatl ʔathi:ʔitq ʔi:qhshiʔatl ʔomʔi:qsakʔi ʔani hininʔatlqa. ʔAhʔa:ʔatlweʔin kamatsap'atl'at ʔohʔat yayaqwinkʔitq ʔotsʔoksopt'a:l Ko:kohw'isaʔi:hʔi. ʔAhʔa:ʔatlweʔin mo:chi:yilʔatltla: wi:napitl wik'atl'atqo:weʔin n'achoʔalʔat ʔohʔat tlatlo:ʔi qoqwa:s. Ha:ho:pamaqshiʔatl ʔomʔi:qsoʔi.

ʔAhʔa:ʔatlweʔin hita:qtl'iʔatltla:, ti:tlti:chiʔatltla. Ts'aʔakʔisma hil ʔahʔa: t'aʔa:qtl'asʔi tl'a:sʔaʔa:l ʔokla: Maʔitqnit[8] wihshiʔatl ts'aʔakʔisʔi ʔa:nachan'olʔitq ʔo:sa:hatl ti:tlti:yatskwi.[9] Ti:tlti:yatlqo:weʔin ʔatlchi:lshiʔatltla: ti:tlti:ya hita:qtl'ash hilh Maʔitqnit to:pshiʔatlqo: wawa:ʔatl ʔoyi:ʔatqo: t'ashi:, tloyachitlokqo: t'ashi: qwi:tsoʔokʔitq, ʔoʔokwink'atl tsitsiqink hina:yilʔi Haw'il, lakso:qistoʔatqo: t'ashi: ʔoyi:ʔat. Sa:ch'inkshiʔatl wawa: ʔoyi:ʔatqo: t'ashi: yatsolnaksap'atqo: tl'athsy'a:holʔi hisap'atimtʔitq hisili:chiʔa:h hininqintl.

N'a:sshiʔatl n'opochilshiʔatlʔitq tlahʔatl ʔi:hʔatl wawa: wiktsokshiʔatlok[10] wawa:. Qwa:ʔatl ʔo:shhʔatqo:,

"Wawe:ʔi," wawa:ʔat.[11]

ʔAtlchi:lsami:chiʔatl ya:tsshitl. ʔAhʔa:ʔatltla: hat'i:sʔatltla: ʔo:y'ip'atl ma:ma:ti histi:p ma:ma:ti ch'aʔakʔi hilhʔi:tq hat'i:s. Hini:p'atl ma:ma:tiʔi, sokwiʔatl tl'o:shiml.[12] Haya:ʔak histaqshitli: ma:ma:tiʔisʔi, sokwiʔatl tlol ma:ma:tiʔisʔi, tlolʔat t'oh̲ts'iti ma:ma:tiʔisʔi. Hat'i:s to:pshitl, ʔah̲ʔa:ʔatl hawi:ʔatl walshiʔatl ʔotsachiʔatl ʔomʔi:qsakʔi.

"Waha:kʔa:qtlah̲ qwitsachitlitqas ʔO:mʔi."

Ya:tsshiʔatl ʔam'i:chiʔatlʔitq ya:tsokw'atl. Weʔichotl ʔah̲ʔa:. Koʔi:chiʔatltla: ya:tsshitltla: ʔam'i:chitltla: hinasiʔatl nochi:ʔi t'a:ʔ̲i:tl'eʔi. ʔOna:k'atl hisyo: ʔaya:k hisyo:. Hininqanoʔatl ya:tsshiʔatl ya:tsokw'atl mo:chilo:ʔokw'atl. Hinasiʔatl tl'ath̲akitʔi t'ashi:ʔ̲iʔatl hininqanoʔatl tlolʔatl t'ashi:ʔi. Hini:p'atl tlolʔi: t'ashi: wik'i:tshiʔatl tl'ath̲akʔi hitapatl p'ishaqʔi t'ashi:ʔi. N'achoʔalʔatl mah̲t'i:, machinoʔatl mah̲t'i:ʔi hine:ʔiʔatl T'i:tsk'in ʔo:tsʔi: mah̲t'i:.

"ʔOʔi:ʔilʔi ya:," wa:ʔat.

ʔAyaweʔin H̲iʔitl'i:k, pisatok H̲iʔitli:k ʔo:shmaqak'ap to:h̲ok ʔo:kwil hisyo:ʔi.

Ha:ʔ̲inchiʔatl Kist'eʔi, **"Hine:ʔiʔatokweʔits mah̲t'a::::."**

Kist'eʔi ʔoh̲ʔatl ha:ʔ̲inchitl.

Ha:ʔ̲inchitltla: Kist'eʔi, **"Hine:ʔiʔatokweʔits mah̲t'a::::, qoʔatstop !"**

Tla:ʔo:ktla: ha:ʔ̲inchitltla: Kist'eʔi, **"Hine:ʔiʔatokweʔits mah̲t'a::::."**

Mo:p'itshitl ha:ʔ̲inchitl.

"Ho::::," t'itskʔ̲atl'at saya:sh̲tʔ̲atl.

Tla:ˀo:ktla: t'itsk̲ˀatl h̲a:m'i:chiˀatl. Tla:ˀo:ktla: h̲a:m'i:chiˀatl ˀana:q̲h̲ˀits'atl, tla:ˀo:ktla: t'itsk̲ˀatl qwa: saya:qo:.

Tsishiˀatl Kist'eˀi, **"ˀOtsachitlchi yi: hoptshitl."**

Hoptshiˀatl qo:ˀasˀi. Hini:ˀatl ma:tli:tsimˀakˀi hisyo:ˀakˀi Kist'eˀi.

"Ho::::," t'itsk̲ˀatl'atl hita:sˀi.

Machinoˀatl qo:ˀasˀi.

"Ha:yiqo:litah̲, qo:ˀasma ye:yil," wa:ˀatl Kist'eˀi.

H̲an'ah̲toˀatl qo:ˀasˀi ˀotsaˀap'atl ya: hi:lsˀatoˀi tlawa: H̲iˀitl'i:kˀi qwitsay'apˀitq k'atsh̲aqokˀi. T'iqpiˀatl qo:ˀasˀi. Tlokwaqak'at qa:ty'apt'a, ˀi:h̲ qo:ˀas.

"Hitatssohtatl'i," wa:ˀatl'at qo:ˀasˀi hopte:ˀi.

Hitatssoh̲tatl qo:ˀasˀi ˀoˀi:ˀilˀatl t'iqpiˀatl. ˀInkokweˀin hil ˀinkolokˀi.

"Haˀokˀa:qtleˀits."

Hini:ˀasˀatl qo:ˀasˀi. Wik qi:kwa:l, hini:s tl'a:q qo:ˀasˀi ˀi:h̲ tl'a:qˀi. Sokwiˀatl ma:qya:kˀi, ˀi:h̲ ma:qyo. ˀAtlqimlokweˀin m'oksy'i hil ˀinkokˀi tl'opa:l sa:ch'ink m'oksy'im'inh̲ˀi. Ch'aqsip'atl ma:qya:kˀi, tl'am'ah̲sip'atl,[13] mox̲shiˀatl tl'imsatsˀi, hitaqsiˀatl tl'a:qˀi ˀi:h̲ˀak tl'am'aqtlˀi. Tl'a:pshiˀatl m'oksy'iˀi tl'am'ah̲sip'atl, ***w::::*** mox̲shiˀatl, hitaqsˀatl tl'a:qˀi tl'ahits'inoˀatl tl'imsatsˀi. Na:w'ah̲atl m'oksy'a:kˀi, qiˀi:p'atl sokwiˀatl tlaˀo:ˀi

m'oksy'i, tl'am'a<u>h</u>sip'atltla: moxshiʔatltla:. ʔAtlqimlok
m'oksy'i. Na:w'a<u>h</u>i:chiʔatl siʔachitlokw'i:kqo:.

"Tloyachitleʔits," wa:ʔatl T'i:tsk'inʔi.

Qo:ʔas ʔo:ty'a:p'atl hisyo:ʔakʔi hini:ʔatl, wa:ʔatl,
**La:kwiqnaka<u>h</u>ʔa:la p'ishaʔa:nita<u>h</u> n'o:w'is
tloyachitlmaʔi:qtla<u>h</u> ʔo:no:tla<u>h</u> ʔotsoʔachitl sow'a, Haw'e:l !
Wi:kmi:kita<u>h</u> chims."**

ʔO:yoqwatl ya: T'i:tsk'in. Wikʔa:tl qo:ʔasʔi T'i:tsk'inʔi
wik tsiqshitl. Sokwiʔatl tl'a:qokʔi hitakwist'a<u>h</u>sʔap'atl[14]
tl'a:qokʔi siʔatl'atlok.[15] Hini:ʔatl'at qoʔasʔi haʔokshiʔatl
qo:ʔasʔi tl'a:qʔi:, wik to:<u>h</u>ok qo:ʔasʔi haʔok ʔi:w'i:sshitl
tl'a:qʔi hawi:ʔatl haʔok.

Tsiqshiʔatl qo:ʔasʔi T'i:tsk'in, **"ʔOyi:ʔa:qtla<u>h</u>
Hiʔitl'i:kʔi qi:tskwi:ʔatl."**[16]

ʔOna:kshiʔatl qo:ʔasʔi hini:ʔatl T'i:tsk'inʔi.

Tsishiʔatl y'oqwa: T'i:tsk'in, **"ʔOna:<u>h</u>ahʔa:la hisyo:tskwi
shi:tlokw'atlqo: maʔas. Cho: walshiʔi:keʔits."**

Hini:ʔasʔatl ma<u>h</u>t'iʔakʔi hiʔi:sweʔin hita:sʔi ʔi:<u>h</u>to:p !

"ʔO:ssikeʔits ʔa<u>h</u>."

"Cho: !" wa:ʔatl qo:ʔasʔi.

Sokwiʔatl ʔaky'akokʔi topkok ʔaky'akʔi, m'oksy'imatakok.
Ch'ichiʔatl qo:ʔasʔi T'i:tsk'in ʔi:<u>h</u>to:pokʔi. Sachkok
ʔaky'ak, lapsa:p ʔi:<u>h</u>to:pʔi. Sokwiʔatl ko<u>h</u>swi:nop
T'i:tsk'in, ʔich'ay'ap'atl T'i:tsk'inʔi ts'isq.w'a:tʔi

tl'a:q.

"Yoxˀits'atlma," wa:ˀatl T'i:tsk'in k'a:lk'oˀ̲itl.

Wik tsiqshitl qo:ˀasˀi to:h̲okw'atl ˀani ˀi:h̲ kwatyi:k. Ch'ihtay'ap'atl T'i:tsk'inˀi tl'a:qˀi, sokwiˀatltla: T'i:tsk'inˀi,

"Yoxˀits'atlma, ni: ?" wa:ˀatltła: ˀo:kwil qo:ˀasˀi.

Wik'atltla sokwitl qo:ˀasˀi wa:ˀatl ˀani kwatyi:k.

"ˀA:nah̲seˀisoko:seˀits. Cho: m'aw'e:ˀi:kah̲ so:til ˀa:nah̲seˀisoko:seˀits tl'a:q."

Machinoˀatl qo:ˀasˀi T'i:tsk'inˀi. Histo:kw'al machi:l ˀi:naxi:chiˀatl m'ochichoˀatl matˀiniˀakˀi. Hini:ˀasˀatl T'i:tsk'in ma:ma:tatl.

"Hilikeˀits ˀah̲ko:," wa:ˀatl'at qo:ˀasˀi ˀa:ˀapsw'inlˀatˀi T'i:tsk'in. **"K'itsink'im,"** wa:ˀatl'at qo:ˀasˀi ˀoh̲ˀat T'i:tsk'in, **"Wik'im napx̲shiˀa:h̲ qah̲shitlo:sin."**

Sokwiˀatl T'i:tsk'in qo:ˀasˀi ˀotsay'ap'atl ˀa:ˀapsw'inlˀatˀi.

"Cho ! K'itsinkshiˀatl'i !"

K'itsinkshiˀatl qo:ˀasˀi. Qwa: ˀappi: hista:tokw'atqo: t'itska: T'i:tsk'inˀi wik h̲asa:tok. Wi:m'a: qo:ˀasˀi naˀa:, wik qwa:ˀap qwa:ˀapˀitq ma:ma:ti mata: ˀa:nah̲i hahaqchim tsi:kmalapi ch'itxwa:. Wi:napoˀatl, hilh̲ˀatl Tl'a:sˀ̲aˀa:l hita:qtl'asˀi. ˀOstˀi:ˀatl qo:ˀasˀi wa:ˀatl'at ˀoh̲ˀat T'i:tsk'inˀi wikqo: napx̲shitl qi:.

"Qaḥshitlo:saḥ," wa:ltaqshiʔatl T'i:tsk'inʔi walshitl matshitl.

ʔOʔi:ʔasʔap'atok tl'a:qʔi: Nanimxsh[18] ʔokle:ʔi nism'a. Wik'atl walshitl qo:ʔasʔi ʔotsachitl ʔomʔi:qsak, mo:chi:y'aqtl'asʔatl. Walshiʔatl ʔatḥi: ʔotsachiʔatl n'ow'i:qsakʔi ʔi:qhokw'atl ʔani ʔotsachitlitqa T'i:tsk'in.

"Hiʔi:sokw'ap'ataḥ tl'a:q Nanimxsh."

"Wikʔa:qtlin haʔok," wa:ʔatl n'ow'i:qsoʔi, "Ch'iḥa:ʔakeʔits," wa:ʔatl n'ow'i:qsoʔi.

Ya:tsshiʔatl ʔam'i:chiʔatlʔitq koʔalḥ ʔotschiʔatl tl'a:qʔi:. N'a:n'a:n'ichshiʔatl tl'a:qʔi: n'ow'i:qsoʔi hayimḥatl qwiqi:, wiky'o: qwayoʔal ʔoy'ichi:lshiʔatl. N'ow'i:qsoʔi ʔoʔoʔi:ḥweʔin tl'anoqmaqsimʔi ʔoy'ichi:l, walshiʔatl. ʔI:qhokw'atl lo:tssma:kʔi, ya:l kamat'ap ʔoḥ ʔomi:qsoʔi ʔoḥi:tqa qwachi:l t'an'a:kʔi qo:ʔatsi:l.

ʔAḥʔa:ʔatlweʔin hashi:chiʔatl'at wikmaqakitʔi ḥa:w'ilatl ʔani ti:chqa: qaḥshitlqatḥʔap'a:nitqa qi:ʔaṭl'a:niy wik'at n'achoʔal. ʔOḥsa:ʔatl'at[19] chims haw'aḥsat, ʔoḥʔat ʔi:ch'imʔi qachts'a. Chichimy'i:ḥshiʔatl ʔotsachitl ʔaʔokʔi.[20] Hitasaʔatl, walshiʔatl ʔatlqimy'aḥs chims. Chimstsa:qshiʔatl ch'iyi:chiʔatl, tl'i:ʔatl w'aqʔo:ʔatl qo:ʔas ḥat.shatak, haʔokshiʔatl chimsʔi. Hawi:ʔatl haʔok walshiʔatl qo:ʔas.

Ha:neʔi:chiʔatl Ko:koḥw'isaʔi:ḥʔi, wik'atl w'aqʔo: hitaḥtis ʔotsachitl ye: top'alʔi. Walshiʔatl qo:ʔasʔi qachts'aqimy'aḥs ko:koḥw'isa. Tl'i:ʔilʔatl y'o:qwa: w'aqʔo:ʔatl qo:ʔas ḥachatak'atltla:, haʔokshiʔatl ʔayeʔi qo:ʔas ko:koḥw'iseʔi qachts'a. Walshiʔatl ʔayeʔi qo:ʔas.

Qiʔatl wiwi:ktaq ʔotsachitlitʔi T'i:tsk'in. Chichimy'i:h̲shiʔatltla:, ʔayi:p'atl chims. H̲ayoqomli:p'atl chims ʔatlchi:lshitlh̲, ch'iyi:chiʔatl tl'oshsa:p'atl h̲ayoqoml motsmh̲aq. Tl'i:ʔilʔatl ch'o:chk'iʔatl cha:kopi:h̲ lo:chsa:mi:h̲ t'a:tn'eʔis, walshiʔatltla: chichimy'i:h̲ʔi qwiyiʔitq[21] chocho:kwaʔinmasʔitq ʔatlqimy'ah̲sʔatltla:, hilh̲ok yi hita:sʔi siqa:. Machinoʔatl siʔ̲atlʔi chims ʔaya, hinh̲awiʔatl qo:ʔas haʔokshiʔatl ʔayeʔi qo:ʔas, ʔi:qh̲okw'atl n'ow'i:qsoʔi ʔani h̲ayoqomlqa chims. ʔAh̲ʔa:ʔatlitweʔin haʔoksap'atl n'ow'i:qsakʔi chims ʔoʔi:sʔap'atl ʔayi:sʔap tl'a:q, tl'a:qok chims. Haʔokwitl'asʔatl ʔani wik'a:nit tlol, haʔokshiʔatl n'ow'i:qsoʔi ʔath̲i:.

"H̲eʔi:sshitlʔa:qtleʔits," wa:ʔatl h̲a:w'ilatlʔi n'ow'i:qsak ʔo:kwil, **"Wi:kmi:kshitlo:sah̲ wiʔi:sshitlqo:k."**

Haʔokshiʔatl, tsoma:noʔatl ʔoʔomh̲ichitl wik'ah̲shitl lo:ʔeʔi tsoma:noʔatlʔitq.[22] ʔAnasila k'ashpa:ts'ol[23] qah̲shiʔatl. Wik hashiy'ani:chitl ʔani qah̲shitlqa nisy'i:h̲a. ʔOy'oksap'atl tl'aʔ̲i:ksap n'ow'i:qsakitʔi ʔatlqiml motsmoh̲aq, n'o:h̲shiʔatl ʔotsaʔap'atl hilat'eʔeʔi toxolʔi. H̲amat.sap'atl'at ʔani qah̲shitlokqa n'ow'i:qso ʔotsachitlitʔi T'i:tsk'in. Wiwi:ktaqshiʔatl qah̲shitlokʔi n'ow'i:qso. ʔAna:tl Kokoh̲w'isaʔ̲i:h̲ʔi Ts'o:maʔasʔath̲ kokoh̲w'isaʔ̲i:h̲ʔatl mo:qomy'ah̲s. Tl'i:ʔilʔatl hitasaʔatlʔitq mo:qomlʔi ko:koh̲w'isa.

ʔAh̲ʔa:ʔatlitweʔin qi:ʔatl wiwi:ktaq qah̲shitlokʔi n'ow'i:qso. ʔOtsachiʔatl Nanimx̲sh hilʔi:tq ʔi:h̲to:pʔi, ʔah̲ʔa:ʔatlweʔin kw'a:li:chʔitap'atl, ʔah̲ʔa:ʔatlweʔin walshiʔatl. ʔ̲IchshiʔatI qi:ʔasʔatlqa. ʔOh̲ʔatlitweʔin n'a:tssa n'ow'i:qsakitqas cha:skwinm'inh̲ich'a hiye:ʔis Nanimx̲sh. ʔAh̲ʔa:ʔatlitweʔin ʔo:ʔinl h̲ayo ʔish n'opoqoml chimsaʔaq, machi:lʔatlok n'opqiml cha:skwin ʔoyima:ʔatl'atl h̲imchitl n'oshshiˀi:kqo:. Chocho:kwaʔ̲inmasˀatl. ˀO:n'akˀa:qtl'atl T'i:tsk'inˀi qwayoˀalitˀitq, ˀoya:tl kwisqˀichshiˀatlˀitq. ˀAh̲ˀa:ˀatlweˀin n'oshshiˀatl w'aqˀo: h̲achatak, hilh̲ˀatl Tl'a:sʔ̲aˀa:l, ˀah̲ˀa:ˀatlweˀin hiy'a:ˀatl t'iʔ̲a:ˀa hitinʔ̲eˀeˀi Tl'a:sʔ̲aˀa:l.

ˀAh̲ˀa:ˀatlweˀin hissimlasts'atlok T'i:tsk'atqt'i:ˀila pits'op ˀoh̲tinˀak hinki:tsim. ˀO:t'i:ˀilap qwa:ˀakˀitq t'oh̲ts'iti yaqoˀalitˀitq T'i:tsk'in. Haya:ˀak'atl'atok qwiqokwi:ˀah̲. Hawi:ˀatl machinoˀatl mah̲t'i:ˀi hine:ˀiˀatl. N'oshshiˀatl motsmoh̲aq ˀo:kwil Ts'o:maʔ̲asˀath̲ Ho:pach'asˀath̲, ˀoh̲ˀatl h̲a:w'ilatlˀi ˀotsachitlitˀi T'i:tsk'inˀi, ʔ̲imtna:ksap'atl lo:chm'o:pokˀi ˀokla:nop To:ti:sʔ̲aˀatoˀaqs.[24] ˀAyi:chiˀatl ʔ̲imti: ˀoh̲ˀatl h̲a:w'ilatlˀi ˀoklintlsintsit ˀoh̲ˀi:chiˀatl ʔ̲imti: Wi:wimtaʔ̲i:k[25] ˀokwachi:lˀatl ʔ̲imti:. ˀAh̲ˀa:ˀatl y'o:qwa: h̲ayoqomy'ah̲s'atl Kokoh̲w'isaʔ̲i:h̲ˀi ˀo:ˀinlˀatl y'o:qwa: cha:ˀoy'inlˀatl[26] ˀoh̲.

ˀAh̲ˀa:ˀatlweˀinˀa:la ˀotsachiˀatlqo: n'ow'i:qsakitqas, ˀayimch'a tich'ak. ˀA:yimkshiˀatl ˀotsich'a tich'ak ˀotsachitlich'a T'i:tsk'in. Histath̲ˀatlokwah̲ ˀah̲ˀa: h̲amatap ˀoˀoˀi:h̲ chims wiktsokw'ap'atl hini:p. Mo:sa:h̲tak tich'im ˀo:sa:h̲atl ˀoyiˀokt'atl waha:ki:ch T'i:tsk'in.